What Is
Scripture?

What Is
Scripture?

Paul's Use of *Graphe* in the Letters to Timothy

L. Timothy Swinson

Foreword by
Ray Van Neste

WIPF & STOCK · Eugene, Oregon

WHAT IS SCRIPTURE?
Paul's Use of *Graphe* in the Letters to Timothy

Wipf & Stock
An Imprint of Wipf and Stock Publishers
199 W. 8th Ave., Suite 3
Eugene, OR 97401

www.wipfandstock.com

ISBN 13: 978-1-62564-100-7

Manufactured in the U.S.A.

Contents

Foreword

Is THE IDEA OF a "canon" biblical? Did the New Testament writers understand themselves to be writing Scripture? How soon were the New Testament writings recognized as Scripture? Did the church later invest authority in certain books, or were these books recognized as authoritative from an early date? These questions and others like them have become increasingly significant in biblical scholarship and in church life in light of the success of the skepticism of James Barr, Bart Ehrman, and others. Timothy Swinson wades into challenging waters as he disputes this skepticism.

Swinson focuses his study on the use of γραφή in 1 and 2 Timothy, specifically contending that 1 Tim 5:18 and 2 Tim 3:16–17 demonstrate that Paul considered some of the apostolic writings extant in his day (particularly the Gospel of Luke) to be on par with the Old Testament as Scripture. Swinson considers the uses of the key term γραφή in extrabiblical literature in order to determine its semantic range, demonstrating that the term (and its Hebrew cognate) refers exclusively to physically written or drawn material. This disqualifies the popular idea that these verses refer to oral tradition or a "sayings" source. Rather, Paul is referring to written sources.

Furthermore, Swinson examines how γραφή, and other terms in its semantic field, function throughout the discourses of 1 and 2 Timothy. He shows that a central concern of these letters is the upholding and preserving of the apostolic message, and that γραφή is used along with other terms referring to this gospel message. The combination of lexical study and discourse analysis produces a cogent argument that γραφή makes most sense in the flow of thought in these letters as referring not only to the Old Testament, but to the apostolic message as well.

If his arguments hold (as I think they do), this book has significant implications in several areas. First, this is an important contribution to scholarship on the Pastoral Epistles. Swinson's careful exegesis, his discourse and semantic analysis, and his lexical study, not to mention his challenge to the typical reading of γραφή, make this a valuable resource for anyone working in these letters. Second, his thesis that apostolic writings were already recognized in the first century as "Scripture" on par with the Law, the Prophets, and the Writings has major implications for our understanding of canon and current debates in that realm.

Careful, detailed, and swimming against the tide, this is a bold, compelling book with significant conclusions for scholarship and the church. I have been privileged to encounter Tim's work in presentations at scholarly conferences along the way and was immediately drawn to the substance and manner of his work—conscientious, cautious, and charitable as it is. I am excited that this work will now be available to a wider audience. This book has challenged and helped me, and I commend it to you.

Ray Van Neste, PhD
Union University

Acknowledgments

SEVERAL PEOPLE MADE THEMSELVES available to me and rendered crucial assistance and support during the writing of this dissertation. The New Testament faculty members of Trinity Evangelical Divinity School gave their time and counsel graciously, especially Dr. Robert Yarbrough (currently at Covenant Theological Seminary in Saint Louis, Missouri), who patiently superintended the entire process and exhibited a great deal of forbearance over the course of several drafts. He and Dr. Ray Van Neste (of Union University in Jackson, Tennessee) have both been highly supportive through the transition from dissertation to publication. Alex Fus graciously lent indispensable assistance through the copyediting process. The brothers and sisters of Heritage Chapel were also quite patient through the years of my doctoral program, and I was deeply touched by the unabashed joy that they demonstrated on my behalf as it drew to a conclusion. Most of all, I thank my wife Beth Ann, who has remained long-suffering throughout and given encouragement and steady support along the way, as well as my children Eric and Maia, who have grown familiar with the enterprise even as they have grown up with it; this truly has proven to be a family endeavor. Thanks be to God for his steadfast mercies in Christ Jesus. "Faithful is the Word!"

Abbreviations

ANTC	Abingdon New Testament Commentaries
BDAG	Bauer, Danker, Arndt, Gingrich, *A Greek-English Lexicon of the New Testament and Other Early Christian Literature*
BDB	Brown, Driver, Briggs, *Hebrew and English Lexicon of the Old Testament*
BNTC	Black's New Testament Commentaries
EBC	Expositor's Bible Commentaries
ECC	Eerdmans Critical Commentaries
Exp	*The Expositor*
JPSTC	Jewish Publication Society Torah Commentaries
LEH	Lust, Eynikel, Hauspie, *Greek-English Lexicon of the Septuagint*
MSJ	*The Master's Seminary Journal*
NA^{27}	*Nestle-Aland Novum Testamentum Graece.* 27th ed.
NTM	New Testament Message
PNTC	The Pillar New Testament Commentaries
PRSt	*Perspectives in Religious Studies*
RevBib	*Revue Biblique*
SBET	*Scottish Bulletin of Evangelical Theology*
SBJT	*Southern Baptist Journal of Theology*
TWOT	*Theological Wordbook of the Old Testament*
UBS^4	*The Greek New Testament.* 4th ed.
WissWeis	*Wissenschaft und Weisheit*
WTJ	*Westminster Theological Journal*
ZBK	Zürcher Bibelkommentare

CHAPTER 1

What Is γραφη? Thesis and Introduction

WITH REGARD TO PAUL's letters to Timothy, analysis of exegetical and historical data suggests that γραφή, as it is employed in each letter, legitimately should be understood not as a reference limited strictly to the Law, Prophets, and Writings, but as a term that includes at least some of the apostolic writings that now appear in the NT. Specifically, this study argues that a written version of the Gospel of Luke stands as the source of the second referent of ἡ γραφή in 1 Tim 5:18, while it also argues that πᾶσα γραφή in 2 Tim 3:16 includes as its referent the apostolic writings extant in Paul's day, most especially Luke's gospel and Paul's own letters. The findings of these parallel lines of analysis will indicate that Paul, the writer of record, ascribes to his own teaching and to that of his apostolic coworkers an authoritative standing equal to that attributed to the sacred writings (τὰ ἱερὰ γράμματα)[1] found in the OT.

In 1 Tim 5:18,[2] the second of two quotations appears to offer a citation of Luke 10:7 as Scripture, though many dispute such an assessment, typically accounting for the apparent correlation with Luke by positing a Logion source. In 2 Tim 3:16–17, Paul comments directly upon the merits of "all Scripture."[3] A significant minority of interpreters maintains that in

---

1. While it is included in this study, the text-critical data make the decision concerning the article difficult, as it is omitted in ℵ, C²ᵛⁱᵈ, D°, F, G, 33, 1175, *pc*, co, and Cl, while it is attested in A, C°, D1, Ψ, 1739, 1881, and M (NA²⁷, 554).

2. λέγει γὰρ ἡ γραφή βοῦν ἀλοῶντα οὐ φιμώσεις, καὶ ἄξιος ὁ ἐργάτης τοῦ μισθοῦ αὐτοῦ.

3. πᾶσα γραφὴ θεόπνευστος καὶ ὠφέλιμος πρὸς διδασκαλίαν, πρὸς ἐλεγμόν, πρὸς ἐπανόρθωσιν, πρὸς παιδείαν τὴν ἐν δικαιοσύνη.

1

this second passage, Paul views the apostolic writings of his day, including his own writings, as Scripture alongside the OT writings. However, the majority opinion insists that whoever the writer may be, he would refer only to the OT writings as "Scripture."[4] The question regarding the referents of these occurrences of γραφή, along with the possibility raised by some interpreters that they designate writings of both the OT and NT as "Scripture," knits these two texts together in this study, the significance of which emerges against the backdrop of the scenario outlined below.

Skepticism Regarding the Canon

Over the past two centuries, Christianity's high view of Scripture, along with the very notion of a NT canon or a true Christian orthodoxy, has endured persistent opposition from those skeptical of the Bible's divine origins and normative function. Increasingly, the legitimacy of a list of "inspired" NT books is dismissed.[5] What premises and observations typically lay behind such disbelief, and are there data that might challenge them? In order to assess these questions, it may prove constructive first to consider briefly the positions of three representatives of this canonical skepticism: namely, James Barr, Lee McDonald, and Bart Ehrman.

In 1983, James Barr offered the observation that there exists "no *scriptural* evidence to decide what were the exact limits of the canon."[6] Essentially, Barr argued that if Scripture were the final authority and arbiter of theological truth, then we would expect to find an explicit assertion of such authority within the scope of Scripture itself. Since we do not, according to Barr, whatever authority we may ascribe to Scripture must derive from outside the Bible, he external sanction of which functions as the real or practical authority over theology and doctrine. Accordingly, Barr maintained,

> It requires no great insight to see that in many cases it is 'conservatism,' or 'Calvinism,' or 'evangelicalism' that is the actual authority,

4. The primary positions regarding both of these passages, along with some of their representatives, will be discussed in detail later in the chapter.

5. Among others, see Barr, *Holy Scripture*, 23, 25; Bauer, *Orthodoxy and Heresy*, xxii–xxv; Ehrman, *Lost Scriptures*, 1–5; Ehrman, *Lost Christianities*, 3–4; Ehrman, *Orthodox Corruption of Scripture*, 7–10; McDonald, *Biblical Canon*, 31–33, 50–55, 416–20; Pagels, *Gnostic Gospels*, xxii–xxiii.

6. Barr, *Holy Scripture*, 24–25. Indeed, he stated further that the idea of the canon is nothing of "first-rate importance to biblical Christianity" (Barr, 63).

and that the authority of the Bible is used and maintained simply because it is supposed to provide the necessary support for the doctrinal authority which is the real dominant power.[7]

Consequently, according to Barr, the entire Protestant edifice rests ultimately not upon biblical authority, but upon a self-authenticating Protestant *tradition* regarding biblical authority, thereby rendering the principles of biblical authority and *sola scriptura* meaningless (a fair inference, if his premise is correct).

In a parallel analysis, Lee McDonald seems to suggest that the relative scarcity of explicit first-century data attesting to a broad recognition of the apostolic writings as Scripture necessarily implies the absence of such recognition.[8] He further supports his position against an early sense of the New Testament as Scripture by pleading that the New Testament writers had few scruples about altering OT teaching.[9] Indeed, he writes,

> Several statements made by Jesus in the Sermon on the Mount (see Matt 5:21, 27, 31, 33, 38, 43) contrast his teachings with— and show their superiority to—those from the OT Scripture, especially the Law of Moses (e.g., "you have heard that it was said . . . but I say to you . . .").[10]

With respect to the apostolic writings, McDonald adds,

> The core of the OT Scriptures was the Mosaic Law. The Law, however, appears to be at variance with much of the NT focus

---

7. Ibid., 31.

8. McDonald, *Biblical Canon*, 22, 248–49. This argument may be overreaching the actual data. In point of fact, the most that one can say is that, in the absence of explicit testimony, we cannot *confirm* externally a wide understanding or agreement in the first-century churches regarding the scriptural status of the apostolic writings. However, this does not necessarily mean that such recognition did not exist. See, for instance, Blum, "Apostles' View of Scripture," 51–53.

9. McDonald, *Biblical Canon*, 198–99.

10. Ibid., 198. However, on this point, even as he refers briefly to Jesus' explicit comments in Matt 5:18 respecting the very inviolability of the Law, suggesting that Jesus himself does not conform absolutely to his own assertion, he fails to consider that Jesus did not set himself against *Moses*, but rather interpreted Moses in opposition to *the Judaism of his day*, the practices of which rested upon the errant construal and misuse of their own Scriptures. See, for example, Matt 5:31–32 (also Mark 10:2–12), in which Jesus censures the Pharisees for how they misuse Deut 24, even as they miss entirely the actual teaching of Moses respecting marriage. Barr exhibits a subtler version of this construal, writing, "Jesus' teaching is about to range far beyond anything that could be justified as an interpretation of these laws" (Barr, *Holy Scripture*, 15).

> on grace . . . The problem of how to live free in Christ and yet
> be subject to the legal codes of the Law was a critical issue for
> the early Gentile Christian community, and it dealt with this
> problem . . . by emphasizing the faith principle that preceded
> the Law (as Paul did in Gal 3–4 and Rom 3–4), which in effect
> created a "canon with the canon."[11]

McDonald's point, assuming that Jesus viewed his own teaching as
superseding that of Moses, and that Paul also considered the Law, Prophets, and Writings as temporary, lies in highlighting the implication that
the very idea of "Scripture" as a fixed and authoritative point of reference
did not exist either for Jesus or for his apostles, and that therefore such a
concept would be unlikely to pertain to the apostles' writings.[12]

Bart Ehrman, also an opponent of an early sense of "Scripture" and
of a legitimately fixed biblical canon, for his part writes,

> Many years passed before Christians agreed concerning which
> books should comprise their sacred Scripture, with debates over
> the contour of the "canon" (i.e., the collection of sacred texts)
> that were long, hard, and sometimes harsh. In part this was
> because other books were available, also written by Christians,
> many of their authors claiming to be the original apostles of
> Jesus, yet advocating points of view quite different from those
> later embodied in the canon.[13]

11. McDonald, *Biblical Canon*, 244–45. Once again, a more careful reading indicates that, in the case of Gal 3–4 at least, Paul does not challenge Moses as incompatible with faith. Rather, he challenges a misappropriation of Moses that does contradict
faith. Moses, on the other hand, even in Paul's words, is completely compatible with
faith, for he says in Gal 3:17, διαθήκην προκεκυρωμένην ὑπὸ τοῦ θεοῦ ὁ μετὰ τετρακόσια
καὶ τριάκοντα ἔτη γεγονὼς νόμος οὐκ ἀκυροῖ εἰς τὸ καταργῆσαι τὴν ἐπαγγελίαν. Indeed,
Daniel P. Fuller points out that Paul's issue here lies between viewing the Law as a
law of faith as opposed to a code stipulating meritorious works of law (legalism). See
Fuller, *Gospel and Law*, 88–105; Shepherd, *Call of Grace*, 54–63.

12. C. F. Evans suggests much the same thesis as McDonald, citing Adolf Deissmann in saying, "Paul had better work to do than the writing of books, and he did not
flatter himself that he could write Scripture" (Evans, "New Testament in the Making,"
237). See also Grant, "New Testament Canon," 286. However, Blum asserts otherwise
(Blum, "Apostles' View of Scripture," 41–47).

13. Ehrman, *Lost Scriptures*, 1. At another point he writes, "If, then, by 'apostolic'
book we mean 'book actually written by an apostle,' most of the books that came to be
included in the New Testament are not apostolic. But if the term is taken in a broader
sense to mean 'book that contains apostolic teaching as defined by the emerging proto-
orthodox church,' then all twenty-seven pass muster" (Ehrman, *Lost Christianities*, 236).

As he develops this idea further, Ehrman refers to others who laid claim to apostleship, maintaining,

> Some of these writings may well have been produced by the original apostles of Jesus. But already within thirty or forty years books began to appear that *claimed* to be written by apostles, which in fact were forgeries in their names (see, e.g., 2 Thess 2:2).[14]

Ehrman's approach in this case functions essentially as a plea to invalidate all notions of a biblical canon, based upon his view of the subjectivity that must have attended multiple and incompatible claims of apostleship, along with multiple and comparable documents from which to "choose." Ehrman's primary target lies in the very idea of an authentic Christian orthodoxy, which, according to him, derived from the triumph of the stronger party in a religio-political conflict as it imposed its particular stamp of Christianity upon the world while rewriting prior history so as to lend legitimacy to its particular variety of orthodoxy. In other words, according to Ehrman, there exists no primordial truth or orthodoxy deriving from Jesus or the apostolic age.[15]

The preceding examples provide only a small sampling of the various scholars and types of arguments that typify much of the skeptical discussion concerning the canon of the NT. Nevertheless, this discussion seems to rest rather heavily upon two major premises. The first maintains that *there exists no direct evidence indicating that any part of what we know as the New Testament was recognized as God-inspired or authoritative until well into the second century.* Consequently, neither the NT writers nor their immediate followers had any sense that they were writing

14. Ehrman, *Lost Scriptures*, 2. He seems to offer these comments as a contraindication against Westcott's canonical standard of apostolicity (see Westcott, *Canon of the New Testament*, 13–14). However, regardless of his intentions, Ehrman's assertion begs yet another question, for if there existed no broad recognition of the unique authority of the apostles and their company, where would lie the attraction and desirability of falsely presenting a work as having been written under apostolic aegis? Indeed, existence of pseudo-apostolic works adduced by Ehrman, inconvenient though it may be for those who advocate a high view of Scripture, in fact *may* indicate that the church observed very early in its existence that the Lord had conferred upon the apostles a unique authority that would transfer naturally to their words, both spoken and written (see Belleville, "Canon of the New Testament," 382; Bovon, "Canonical and Apocryphal Acts," 175; Harding, "Disputed and Undisputed Letters," 149). Terry Wilder also argues for such an understanding, adducing it as one reason that the early church would not have countenanced pseudonymous writings attributed to the apostles (Wilder, *Pseudonymity, the New Testament, and Deception*, 165–216, esp. 168–69).

15. Ehrman, *Lost Christianities*, 180, 235.

Scripture, or that their words stood on par with or shared the God-given authority ascribed to the OT Scriptures.[16]

A second premise accompanies the preceding claim and is widely viewed as axiomatic in discussions of the NT canon in particular; namely, that several of the books currently comprising our New Testament, among them 1 and 2 Timothy, *did not enjoy apostolistic authorship or authorization*.[17] The relegation of such writings to pseudepigraphic standing effectively levels the playing field when comparing these documents with those customarily considered apocryphal, for it permits the alleged apostolic origin of other acknowledged pseudepigraphic writings to stand alongside the corresponding claims of the canonical works.[18] With respect to this skeptical stream of thought concerning Scripture and its implications, A. T. B. McGowan writes,

> At the present time, [no issue] is more vital than the doctrine of Scripture. I say this because what we believe about Scripture determines what we believe about everything else. If we take the view that the Scriptures are God-given and without error, then our views on every other subject will be determined with reference to Scripture. It stands to reason that, if God has spoken and if what he said has been written down under the supervisory action of the Holy Spirit, then the Scriptures become the final

16. Regarding this, McDonald writes, "Only the book of Revelation (ca. 90–95) claims for itself such a lofty position that would come close to the notion of inspiration and Scripture . . . Although Paul was mindful that he was communicating the authoritative words of Jesus on occasion (1 Cor 7:10–11; 9:14; 11:23–26), he apparently was unaware of the divinely inspired status of his own advice (7:12, 25). He never wrote as if he himself were setting forth Scripture, although he did acknowledge the superior authority of the words of Jesus in settling matters of Christian ethic and did emphasize his own apostolic authority in resolving disputes in the churches that he founded (e.g., 1 Cor 4:14—15:5; 7:12–16; 2 Cor 13:10), and is the first NT writer to make a qualified claim to inspiration by the Spirit regarding what he said" (McDonald, *Biblical Canon*, 31–32). D. A. Carson and Douglas Moo adopt a neutral position on this particular point, for they state, "Nowhere does Paul make it clear that he thought his letters to be inspired Scripture," and that he was "not perhaps conscious of writing inspired Scripture" (Carson and Moo, *Introduction to the New Testament*, 370).

17. Among others, see for instance Barrett, *Pastoral Epistles*, 4–12; Collins, *Timothy and Titus*, 3–5; Dibelius and Conzelmann, *Commentary on the Pastoral Epistles*, 1–5; Hanson, *Pastoral Letters*, 6–7.

18. Ehrman in particular plays upon this point, presuming the pseudepigraphy of the Pastoral Epistles, for instance, which diminishes their standing, while implicitly elevating that of the Gospel of Thomas since, by comparison, it is equally "apostolic" (Ehrman, *Lost Christianities*, 31, 58–59, 64–65, 235–36).

authority for decision-making and the ultimate arbiter of truth. If, on the other hand, we believe that the Scriptures are simply an interesting record of what Jews and Christians have believed over the centuries but that these beliefs are not binding upon believers today, then we may reach quite different decisions in respect of doctrine, ethics and the life of faith.[19]

The impetus for the present study lies, in large part, in a conviction similar to McGowan's. Specifically, the question of the nature and significance of Scripture entails a good deal more than a mere academic exercise. In fact, nothing less is at stake than the capacity to discriminate truth from falsehood, with respect to both God and humanity.

The previously outlined scenario of canonical skepticism, though briefly presented, entails a tangle of complicated details, exchanges, and issues, the entirety of which vastly exceeds the scope of this study. However, it is feasible to isolate particular matters and concerns that assume strategic importance over the course of the larger discussion. Among them, the question of just how Jesus' apostles viewed their own teachings and writings is a foundational concern, and this study represents an effort to offer at least a partial solution to that question. To that end, the present work concentrates upon 1 and 2 Timothy for two distinct but related reasons.

First, apart from 1 Cor 2:12–13 and 2 Pet 3:14–16, no text in the New Testament speaks so directly to the question of a Scriptural consciousness in the apostolic age as 1 Tim 5:18 and 2 Tim 3:16.[20] Of these, only in 2 Tim 3:16–17 is there any statement that explicitly speaks to the standing and perceived worth of a body of material recognized as γραφή.

Second, while the majority of opinions and interpretations concerning 2 Tim 3:16–17 maintain that Paul had nothing in mind beyond a received form of the OT,[21] none of the sources consulted to date have attempted to trace a coherent theology of Scripture and the apostolic tradition, either through each letter read independently or in the two letters read consecutively.[22] Furthermore, none of these sources

19. McGowan, "Divine Spiration of Scripture," 199.

20. The matter of 1 Corinthians 2:12–13 has been addressed in both a 2001 ThM thesis and a paper read at the annual meeting of the Evangelical Theological Society in 2005 (Swinson, "'Words Taught by the Spirit'"; Swinson, "'We' Effect, and Its Implications"). See also Kaiser, "A Neglected Text," 301–19.

21. As surveyed below.

22. The closest example of such an attempt would be that offered by Philip Towner

has offered a thorough inductive assessment of the uses of ἡ γραφή, ἡ διδασκαλία, ὁ λόγος, ὑγιαίνω and other related terms in these letters.[23] Among these, tracing Paul's use of ὁ λόγος in the letters to Timothy provides the most stable and consistent point of reference, especially in view of the recurring elliptical clause, πιστὸς ὁ λόγος, for in most cases, it may be argued that ὁ λόγος serves as a designation for the apostolic gospel proclamation.[24] Considering what lies at stake in the interpretive decisions relative to the letters to Timothy, one contention behind this discussion is that these heretofore neglected lines of analysis offer some vital exegetical anchoring points upon which continuing discussions regarding Scripture and canon may build.

In framing the central research question of the study, exactly how much Paul may claim in these texts will be examined. Specifically, what does he mean by ἡ γραφή and πᾶσα γραφή? As part of the investigation of the use and meaning of γραφή, it will be demonstrated that terms such as ἡ διδασκαλία, τὸ εὐαγγέλιον, ὁ λόγος, and ἡ παραθήκη (among others) modified occasionally by some form of καλός, ὑγιαίνω, or ἡ ἀλήθεια,[25] often function synonymously with each other and with γραφή throughout the letters to Timothy. These occurrences indicate that Paul has a very specific body of material or teaching in mind that he wishes Timothy to guard for the sake of the church. Accordingly, Paul's use of γραφή assumes considerable importance relative to that concern.

(Towner, *Goal of Our Instruction*). However, even here, while Towner correctly observes that the primary issue of the Pastoral Epistles concerns the apostolic proclamation of the gospel, he does not follow this argument so far as to offer any conclusions respecting Paul's use of γραφή. See Towner, *Goal of Our Instruction*, 75–119.

23. Again, Towner (along with Ray Van Neste) comes the closest to this, essentially providing an assessment similar to that proposed here, though featuring a different focal point and employing an alternate approach (Towner, *Goal of Our Instruction*, 123–25; Van Neste, *Cohesion and Structure*, esp. 109–11 and 216–17). See also Knight, *Faithful Sayings*, esp. 14–15.

24. See Rendall, "Faithful Is the Word," 314–20; Van Bruggen, "Vaste grond onder de voeten," 38–45; Swinson, "Πιστὸς ὁ λόγος: An Alternative Analysis." Concerning ὁ λόγος in the PE, see Towner, *Goal of Our Instruction*, 123–24. Also, while it might be desirable to show that ὁ λόγος functions as a typical reference to the gospel message in all of Paul's writings, the immediate question of this study concerns usage specifically in 1 and 2 Timothy.

25. See, for instance, 1 Tim 1:10; 4:6; 6:3; 2 Tim 1:13; 2:15; 3:10, 14; 4:3.

Construals of γραφή: Status Quaestionis

The foundational task in this study lies in determining the most suitable interpretations of ἡ γραφή and πᾶσα γραφή as they occur in 1 Tim 5:18 and 2 Tim 3:16, respectively. While the scholarly sources consulted adopt their own unique approaches in the interpretation of these texts, most of them tend to point in the same basic direction.

For example, Jouette Bassler, Raymond F. Collins, Lorenz Oberlinner, and Jürgen Roloff all propose an epistolary environment in which the Pastoral Epistles were composed sometime after A.D. 80 but before the middle of the second century, and maintain that someone other than Paul wrote them.[26] Within this framework, Bassler and Collins then argue that the second citation of 1 Tim 5:18, which they understand as a part of the intended referent of λέγει γὰρ ἡ γραφή, derives from a statement made by Jesus that Luke cast into writing at a later time.[27] Oberlinner, while acknowledging that the "conspicuous correspondence with Luke 10:7" could certainly be explained by appealing to a Logion source,[28] suggests that a saying such as that found in the second citation of 5:18 also could be explained simply by positing a common proverbial tradition.[29] In view

26. Among others, Bassler suggests a *terminus a quo* of A.D. 90, and Collins suggests A.D. 80, while Oberlinner specifies only the late first century (Bassler, *1 Timothy, 2 Timothy*, 20; Collins, *Timothy and Titus*, 9; Oberlinner, *Erster Timotheusbrief*, xlvi). See also Fiore, *Pastoral Epistles*, 20; Roloff, *Der erste Brief an Timotheus*, 38–39.

27. Collins offers a more explicit explanation, asserting that the citation derives from "a logion from Q that Matthew and Luke have incorporated into their respective versions of Jesus' missionary charge" (Collins, *Timothy and Titus*, 145). See also Bassler, *1 Timothy, 2 Timothy*, 100. Despite an early remark that it is "virtually impossible to determine the date of composition of the Pastoral Epistles" (Collins, *Timothy and Titus*, 9), Collins nevertheless writes, "The Pastor seems to identify both the passage from Deuteronomy and the logion as 'Scripture' (*he graphe*), but Christian writings were not yet regarded as Scripture at this point in the history of the early church. It is moreover, quite unlikely that the Pastor had available a written version of Q, Matthew, or Luke . . . Since Deut 25:4 is certainly a 'Scripture,' the adage might have been taken as a paraphrase of Moses' charge to the Israelites with regard to the material welfare of Levites (Num 18:31; see 2 Chr 15:7)" (Collins, *Timothy and Titus*, 146).

28. Oberlinner, *Erster Timotheusbrief*, 254.

29. Indeed, he writes, "Not only can such dependency not be documented, it also is unnecessary, for our author could just as well have taken this word from oral tradition" (ibid., 254–55). At the same time, Benjamin Fiore states, "It is more likely that the designation of 'Scripture' applies only to Deuteronomy." He also allows that "the Q saying may have circulated with scriptural authority even at the time of the PE, or the author might have known Luke" (Fiore, *Pastoral Epistles*, 111). For Oberlinner and all other non-English sources, all translations are my own unless otherwise noted.

of this possibility, Oberlinner then suggests that ἡ γραφή in 5:18 may in fact refer only to the first citation, which comes from Deuteronomy.[30] In a similar statement, Roloff suggests that the text that reflects Luke 10:7 actually derives from a Logion source that likely corresponds with Q.[31]

In their expositions of 2 Tim 3:15–16, Bassler, Collins, and Oberlinner contend that [τὰ] ἱερὰ γράμματα functions as a typical Hellenistic label for the Hebrew Scriptures.[32] When the discussion then shifts to include πᾶσα γραφή of 3:16, Bassler and Collins comment very briefly on ἡ γραφή, affirming only that it serves as an alternative designation for those same Hebrew Scriptures, now being discussed in a context in which the writer affirms their usefulness on the basis of their having originated with God.[33] Oberlinner essentially concurs with Bassler and Collins in his interpretation of 2 Tim 3:16–17.[34] However, in his exposition of πᾶς in the expression πᾶσα γραφή, which he construes as "every Scripture," Oberlinner acknowledges that the text makes at least theoretically possible the inclusion of NT writings as ἡ γραφή.[35] Alfons Weiser, while also maintaining that [τὰ] ἱερὰ γράμματα and ἡ γραφή both likely refer to the OT, suggests that the first reference, [τὰ] ἱερὰ γράμματα in 3:15, has a soteriological significance, while the second, γραφή in 3:16, is ecclesiological in its force, pertaining to the life of the congregation.[36]

Thus, minor variations between them notwithstanding, Bassler, Collins, Oberlinner, Roloff, and Weiser all reflect fundamentally the same frame of reference when approaching the letters to Timothy and draw essentially the same conclusions regarding λέγει γὰρ ἡ γραφή and πᾶσα γραφή. Their positions are shared by most of the scholars consulted, such

---

30. Oberlinner, *Erster Timotheusbrief*, 255. Bassler offers a variation on this point, suggesting that the use of the term "Scripture" does not require the existence of a New Testament canon, but could reflect the practice of reading Christian writings alongside the Jewish Scriptures in a liturgical setting. However, she stops short of suggesting that these writings may have been recognized as Scripture (Bassler, *1 Timothy, 2 Timothy*, 100). See also Kelly, *Pastoral Epistles*, 126.

31. Roloff writes, "The Jesus logion cited in the version from Luke 10:7 may correspond to that of Q" (Roloff, *Der erste Brief an Timotheus*, 306).

32. Bassler, *1 Timothy, 2 Timothy*, 166–67; Collins, *Timothy and Titus*, 261; Oberlinner, *Zweiter Timotheusbrief*, 145.

33. Bassler, *1 Timothy, 2 Timothy*, 167–68; Collins, *Timothy and Titus*, 263.

34. Oberlinner, *Zweiter Timotheusbrief*, 147.

35. Ibid.

36. Weiser, *Der zweite Brief an Timotheus*, 279.

as Jerome Quinn and William Wacker,[37] Donald E. Cook, and David G. Dunbar, among others.[38] However, while the projected historical setting and understanding of authorship frequently *does* influence the exegetical decisions, it would be inappropriate to view such reconstructions as *necessarily* determinative for the interpretive outcome. In other words, if one were to incorporate into the list of interpreters those who maintain an earlier date of composition for the Pastoral Epistles and genuine Pauline authorship while arriving at the same interpretive conclusions with respect to 1 Tim 5:18 and 2 Tim 3:16, the list could be expanded to include Gordon D. Fee,[39] Daniel P. Fuller,[40] J. N. D. Kelly, Luke Timothy Johnson, William D. Mounce, and Philip Towner, among others.[41] Further complicating the array of interpretive configurations, I. Howard Marshall

---

37. A divergence in Quinn and Wacker lies in the observation that, if the Pastoral Epistles had been written in the second century, then "it is striking that they, intent on transmitting the Pauline heritage, do not quote the apostle's own words." Accordingly, they place the date of composition within the range of A.D. 80 to 85 (Quinn and Wacker, *Letters to Timothy*, 19).

38. Cook, "Scripture and Inspiration," 58; Dunbar, "Biblical Canon," 318; Quinn and Wacker, *Letters to Timothy*, 450–51, 748–50, 758–60. See also Brox, who maintains that the writer may view Luke's gospel as Scripture, but that placing such remarks in a pseudo-Pauline setting results in an anachronism (Brox, *Die Pastoralbriefe*, 199–200).

39. Fee, *Timothy and Titus*, 129, 278–79. In his discussion of 1 Tim 5:18, Fee's remark does not present quite as strong a claim as that put forward by the others, for he states only, "This is a saying of Jesus, exactly as it appears in Luke 10:7" (ibid.).

40. Fuller's position on record concerns only 2 Tim 3:16 (Fuller, *Unity of the Bible*, 24, 28).

41. Kelly, *Pastoral Epistles*, 126, 201–3; Johnson, *Letters to Timothy*, 278, 422–23; Mounce, *Pastoral Epistles*, xlvii, 310–11, 563–65; Towner, *Letters to Timothy and Titus*, 83–84, 366–67, 587. In his discussion of 2 Tim 3:14–17, Mounce initially suggests that ἱερὰ γράμματα, instead of πᾶσα γραφή, may indicate a referent expanded to include the apostolic gospel message. While this proposal warrants careful evaluation in view of its uniqueness, his rationale seems more theological than exegetical, for Mounce writes, "While issues of faith and the message about a coming Messiah are part of the OT, it seems doubtful that Paul would say that the OT by itself could instruct Timothy in a salvation that was by faith in Christ Jesus; this would be anachronistic." However, in the next sentence, he allows, "Of course, in his childhood Timothy would only have known the Hebrew Scripture. It may be concluded that the expression 'sacred writings' is drawn solely from the vocabulary describing the Hebrew Scripture" (Mounce, *Pastoral Epistles*, 564). Offering a unique version of the general position so widely represented, Ben Witherington, maintaining Pauline authorization and Lukan composition, views the citation of 1 Tim 5:18 as Luke's version of a Jesus saying (which is why it reflects so neatly the text of Luke 10:7), while he treats 2 Tim 3:16 as a reference to the Old Testament only (Witherington, *Letters and Homilies*, 60, 275, 361).

approximates concurrence[42] with the majority opinion regarding the non-Pauline authorship of these letters and the construal of 2 Tim 3:16 as a further referent to the OT only,[43] diverging from the majority interpretation of 1 Tim 5:18 by cautiously proposing that "it is quite possible that both quotations are envisaged as coming from 'Scripture.'"[44] At the same time, Donald Guthrie, maintaining the genuine Pauline authorship of the Pastoral Epistles against the majority opinion, nevertheless interprets 1 Tim 5:18 and 2 Tim 3:16 along lines that run similarly to Marshall's treatment.[45] Common to all of the sources surveyed thus far is a fairly strict interpretation of 2 Tim 3:16 as a reference to the Law, Prophets, and Writings, and an apparent preference for construing the second citation of 1 Tim 5:18 as deriving from a Logion source. Occasional variations among their positions notwithstanding, it consequently may be said that each of these sources holds to some form of the majority interpretation.

Representing a different point along the interpretive continuum, near the end of an article focused chiefly upon the nature of inspiration (θεόπνευστος) in 2 Tim 3:16, Antonio M. Artola asserts that Paul, as one who experienced the gift of prophecy, serves as a paradigm for writers of inspired material and that his writings represent a bridge from the OT to the NT. Artola therefore holds that the affirmation of 2 Tim 3:16 speaks to the totality of Scripture.[46] However, he arrives

42. On the one hand, Marshall exhibits distaste for the "uncritical acceptance" of the prevailing hypothesis. At the same time, his own position effectively amounts to pseudonymity, since under the conditions of the "allonymity" that he hypothesizes, ultimate responsibility for the composition and dispatch of these letters still passes to someone other than Paul (Marshall, *Pastoral Epistles*, 58, 92).

43. Ibid., 92, 616–17, 790–93. While Marshall does acknowledge the possibility that πᾶσα γραφή could represent an expansion to include gospel accounts and Paul's own writings (ibid., 792), his clearest statement on the matter occurs relative to ἱερὰ γράμματα, already understood as a designation for the Old Testament, as he writes, "The statement about Scripture is backed up by a fuller explanation of its nature and purpose" (ibid., 790).

44. Ibid., 615. In addition to this remark, Marshall states near the end of his exposition of vs. 18, "A written source is surely required, and one that would have been authoritative" (ibid., 616).

45. His comments on 2 Timothy cut straight to the point, as he writes, "*Graphe* could mean any writing, but the uniform New Testament use of it with reference to Scripture (i.e., the Old Testament) determines its meaning here" (Guthrie, *Pastoral Epistles*, 175). However, while cautioning that the favorable comparison of the second citation in 1 Tim 5:18 to Luke 10:7 does not necessarily require a canonical written source, he yet adds that such an explanation "cannot be entirely ruled out" (ibid., 117).

46. Artola, "El Momento de la Inspiración," 72–74.

at this conclusion not by an exegetical analysis of 2 Tim 3:14–17, but by appealing to 2 Pet 1:21 and postulating the inspired nature of "the prophetic word" as found in the OT and in some of the NT oracles.[47] Meanwhile, in his discussion of 2 Tim 3:16 on its own terms, Artola characterizes it only as a text in which "the New Testament affirms the inspiration of the Old Testament."[48] At one point, Antonio Piñero offers a similar assessment of 2 Tim 3:16, writing, "It is a testimony of a canonical book of the NT concerning the inspiration of the Old."[49]

Addressing the significance of 2 Tim 3:16 with respect to canonization, Yves-Marie Blanchard proposes that two groups of writings may fall under the designation πᾶσα γραφή. The first consists of those writings that made up the Christian Bible: namely, the texts "inherited from ancient Judaism,"[50] while the second entails "those of the New Testament, [a] collection of apostolic writings."[51] While Blanchard defends his proposal by claiming that inspiration applies as much to the first generation of Christian missionaries as to the OT prophets, and thus embraces the "embryonic state" of the NT,[52] this assertion seems to rest largely upon the witness of Irenaeus and the Muratorian Canon in conjunction with Blanchard's apparent assumption of the post-Pauline composition of 2 Tim.[53] Reinhold Reck reflects a similar position,

47. Ibid., 68–69. See also ibid., 68–69, n. 22.

48. Artola, "El Momento de la inspiración," 70. Consequently, Artola's final interpretation of 2 Tim 3:16 probably has more to do with the theological significance that he projects upon the text than with actual meaning inhering in the text. See also Piñero, "Sobre el Sentido de θεόπνευστος," 143–53.

49. Piñero, "Sobre el Sentido de θεόπνευστος," 146. However, a later comment seems to temper his exclusive reading of 2 Tim 3:16, for he cautions, "In theory, the syntactical scope of πᾶσα γραφή cannot be reduced to the OT . . . Consequently π. γ. could refer to any writing that Christians considered inspired, not only to the OT." Nevertheless, in the final analysis, Piñero equates πᾶσα γραφή with ἱερὰ γράμματα, for he writes, "However, the preceding verse (". . . since from infancy you knew the Sacred Writings . . .") limits this γραφή to the OT" (ibid., n. 13).

50. Blanchard, "'Toute écriture est inspirée,'" 499.

51. Ibid., 502. Once again, the determination that the New Testament writings are included in the referent πᾶσα γραφή has the appearance of a theological-historical determination rather than an exegetical one.

52. Ibid., 509.

53. Ibid., 503. Indications of Blanchard's view of authorship are inferred from remarks such as, "the affirmation of the Pauline redactor" and "suggested by the Pauline citation" as well as his reference to "the epistles of Paul and throughout the gospels," in an apparent contra-distinction from 2 Tim (ibid., 497–99).

although he points out that while the early believers attributed scriptural status to the NT writings alongside the OT, they did so "without it being asked what the author probably could have meant originally."[54] In his discussion of the inspiration of Scripture and its relationship to the efficacy of Scripture,[55] Giuseppe De Virgilio proposes a chiastic arrangement of the material in 2 Tim 3:14–17. In his configuration, vv. 14 and 17 comprise the outer elements, A and A'.[56] He places the remaining elements in the following array:

B   3:15a καὶ ὅτι ἀπὸ βρέφους τὰ ἱερὰ γράμματα οἶδας, τὰ δυνάμενά σε σοφίσαι

C   3:15b εἰς σωτηρίαν διὰ πίστεως τῆς ἐν Χριστῷ Ἰησοῦ

B'   3:16 πᾶσα γραφὴ θεόπνευστος καὶ ὠφέλιμος πρὸς διδασκαλίαν, πρὸς ἐλεγμόν, πρὸς ἐπανόρθωσιν, πρὸς παιδείαν τὴν ἐν δικαιοσύνῃ[57]

De Virgilio then argues that the two divisions (B and B'), marked by ἱερὰ γράμματα and πᾶσα γραφή represent two phases of revelation. The first signifies a more primitive form of written instruction and pertains to the early writings of the OT, characterized as ἱερά. The second phase signifies a final form in which the initial stages of a fixed canon may be observed, at which point the writings are θεόπνευστοι and comprise the NT, the emergence of which has its roots in the Christ event.[58] John P.

54. Reck, "2 Tim 3,16 in der altkirchlichen Literatur," 105.

55. De Virgilio, "Ispirazione ed efficacia della Scrittura," 494.

56. Ibid., 490.

57. Ibid.

58. De Virgilio writes, "*Hiera grammata–pasa graphe* constitute the structural correspondence of this second passage. An ulterior transition in the same Scripture is recorded: from *grammata hiera* (semantic-literal level) to *pasa graphe* (final level of the written revelation) . . . Structurally, one obtains the correspondence between *grammata* and *pasa graphe* from one part and *hiera* and *theopneustos* from the other. Such elegant correspondence of reported epithets to the Scripture carries with it the theological consideration [present in the Pauline theology] of the distinction between the AT and NT, the veiled sense of *hiera* (AT) and that revealed in *theopneustos* (NT), beginning from the event of Christ" (ibid., 490–91). De Virgilio's literary analysis aside, his proposal appears to ride the momentum of a prior theological stream in which perceived contrasts between the Old and New Testaments play a crucial role. Furthermore, while the structural array may have some merit, the exegetical base is not obvious. Indeed, even though Artola, Piñero, Blanchard, and De Virgilio all address 2 Tim 3:16 directly and maintain a final position that agrees with at least part of the thesis of this study, the exegetical bases for these conclusions remain opaque, which makes it difficult to evaluate both the conclusions and their merits as supporting data.

Meier and B. Paul Wolfe, both of whom write from within the framework of non-Pauline authorship,[59] also interpret ἡ γραφή in 1 Tim 5:18 and 2 Tim 3:16 in a manner compatible with that proposed in the present work. According to Wolfe, denying that πᾶσα γραφή in 2 Tim 3:16 comprises a reference to both OT and NT writings constitutes a failure to attend to the "consistent use and meaning" of ἡ γραφή in the NT.[60] Wolfe offers four arguments in defense of his thesis. First, Wolfe appeals to the writer's comment in 1 Tim 5:18 in which he speaks of Scripture (ἡ γραφή) and then appears to cite Luke 10:7 verbatim. Wolfe contends that the most natural reading of the verse, which begins with the formula, λέγει γὰρ ἡ γραφή, would yield a statement referring to both citations as Scripture.[61] Second, drawing upon the testimony of 1 Tim 6:3, in which the writer speaks of ὑγιαίνουσιν λόγοις τοῖς τοῦ κυρίου ἡμῶν Ἰησοῦ Χριστοῦ, Wolfe

---

Nevertheless, it may be significant that such work at least indicates an intuitive inclination toward an expanded construal of γραφή. See also Eckhard J. Schnabel, who asserts that inspiration, as presented in 2 Tim 3:16, applies equally to the New Testament as to the Old (Schnabel, *Inspiration und Offenbarung*, 34, 35, 150, 159).

59. John P. Meier is unequivocal in his statement, "a member of the Pauline school, an author scholars call 'the Pastor,' threw over his shoulders the pseudonymous cloak of Paul" (Meier, "What Counts as Scripture?" 73). B. Paul Wolfe, while not explicitly declaring himself on the matter of authorship, nevertheless telegraphs in earlier works the same tendency with his frequent references to "the Pastor," along with his assertion that in 1 Tim 5:18, "The Pastor does not follow the exact wording of Paul" (Wolfe, "Scripture in the Pastoral Epistles," 12). Several other remarks through the article reflect the same posture. Also, early in his 1990 dissertation, Wolfe asks, "Has the author of the PE maintained intact the Pauline perspective on Scripture? Is his view a faithful extension of Paul's views on this, or do we see a distortion of the Pauline tradition with regard to Scripture?" (Wolfe, "Place and Use of Scripture," 10). Furthermore, one must note his observation with respect to 1 Cor 9:9 and 1 Tim 5:18, that "the Pastor and Paul were drawing on a common tradition for their understanding and application of this passage" (ibid., 25). These observations notwithstanding, Wolfe seems to presume the Pauline authorship of the PE in his 2010 essay, "Sagacious Use of Scripture," 199–218). Indeed, the essay opens with the remark, "Paul concludes his writing ministry with a strong affirmation of the character and usefulness of Scripture" (ibid., 199).

60. Wolfe, "Scripture in the Pastoral Epistles," 11. Meier mirrors the essential elements of Wolfe's position (Meier, "What Counts as Scripture?" 71–78).

61. Wolfe, "Scripture in the Pastoral Epistles," 13–14; Wolfe, "Sagacious Use of Scripture," 201. See also Meier, who states, "Some claim that the Pastor is not using Luke's gospel but only oral tradition; that hardly fits the designation of *graphe*. Normative or not, Scripture or not, the saying is said to be written . . . it is the second citation, not the first, that fits the Pastor's argument in a smooth and natural way. The second text, not the first, is announced in v. 17 by the choice of the verb 'deem worthy' [*axiousthosan*]" (Meier, "What Counts as Scripture?" 77).

asserts that this writer views Jesus' words as Scripture.[62] Third, Wolfe
then proposes that within the Pastoral Epistles "there is no discrepancy
between the authority attributed to Scripture and that attributed to the
kerygma, of both Jesus and the apostles."[63] Finally, as Wolfe reflects upon
the occurrences and usage of παράδοσις, ὑγιαίνω, and similar terms in
these letters, he determines that "this terminology indicates a Christian
παράδοσις (tradition) which has come to be recognized as having inherent authority equal to that of Scripture itself."[64]

By comparison with most of the views surveyed thus far, H. Wayne
House and Eckhard J. Schnabel together represent a mediating position.
Neither one opposes the possibility that 1 Tim 5:18 and 2 Tim 3:16 may
include NT writings in their references to ἡ γραφή and πᾶσα γραφή. In
an article discussing basic canon issues, Schnabel observes of 2 Tim 3:16
and 2 Pet 1:20–21, "The authority of the Hebrew Bible was grounded
in the conviction that its content, indeed its very words, were divine
revelation."[65] In the next paragraph, Schnabel then suggests, "It is by no
means impossible that the notion of a new and additional set of normative Scripture for the 'new covenant' on a par with the Scriptures of the
'old covenant' was born already in early apostolic times."[66] With respect
to the possibility that Paul may cite the Gospel of Luke, Adolf Schlatter
maintains the likelihood that Paul was well acquainted with our written gospels.[67] Ceslas Spicq stands in company with House, Schnabel, and
Schlatter, though he does take a more definitive position relative to 1 Tim
5:18, describing the second clause as "The oldest citation of a gospel word
as 'Scripture.'"[68]

Of the scholarly literature consulted to date, George W. Knight's
work reflects a position most closely resembling the thesis proposed in

62. Wolfe, "Scripture in the Pastoral Epistles," 14; Wolfe, "Sagacious Use of Scripture," 214.

63. Wolfe, "Scripture in the Pastoral Epistles," 14.

64. Ibid.

65. Schnabel, "History, Theology, and the Biblical Canon," 18a. See also, House,
"Biblical Inspiration," 56–57.

66. Ibid. Schnabel then follows with, "It would therefore not be necessary to assume that Christians used the term 'Scripture' (*graphe*) for their own normative
tradition only after their final break with the synagogue" (ibid.). See also Schnabel,
Inspiration und Offenbarung, 118.

67. Schlatter, *Die Kirche der Griechen*, 151.

68. Spicq, *Les Épitres Pastorales*, 177, 377.

this study. With respect to λέγει γὰρ ἡ γραφή in 1 Tim 5:18, Knight anchors his argument in the assertion that forms of the clause ἡ γραφὴ λέγει occur "almost exclusively in Paul," and that ἡ γραφή functions throughout the NT "exclusively with a sacred meaning, of Holy Scripture."[69] He then observes that the second citation of verse 18 is "identical to Jesus' words in Luke 10:7," maintaining further that Paul attributes to Jesus' teachings the same authority ascribed to Moses and the OT writings.[70] Knight's discussion of πᾶσα γραφή in 2 Tim 3:16 has its roots in the observation that, since it occurs in a text parallel to 3:15, in which we find τὰ ἱερὰ γράμματα as a virtually certain reference to the OT writings, πᾶσα γραφή must signify at least these same writings. Furthermore, such an understanding reflects the typical New Testament usage of γραφή.[71] Knight then proposes that, in his use of ἡ γραφή instead of τὰ ἱερὰ γράμματα, Paul may signal a more expansive body of writings, inclusive of but extending beyond the OT. If such is the case, this expansion would entail "those accounts of the gospel that may have been extant and perhaps also his own and other apostolic writings that have been 'taught by the spirit.'"[72]

As the preceding review demonstrates, prior stances regarding provenance do not necessarily exert as much determinative influence over the interpretations of these letters as might be expected. While Fee, Johnson, Mounce, and Towner, among others, all disagree with Bassler, Collins, Cook, Oberlinner, Roloff, Weiser, and others with

69. Knight, *Pastoral Epsitles*, 233. For the record, forms of ἡ γραφὴ λέγει occur in the New Testament twelve times, four of which appear in John's gospel and two of which may be found in James. Of the remaining six, four appear in Romans and one each occurs in Galatians and 1 Timothy.

70. Ibid., 234. Knight further argues that since γραφή typically refers to something written, and the citation precisely reflects not only the sense but also the form of the text of Luke 10, "the source of these words would seem to be Luke's gospel" (ibid.).

71. Ibid., 445.

72. Ibid., 448. While Knight emphasizes that "we can only say that this is a possibility that should be considered alongside the other" (ibid.), he also points out that the expanded understanding at least suits the context, for it "provides a reason for Paul's use of γραφή and for his change from ἱερὰ γράμματα, an OT designation to πᾶσα γραφή, a possibly more inclusive term" (ibid.). It probably would be more profitable to ask why Paul would use τὸ γράμμα to refer to the OT (a usage unique in the NT), instead of the more characteristic γραφή. An additional piece of Knight's argument entails a brief survey of other expressions in 2 Timothy that he views as parallel to γραφή, such as references to the writer's teaching (3:10), what Timothy has learned from Paul (3:14), the pattern of "sound words" (1:13), and "the word of truth" (2:15) (ibid.). This suggestion seems correct, although it still requires a careful and systematic development in order to prove compelling.

respect to the authorship and compositional date of the letters to Timo-thy, they essentially agree in their interpretations of ἡ γραφή and πᾶσα γραφή in 1 and 2 Timothy. At the same time, while Oberlinner does not attach much importance to any particular source for ἄξιος ὁ ἐργάτης τοῦ μισθοῦ αὐτοῦ, he acknowledges that the context at least permits πᾶσα γραφή to include NT writings alongside the Hebrew Scriptures as its referent. In a similar vein, while Meier and Wolfe both write from the standpoint of the pseudonymity of the letters to Timothy,[73] they also manifest a more determined commitment than House, Knight, or Sch-nabel to a construal of γραφή in 1 and 2 Timothy that would imply that scriptural standing was attributed to at least some writings now com-prising the NT. It is difficult to say whether such a scenario indicates the elusiveness of firm historical data respecting the letters to Timothy or the potentially circular nature of the interplay between assumptions and interpretive decisions. However, the fact of such divergent points of view respecting both provenance and interpretation does hint at a fairly open field of possibilities in which the most stable, objective, and sharable data may be found in the texts themselves.[74]

Method and Contribution of This Study

Whether electing to trust the most transparent reading and apparent situation of the letters to Timothy or not, we still must come to terms with the material as it presents itself in the texts. Thus, the point of departure for this investigation lies in the premise of the value and pri-macy of the text—the most immediate and accessible data.[75] Further-more, while the positions represented by Artola, Blanchard, Kaiser, and Piñero are compatible with the thesis of this work, their predominantly

73. It already has been acknowledged, however, that Wolfe does not explicitly declare a position on authorship, and in different works, he seems to reflect both main views.

74. "Sharability" provides a key element in determinative meaning and is a term explained by E. D. Hirsch, who proposes, "A single principle underlies what we loosely call 'the norms of language.' It is the principle of sharability . . . the capacity of language to represent all conceivable meanings is ultimately limited only by the overarching prin-ciple of sharability" (Hirsch, *Validity in Interpretation*, 31). See also ibid., 47, 49, 67.

75. Such data would include the establishment and stability of the text itself, the most apparent intent of the author as expressed in the text (as opposed to attempts to read a hidden message behind the text), and the self-testimony of these letters regard-ing their author and addressee.

theological approach—as opposed to textual or exegetical—renders them susceptible to Reck's commentary regarding the early churches' lack of attention to the intent of the author in their appropriation of these texts, especially 2 Tim 3:16.[76] Setting up the main body of the study, chapter 2 shall offer a brief assessment of the issues of Pauline authorship, an examination of Pauline eschatology and its relationship to authorship and the very idea of a biblical canon, and a discussion of the unity of both letters to Timothy.[77]

The heart of this work, appearing in chapters 3 through 6, consists of a study that exegetically traces the ideas attending γραφή and its related terms through the letters to Timothy. It shall treat each document independently and as an organic whole in its own right, devoting two chapters to each book: one that traces the discourse and semantic development through each letter in its entirety as it pertains to γραφή and its usage, and one that argues for a specific construal of γραφή in the immediate literary context containing each occurrence. These chapters will employ a grammatical-historical approach that will seek to discern and work in correspondence with the most apparent intent of the writer.[78] Accordingly, this study will not present itself as a thorough commentary upon the epistles. Rather, it will identify and follow the primary concern and thesis running through each letter by means of tracking the syntax and the relationships between discrete ideas. In the process, the examination will mark the occurrences and development of the various terms that Paul uses to refer to the teachings he seeks to commend and guard, and it will investigate the usage of each, paying special attention to the semantic overlap and correspondence between such terms.[79]

76. Reck, "2 Tim 3,16 in der altkirchlichen Literatur," 105.

77. While it has already been suggested that Pauline authorship need not be determinative in the discussion of γραφή, the fact remains that the supposition of the pseudepigraphy of the PE stands as one conventional objection to the position of this study. Thus, a brief defense of Pauline authorship is offered so as to answer that objection.

78. As distinct from the classic "Historical-Critical Method." See, for instance, Balla, *Challenges to New Testament*, 3–4, 16; Bray, *Biblical Interpretation*, 354–56; Hirsch, *Validity in Interpretation*, 8, 10, 26; Soulen and Soulen, *Handbook of Biblical Criticism*, 78–80.

79. This includes terms such as γράμμα, γραφή, διδασκαλία, διδάσκω, διδαχή, εὐαγγέλιον, λόγος, παρατίθημι, ὀρθοτομέω, and ὑγιαίνω, among others, along with the recurring elliptical clause πιστὸς ὁ λογός. The kind of inductive analysis proposed here also traces what Van Neste calls "semantic chains," a term designating "a set of words in a discourse which are related to each other semantically because they refer to the

In chapter 7, the study shall survey the uses of γραφή in the writings of Philo, Josephus, the Greek translation of the OT (LXX), the NT, and the Apostolic Fathers. An assessment of כתב in the MT will appear alongside the survey of the LXX. Since the present work is based upon the primacy of exegesis and word treatment in context for determining the most likely intent behind Paul's use of γραφή, the word study occurs after the exegetical chapters so that it may not be seen to circumscribe the exegetical conclusions prematurely.

The study will conclude in chapter 8 with a final reflection upon γραφή in each of the two passages mentioned at the outset, 1 Tim 5:18 and 2 Tim 3:16–17. This final discussion shall address the function of γραφή in the overall aim of each letter, along with some of the implications of the broad study for the larger question of Scripture and canon.

Three aspects of this study mark it as unique. First, the notion that Paul likely used interchangeable terms such as ἡ γραφή, ἡ διδασκαλία, ἡ διδαχή, τὸ εὐαγγέλιον, ὁ λόγος, and ἡ παραθήκη, among others, serves as a strategic hypothesis that will be tested throughout. Second, in view of that possibility, this study will attempt to ascertain a consistent understanding of Scripture (γραφή) shared by both letters, while treating each letter as its own distinct document. Third, the method employed here will render the establishment of a *prior* and *fixed* position regarding authorship and background unnecessary to the interpretation of the textual material, even though it will be impossible to avoid implications regarding this issue. At the same time, it will honor the most apparent intent of the human author. As a result, this study will offer a demonstrably historical, critical, and exegetical treatment of the letters to Timothy, focused especially on 1 Tim 5:18 and 2 Tim 3:16–17.

---

same person/concept or to the same general class of people/concepts" (Van Neste, *Cohesion and Structure*, 16). Over the course of the present work, these also are referred to as "semantic streams," "semantic threads," or collectively as "discourse flow." See also Reed, "Cohesive Ties in 1 Timothy," 131–47; Reed, "Discourse Features," 228–52.

CHAPTER 2

The Authorship and Unity of the Letters to Timothy

As STATED IN THE first chapter, while authorship in itself neither confirms nor discredits the interpretation proposed for γραφή, the widely supposed pseudepigraphy of the PE stands as one conventional objection to the wider conclusion of this study. Similarly, the unity of these letters also affects the broader discussion, specifically in terms of the significance of the findings concerning γραφή and the implications of these findings for matters of biblical authority and the biblical canon. In the case of authorship, the sense and function of γραφή bear more critical implications if Paul himself wrote these letters, and if they were familiar to believers of the first generation, than if they were written pseudonymously. If, as this study argues, the referents of γραφή in both 1 Tim 5:18 and 2 Tim 3:16 include both the OT writings and some of the apostolic writings, Pauline authorship would indicate that Paul consciously viewed his writings and at least one of the gospels as standing alongside the Law, Prophets, and Writings as God-inspired and authoritative documents. A second factor follows upon the first, for a strong case for Pauline authorship and Paul's consciousness of having written Scripture presents a significant challenge to those who question the legitimacy of an authoritative Bible or a biblical canon at all.[1]

At the same time, the unity (or otherwise) of the two letters to Timothy has considerable bearing upon the force of their composite

---

1. This recalls the brief discussion in chapter 1 concerning Barr, Ehrmann, McDonald, Pagels, and more recently, Allert, *High View of Scripture?*, among others.

testimony regarding Paul's use and understanding of γραφή. In this study, unity shall not be assumed. This way, neither work may be permitted to exert determinative influence on the interpretation of the other; the best that such an approach could achieve would amount to a kind of exegetical circularity. However, once each document has been surveyed and each discrete construal of γραφή has been proposed, the findings will be considered side-by-side, as it were, for comparison and further reflection upon their composite significance. Should it be shown that the author does indeed use this term consistently as a reference to both apostolic writings and the OT writings, it then will be possible to extrapolate from the findings of the exegetical study the general assertion that γραφή in fact does acquire a widely recognized and virtually technical function as early as the apostolic age, at times denoting as authoritative Scripture even some of the apostolic writings. This point in turn would challenge the idea that all sense of an authoritative "canon" derived only during or after the second century.

The Question of Authorship

For the purposes of this study, Pauline authorship serves as a working premise. Accordingly, while discussion of authorship will not be exhaustive, a brief defense of the affirmation of Pauline authorship follows below so as to demonstrate that this working premise is not without warrant. Extended analyses of the authorship of the letters to Timothy appear in several modern works, some of which offer thorough arguments in defense of the authenticity and Pauline composition of the two epistles.[2] Thus, while some of these arguments will be summarized here, they will not be reproduced in their entirety. Following these summaries, several additional details—some of them emerging as subtle and apparently incidental features nearly hidden in the fabric of the documents

---

2. Among those arguing for Pauline authorship, see Fee, *Timothy and Titus*, 1–31; Johnson, *Letters to Timothy*, 20–97; Knight, *Pastoral Epistles*, 4–52; Mounce, *Pastoral Epistles*, xlvii–cxxix; Spicq, *Les Épîtres Pastorales*, xcv–cxxx; Towner, *Letters to Timothy and Titus*, 1–89; Witherington, *Letters and Homilies*, 23–75. However, Witherington does qualify his position, proposing, "The voice is the voice of Paul, but the hand is the hand of Luke" (ibid., 60). It also should be noted that Marshall, while attempting to establish a position of "allonymity," more than once observes that the context, apparent historical setting, ecclesiastical structure, and even writing style and lexis are not necessarily incompatible with Pauline authorship (Marshall, *Pastoral Epistles*, 47, 52, 71, 78).

themselves—will be brought forward for consideration. These details will serve to strengthen the case for Pauline authorship.

To begin with (and often an undervalued factor in discussions of the authorship of 1 and 2 Timothy), these letters present themselves from the outset as genuine Pauline compositions and as occasional documents written into actual historic situations and prepared for actual addressees.[3] Thus, even if the opening words of the epistle reflect precisely what one might expect were it the product of a writer attempting to assume a Pauline persona so as to write under his name and authority,[4] they also are what one would expect if the writing is genuinely Pauline.[5] Similar opening salutations may also be found at the beginnings of several Pauline epistles: specifically, Romans, 1 and 2 Corinthians, Galatians, Ephesians, Philippians, and Colossians.[6] Consequently, apart from a compelling

3. Knight writes, "The letters all claim to be by Paul the apostle of Christ Jesus, and this assertion is made in salutations similar to those in the other Pauline letters . . . The letters refer to specific events and places and are written in relation to these events . . . The self-testimony of the letters is most explicit in the identification of the author in the first verse of each letter, but it is also found in the repeated and pervasive personal references that the author makes about himself and about his relationships with the addressees and other individuals" (Knight, *Pastoral Epistles*, 4, 6). See also Johnson, *Letters to Timothy*, 98; Mounce, *Pastoral Epistles*, xlvii; Witherington, *Letters and Homilies*, 50. Terry Wilder also argues that the false attribution of a document to an apostolic writer would not have been an acceptable practice in the first century, since there was a sense of "literary property, which could not be violated" (Wilder, *Pseudonymity, the New Testament, and Deception*, 60).

4. Dibelius and Conzelmann would seem to reflect this position as they state, "The form of the prescript is taken from the Pauline epistles" (Dibelius and Conzelmann, *Commentary on the Pastoral Epistles*, 13). Cesare Marcheselli-Casale, an adherent of pseudepigraphy, nevertheless observes, "Surely, this is typical of the great Pauline letters, it is of the flavor of Paul, but not by the hand Paul" (Marcheselli-Casale, *Le Lettere Pastorali*, 77). See also ibid., 25. Marshall suggests, "The greeting itself is the normal Pauline one. . . . If the letter is not directly from Paul, the effect is still to enhance the authority of what is taught and hence of any church leader who tries to lead his congregation according to Pauline teaching" (Marshall, *Pastoral Epistles*, 353–54). Later, Marshall adds, "The opening is intended to give an impression of authenticity and get down to the evils to be confronted without delay" (ibid., 360). See also Oberlinner, *Erster Timotheusbrief*, 1; Wolter, *Die Pastoralbriefe als Paulustradition*, 27.

5. Bassler observes, "The letter's salutation conforms to Paul's established formula (itself derived from Hellenistic and Jewish letter-writing conventions)" (Bassler, *1 Timothy, 2 Timothy*, 35). Spicq also states, "In accordance with his almost general usage, Paul begins his letter by underlining his authority of apostle, which comes to him from God" (Spicq, *Les Épîtres Pastorales*, 1).

6. Johnson, *Letters to Timothy*, 157; Knight, *Pastoral Epistles*, 57; Mounce, *Pastoral Epistles*, 4; Pirot and Clamer, *La Sainte Bible*, 205; Spicq, *Les Épîtres Pastorales*, 1;

demonstration of the improbability of Pauline authorship, a summary dismissal of the *prima facie* evidence of the self-attestation of these letters seems hasty and without reason. Indeed, it all too frequently goes unmentioned that all of the positive data currently available ratify rather than challenge the internal testimony of the letters.

Second, the overwhelming tide of interpretive history from the Apostolic Fathers until 1807 treats all three of the PE as authentic letters, each having its own unique message and composition tailored to its own set of circumstances.[7] For example, in addition to indications that Polycarp of Smyrna knew and used Paul's letters to Timothy in his own correspondence,[8] one may find details that suggest not only that Polycarp may have *used* 1 Timothy, but also that he probably *intended to cite Paul*, as he writes,

> οὔτε γὰρ ἐγὼ οὔτε ἄλλος ὅμοιος ἐμοὶ δύναται κατακολουθῆσαι τῇ σοφίᾳ τοῦ μακαρίου καὶ ἐνδόξου Παύλου, ὃς γενόμενος ἐν ὑμῖν κατὰ πρόσωπον τῶν τότε ἀνθρώπων, ἐδίδαξεν ἀκριβῶς καὶ βεβαίως τὸν περὶ ἀληθείας λόγον, ὃς καὶ ἀπὼν ὑμῖν ἔγραψεν ἐπιστολάς.[9]

Furthermore, Polycarp's reference to Paul, and his use of τὸν περὶ ἀληθείας λόγον in *Phil.* 3:2—reminiscent of τὸν λόγον τῆς ἀληθείας of 2 Tim 2:15, and falling as it does in such close proximity to almost certain allusions to 1 Tim 6:7 and 6:10—is also suggestive, and may indicate a

---

Towner, *Letters to Timothy and Titus*, 94–95.

7. Spicq argues, "But as these epistles are surely cited by saint Ignatius and Polycarp, one cannot put off their composition to later than the year 110" (Spicq, *Les Épîtres Pastorales*, lxxiii). See also Witherington, *Letters and Homilies*, 50. With respect to the subsequent ages, Johnson writes, "Until the nineteenth century, it was possible to touch on interpretations of 1 and 2 Timothy without reference to Titus. This is because although the resemblance among the letters was known, they were regarded as real letters written to real people, and therefore to be interpreted, as the rest of Paul's letters, with reference to the situation described in the letters and to the rest of the Pauline corpus" (Johnson, *Letters to Timothy*, 98).

8. Such as allusions to 1 Tim 6:10 (ῥίζα γὰρ πάντων τῶν κακῶν ἐστιν ἡ φιλαργυρία) and 6:7 (οὐδὲν γὰρ εἰσηνέγκαμεν εἰς τὸν κόσμον, ὅτι οὐδὲ ἐξενεγκεῖν τι δυνάμεθα) in his letter to the Philippian believers, where he writes, Ἀρχὴ δὲ πάντων χαλεπῶν φιλαργυρία. εἰδότες οὖν ὅτι οὐδὲν εἰσηνέγκαμεν εἰς τὸν κόσμον, ἀλλ'οὐδὲ ἐξενεγκεῖν τι ἔχομεν (Polycarp, *Phil.*, 4.1).

9. Ibid., 3.2–3. Furthermore, after Johnson remarks upon this very point, he proceeds to the next implication: "If Polycarp knew and used these letters and considered them to be by Paul, then their composition has to substantially precede his own" (Johnson, *Letters to Timothy*, 20, 299).

familiarity with 2 Timothy as well.[10] These factors are noteworthy relative to both authorship and date of composition.

Third, while the historical situations that seem to lie behind these letters fall outside the evidence found in other canonical writings, they are not thereby necessarily incompatible with those writings. In fact, at least partial corroboration for these historical situations may be found in the writings of Eusebius and the Apostolic Fathers. For instance, Eusebius, probably writing in a period between 311 and 315, reports of Paul's imprisonment in Rome,

> Tradition has it that after defending himself the Apostle was again sent on the ministry of preaching, and coming a second time to the city suffered martyrdom under Nero. During this imprisonment he wrote the second Epistle to Timothy, indicating at the same time that his first defense had taken place and that his martyrdom was at hand ... We have said this to show that Paul's martyrdom was not accomplished during the sojourn in Rome which Luke describes.[11]

Prior to this writing, Clement of Rome also testified of Paul's ministry, referring to journeys and trials that do not appear in Acts or the other Pauline writings. He writes,

> Seven times he bore chains; he was sent into exile and stoned; he served as a herald in both the East and the West; and he received the noble reputation for his faith. He taught righteousness to the whole world, and came to the limits of the West, bearing his witness before the rulers ...[12]

10. Polycarp, *Phil.*, 3.2. Kenneth Berding's observations concerning Polycarp's tendency to cluster references to Paul has bearing on this point as well. He writes, "If ... Polycarp tends to group references from the Pauline Epistles around explicit namings of Paul, and there is a quotation from 1 or 2 Timothy in two of these clusters, it can be plausibly argued that Polycarp (rightly or wrongly) understood Paul to be the author of these two epistles" (Berding, "Polycarp of Smyrna's View," 349). See also ibid., 356.

11. Eusebius, *Ecclesiastical History*, 2:22.1–5, 7. Knight comments upon Eusebius' remarks, adding that there exists no evidence to contradict his testimony (Knight, *Pastoral Epistles*, 19–20).

12. *1 Clem.*, 5.6–7.

In addition, Johnson points out that the undisputed Pauline letters of Romans, 2 Corinthians, and Galatians all report some details of Paul's ministry not found in Acts or in other biblical material.[13]

Fourth, with respect to the historical circumstances from which the letters derive, no one has yet offered a positive reconstruction for the setting and composition of these letters that surpasses their own internal testimony in plausibility.[14] Not only so, the supposed advanced development of ecclesiastical structure does not fit with the evidence as found even in other Pauline writings.[15] Also related to setting, the claim that the PE reflect a transition in the life of the church from an ethos of vital charismata and the expectation of an imminent *parousia* to a state of more settled and institutional existence fails to reflect the heart of Pauline eschatology.[16] Indeed, upon surveying the eschatology of Paul, it seems that the supposed expectation of an imminent return may be overstated in the first place. For example, while Hermann Ridderbos observes that Paul likely did expect to be alive when Christ returned, he nevertheless points out,

13. Johnson, *Letters to Timothy*, 68. As Mounce also observes, "It is argued that the historical events referred to (in) the PE do not fit into the time frame of Acts and are therefore fictitious . . . This argument has significance only if Acts must tell the entire story . . . In light of the frequent scholarly distrust of the reliability of Acts, it is interesting that here its reliability becomes the standard against which the PE are judged" (Mounce, *Pastoral Epistles*, lxxxiv–lxxxv). Spicq also suggests "One will see that, if these historical and personal notations of the Pastorals cannot be explained from the life of Saint Paul between 57 and 63, they keep all of their merit with respect to realism between the years 63 and 67" (Spicq, *Les Épîtres Pastorales*, lxxiv). See also Mounce, *Pastoral Epistles*, liv–lvi.

14. Johnson summarizes his assessment of conventional solutions to the origins of the Pastoral Epistles accordingly: "One of the major challenges to the majority view has been the inability to provide a truly convincing setting for the production of these three letters" (Johnson, *Letters to Timothy*, 86).

15. Johnson, *Letters to Timothy*, 75–76; Knight, *Pastoral Epistles*, 29–31; Spicq, *Les Épîtres Pastorales*, xliii–li; Towner, *Letters to Timothy and Titus*, 50–52.

16. Among those adducing the supposed shift in eschatology as evidence of the non-Pauline authorship of the PE, see Collins, *Timothy and Titus*, 11–13; Dibelius and Conzelmann, *Commentary on the Pastoral Epistles*, 1; Fiore, *Pastoral Epistles*, 5–6. For example, Collins asserts, "Now that the expectation of an imminent Parousia was no longer theirs, believers were constrained to organize themselves" (Collins, *Timothy and Titus*, 13). Similarly, Fiore claims, "The *parousia* is still awaited, but not with Paul's original urgency" (Fiore, *Pastoral Epistles*, 5). Marshall, while not offering the same kind of terse declaration, nevertheless suggests, "The PE . . . represent . . . a more realistic response to the needs of a church which could not live indefinitely on the high level of Spirit-inspired enthusiasm which Paul had envisaged . . . There has been a loss of vitality compared with Pauline Christianity" (Marshall, *Pastoral Epistles*, 97).

One will thus be allowed to conclude that living to see the parousia was for Paul indeed a real possibility, we may perhaps say the object of his hope and expectation, but that both for his own faith and for his paraenesis this expectation was in no way a *conditio sine qua non.* The force of his expectation for the future and of his paranaesis is to be sure dependent on the appearing of Christ in glory, and on its significance for the present, but not on still being alive to see this appearing.[17]

Also, even considering the proposal that Paul's perspective actually changed during his own lifetime, in a possible shift that may be tracked through the two letters to the Corinthians, Ridderbos again acknowledges that such a shift would have occurred in a one-year or two-year time span, hardly a situation that signals a radical departure from a fixed eschatological point of view.[18] Thomas Schreiner also weighs in on the matter of Paul's perspective, arguing,

Obviously Paul died before the Lord returned, and thus it appears that he was mistaken, for he speaks of remaining until the parousia. The problem is more apparent than real . . . First, Paul would probably have been astonished to find that two thousand years have passed since he wrote 1 Thessalonians. He did expect the Lord to return relatively soon. Saying this, however, is not to say that Paul erred in what he said about Christ's coming. Second, nowhere does Paul actually specify a timetable that delimits when the Lord will return. He expected the Lord to come soon, but he had no certainty as to when the Lord would return . . . Third, when Paul wrote 1 Thessalonians he did not know if he would live or die before the second coming. By speaking of "we," he identifies himself with those who will be alive when the Lord returns . . . When the Thessalonians are summoned to sobriety and to alertness (1 Thess 5:6), Paul is not telling them to calculate, through the reading of signs, the day of the Lord's return. The alertness demanded here is moral, not chronological. Believers show that they are

17. Ridderbos, *Paul: An Outline*, 492. Bruce also notes, with respect to 1 Thess 5, "As for the latter and more general question, *when* the parousia would take place, Paul does little more than repeat the words of Jesus, that it would come unexpectedly, 'like a thief in the night'" (Bruce, *Paul: Apostle of the Heart*, 306).

18. Ridderbos, *Paul: An Outline*, 491–92. Bruce also writes, "Be it noted . . . that while it affected his personal perspective, the 'deferment of the parousia,' caused no such fundamental change in his thought as it is sometimes held to have caused in the thought of the church as a whole" (Bruce, *Paul: Apostle of the Heart*, 305–10).

alert and prepared for the Lord's coming by living in a way that
pleases him every day.[19]

In addition, Robert Yarbrough marks one highly specific detail that
reinforces the notion of a basic continuity in Paul's eschatology (or at
least in the eschatology between the PE and the undisputed Pauline writings). As Yarbrough observes, there is a remarkable correspondence in
content and form between Paul's assertion in Rom 6:8, εἰ δὲ ἀπεθάνομεν
σὺν Χριστῷ, πιστεύομεν ὅτι καὶ συζήσομεν αὐτῷ, and that found in 2 Tim
2:11, which reads, εἰ γὰρ συναπεθάνομεν, καὶ συζήσομεν.[20] The significance
of this observation lies in the fact that, in both instances, the promise of
sharing in Christ's resurrection derives from identifying with him in his
death—an identification that is manifested in one's ethical response to the
gospel message. Considering these points, the eschatological perspective
of the PE does not seem so incompatible with the rest of Paul's eschatology after all, with the result that the historical aspect of Pauline authorship is much less vulnerable on this front than is sometimes alleged.[21]

Fifth, the matters of vocabulary and writing style that often are
deemed unique to the PE cannot be said to prove anything of substance.
Any observable difference between these letters and the remaining Pauline writings in terms of purpose and subject matter, and in terms of their
association with close ministry partners (as opposed to congregations),
surely must be taken into consideration when attempting to evaluate lexis
and writing style.[22]

19. Schreiner, *Paul: Apostle of God's Glory*, 461–62.

20. Yarbrough, "Theology of Romans," 51.

21. Thus, Fee writes, "It is sometimes argued that the eschatological perspective of
the PE is different from this, that Paul now expects to die before the Parousia . . . It would
seem, however, that much of this objection is the result of a prior commitment to a point
of view. For, in reality, the eschatology of these letters is thoroughly Pauline. As in other
settings (cf. 2 Thess 2:3, 7), the present apostasy is seen in terms of the eschatological
woes of the End (1 Tim 4:1; 2 Tim 3:1)" (Fee, *Timothy and Titus*, 19). See also Canoy,
"Teaching Eschatology," 249–60; De Boer, "Paul, Theologian," 21–33; Green, "La muerte
y el poder del Imperio," 9–26; Hafemann, "Eschatology and Ethics," 161–92; Harrison,
"Paul and the Imperial Gospel," 71–96; Kuck, "The Freedom of Being in the World 'As
If Not,'" 585–93; Ladd, *Theology of the New Testament*, 595–602; Schreiner, *Paul: Apostle
of God's Glory*, 455–63; Thomas, "Imminence in the NT," 191–214; Towner, *Goal of Our
Instruction*, 72–74; Yarbrough, "Theology of Romans," 46–60.

22. Even Marshall, after presenting a survey of the language of the PE, observes,
"The use of non-Pauline words tends to be most evident when the writer is dealing
with topics, such as the heresy or the qualifications for church leaders, which are
not addressed in the accepted letters of Paul; the unusual vocabulary is thus in some

In addition to this, in *The Problem of the Pastoral Epistles*, the most prominent modern analysis of the peculiar lexis of the PE to date, P. N. Harrison appears to overreach himself and undermine his own argument. Specifically, while Harrison is adamant in his denial of the generally Pauline authorship of the PE, he demonstrates an equally vigorous certainty that the personal remarks found in these letters do in fact come from Paul's own writings, though in the form of textual borrowing from documents no longer available to scholars.[23] In the process of accounting thusly for these personal remarks, Harrison undermines his own thesis in two ways. First, he supposes that a writer had the perspicacity to borrow from genuine Pauline material in order to affect the Pauline feel of the personal remarks, but was so otherwise negligent that he did not think to borrow material for the rest of these letters. Such an argument begs the question as to which scenario truly is more likely: a thoroughly un-Pauline pseudonymous letter sprinkled with genuine Pauline personal remarks, or a genuine Pauline letter with didactic and polemic material previously unseen in his other extant letters.[24] Second,

---

measure due to the unusual subject-matter" (Marshall, *Pastoral Epistles*, 61). Later, Marshall writes, "There is nothing here that Paul himself could not have done with his broad background in both Palestinian and Hellenistic Judaism" (ibid., 78). Dibelius and Conzelmann, though assuming the pseudonymity of the Pastoral Epistles, also caution, "One must be careful in drawing conclusions as to authenticity or imitation, since there are no other Pauline letters addressed to a single person" (Dibelius and Conzelmann, *Commentary on the Pastoral Epistles*, 14). See also Knight, *Pastoral Epistles*, 23–24; Johnson, *Letters to Timothy*, 71; Mounce, *Pastoral Epistles*, xcix; Witherington, *Letters and Homilies*, 55, 67. Among those addressing Harrison's argument directly, see Carrington, "Problem of the Pastoral Epistles," 32–39; Guthrie, *Pastoral Epistles*, 53–55; Guthrie, *Mind of Paul*, 5–15; Roberts, "Bearing of the Use of Particles," 132–37.

23. Indeed, he writes, "This author must have had before his eyes, and has incorporated bodily into his epistles and so has preserved for all time, a certain amount of genuine Pauline material, which cannot be identified with any of the surviving epistles, and would otherwise, in all human probability, have been lost beyond recall . . . These Personalia are so vivid, so concrete, so entirely in the vein of the references to be found in every letter that Paul ever wrote, that, we may safely assert, no one would ever have dreamed of doubting their authenticity, had it not been for the context in which they occur" (Harrison, *Problem of the Pastoral Epistles*, 93). See also ibid., 93–135.

24. Johnson expresses the same idea accordingly: "The hypothesis invites us to contemplate a forger sufficiently attuned to stylistic niceties to be able to seek the use of the proposed fragments as a way of conveying to others the 'Pauline' character of his pseudepigraphy, yet so stylistically inept as to be unable to replicate that style in the portions he writes himself" (Johnson, *Letters to Timothy*, 72). Miller marks the same problem, observing, "With the models of ten Pauline letters before him, and

by positing other "genuine Pauline material" that is no longer available (requiring at least five separate documents by his own reckoning), Harrison enlarges the stylistic and lexical "fingerprint" by at least half again as many documents with which he must work as before, without having the means to survey and evaluate this additional hypothetical material. At this point, it becomes even more meaningless to propose a representative Pauline lexis and style, since this additional hypothetical material very well could reflect a lexical and idiomatic style commensurate with the material found in the PE.[25]

These items aside, the fact remains that the currently prevailing position, notwithstanding the complete absence of positive data attesting to any author other than Paul,[26] maintains that someone other than Paul actually wrote them, and that he did so some years after the death of the apostle. As one example of the intractability of this position, one must consider the case of Fiore, who affirms the pseudepigraphy of these letters with relatively little argument in spite of observing at the very outset of his introduction,

the concern to make his pseudepigraphic writings appear authentic, it is hard to understand why a pseudonymous author would not take more care in conforming the epistolary format of the Pastorals to that of the other Paulines . . . Conforming the Pastorals to the style of the other Paulines would contribute, one would think, to the verisimilitude needed in a pseudonymous undertaking of this kind" (Miller, *Composite Documents*, 8–9). James Aageson also remarks, "Paul, of course, would not emulate himself, as would someone writing pseudepigraphically in the name of Paul" (Aageson, "Pastoral Epistles, Apostolic Authority," 6). David Cook, on the other hand, argues for the first scenario (Cook, "2 Timothy 4:6–8," 168–71; Cook, "Pastoral Fragments Reconsidered," 120–31).

25. This problem attends every composite theory relative to the authorship of the PE. With respect to Harrison's core hypothesis, E. Earle Ellis also points out, "Harrison found an excessively high number of 'Hapaxes per page' in the Pastorals; but he neglected to mention that these letters have a high number of 'words per page'; and that in proportion to 'words per book' the percentage of Hapaxes in the Pastorals was not greatly different from other Pauline letters" (Ellis, *Paul and His Recent Interpreters*, 54).

26. Relative to Schleiermacher, Johnson remarks, "What impresses the reader who has moved through all the prior history of interpretation is the sheer self-confidence to declare, with very little substantial argumentation—Schleiermacher's book, after all, is quite short—against the entire preceding tradition" (Johnson, *Letters to Timothy*, 43). Mounce points out, "Nowhere does the author of the PE say something that is necessarily contradictory to Paul's teaching" (Mounce, *Pastoral Epistles*, xcviii). Towner also offers an important observation regarding method, noting, "It is far too convenient for the majority view to elevate the areas of alleged Pauline dissimilarity as evidence of discontinuity while dismissing the points of similarity as part of a fiction. This is a methodological flaw" (Towner, *Letters to Timothy and Titus*, 24).

Paul ordinarily wrote his letters to Christian communities in a particular city or region. Even the letter to Philemon includes other named individuals and the entire house church among the addressees. The Pastoral Epistles stand out as exceptions in that they are addressed to individual recipients: Timothy, for two letters, and Titus. Moreover, the recipients have the same relationship to the sender. They are his dear children in the faith, and they are given the responsibility of organizing and supervising Christians across a large geographic area (Crete) or metropolitan region (Ephesus). As such, these relatively young church leaders have doctrinal and jurisdictional authority unlike the authority of the church leaders identified in Paul's other letters, and even Timothy himself in those letters.[27]

Even with such observations regarding the unique complexion of the PE, the non-Pauline authorship of these letters has attained the status of virtual axiom across the discipline of biblical studies, no longer requiring an argument, but practically demanding universal subscription by virtue of critical mass.[28] However, while the non-Pauline authorship of the letters to Timothy enjoys widespread and frequently uncritical acceptance, the variations of this basic position all raise additional issues that lack plausible or satisfactory solutions.

Beyond the familiar arguments in defense of Pauline authorship summarized above, several additional features emerge from the text and manuscripts of the documents themselves over the course of exegetical analysis that tend to corroborate the self-attestation of the documents. These details, a few of which appear below, are more subtle and narrow in scope than those presented in the more conventional arguments. However, it is proposed here that they must be given substantial weight in the overall assessment, for some of these details fall well outside the control of the original writer, while others lie embedded within the very conceptual and literary fabric of the writings themselves, and likely betray habits

27. Fiore, *Pastoral Epistles*, 5. See also ibid., 6, 16.

28. See Carson and Moo, *Introduction to the New Testament*, 555. Especially pointed is Johnson's comment, to the effect that "the conventional wisdom concerning authenticity moves farther and father from any grounding in evidence and argument, farther and farther from the best and most recent scholarship on Paul himself, and perpetuates itself mainly by force of inertia based on an unexamined majority vote by an increasingly uninformed electorate" (Johnson, *Letters to Timothy*, 90). Knight also states, "Since [the emergence of the 'Tübingen School'] repudiation of the Pauline authorship of the PE has become a mark of critical orthodoxy" (Knight, *Pastoral Epistles*, 21).

of thinking that transcend mere mimicry, borrowing, or other aspects of pseudepigraphy.

Among the many sources that preserve the historical traditions of the church, one that proves surprisingly suggestive consists of the superscriptions found in several of the manuscripts that contain 1 and 2 Timothy. A survey of the data concerning the manuscripts from which the texts of the letters to Timothy derive, as they appear in the NA[27] and the UBS[4], shows that every one of the manuscripts that features some superscription notation—more than twelve hundred documents spanning the fourth to the fourteenth centuries—reflects a preserved tradition of Pauline authorship alone.[29] Put another way, alongside this positive testimony there exists no data, originating from any century, that attests to any other authorship tradition relative to Paul's letters to Timothy. In addition to this, at least two pieces of incidental information that suggest Pauline authorship appear in 1 Tim 1:1–11.

The first bit of data concerns the favorable perspective on the Law, Prophets, and Writings that is found in the letters to Timothy. Specifically, in the assertion that the law has a "lawful" use even though "certain men" appear to misuse and misunderstand it, as in 1 Tim 1:8–11, one may note a concern similar to that found in both Romans and Galatians. In each of these epistles, universally recognized as authentically Pauline, Paul inveighs against Judaism as a system built upon the wrongful pursuit and use of the Law of Moses, while he upholds the worth of that revelatory law in itself when it is rightly, or "lawfully," construed.[30] At the same time,

29. NA[27], 44–83, 684–720; UBS[4], 7–19; Birdsall, "New Testament Text," 308–77; Metzger, *Textual Commentary*, 577–78, 583; Swinson, "Textual Criticism and Authorship Traditions."

30. Concerning 1 Tim 1:8, Aageson remarks, "The writer says that the law is good . . . if one understands that the law is set forth for the lawless and not the innocent (1:8–10). Galatians 3:19, read on its own terms in the context of Galatians, appears to suggest a view of the law that is similar . . . In both texts, the function of the law is to deal with lawlessness and transgressions" (Aageson, "Pastoral Epistles, Apostolic Authority," 23). Dibelius and Conzelmann also observe, "The author reproduces literally a phrase from Paul's reflections on the law (see Rom 7:16, 12), and introduces it with the phrase 'we know' (οἴδαμεν) as an acknowledged principle" (Dibelius and Conzelmann, *Commentary on the Pastoral Epistles*, 22). With regard to 1:8a, Towner writes, "The whole phrase may echo the earlier discussion of one of the law's uses in Rom 7:12–25, and it may consciously recall what Paul said in that discussion about the moral function of the law: 'I agree that that the law is good.' For Timothy and presumably the Ephesian Christian community, such an allusion to Paul's teaching would certainly count as an appeal to apostolic tradition" (Towner, *Letters to Timothy and Titus*, 123).

in the case of pseudepigraphy, one might expect a writer attempting to project a Pauline persona to draw judiciously upon recognizable Pauline expressions in making this point. However, the formulation of the ideas in this passage, while reflecting a patently Pauline *position* concerning the Law of Moses, nevertheless exhibits no sign of *literary dependence* upon the other Pauline epistles. Rather, the language of 1 Tim 1:1–11 assumes the fluid and natural discourse of one at ease with the issue and practiced in the discussion of it.[31]

A similar feature may be observed in 2 Timothy, though it is less direct than in 1 Timothy. After his discussion in 3:14 regarding "the things [Timothy has] learned and come to believe," Paul writes of [τὰ] ἱερὰ γράμματα . . . τὰ δυνάμενά σε σοφίσαι εἰς σωτηρίαν διὰ πίστεως τῆς ἐν Χριστῷ Ἰησοῦ. In this remark, even if the occurrence of πᾶσα γραφή in the following verse may include an understood reference to the apostolic writings, [τὰ] ἱερὰ γράμματα in 3:15 surely denotes the Law, Prophets, and Writings collectively. Consequently, as with 1 Timothy, in 2 Timothy Paul affirms the perpetual authority and legitimacy of Moses and the Prophets, even as he challenges Timothy to uphold the gospel with diligence and courage.[32]

The second matter is of greater complexity than the first, and it arises when one examines more closely how Paul actually handles the text of the OT writings. It lies deeply embedded within the text of these letters, which makes it more likely to reflect a native (and therefore non-imitative) idiom and perspective. As a result, it is both subtler and more compelling than the preceding observation. One significant aspect of this line of analysis lies in marking the distinctive contours that Paul's approach assumes when he cites OT writings as opposed to those instances in which he simply alludes to them.

This discussion begins with a close examination of 1 Tim 1:8–11. In these verses, Paul writes of the "lawful" use of the law, as it stands appointed for various classes of sinners. While examining the types of persons who stand under the scrutiny of the Law, according to Paul, one should attend closely to the vices associated with them, noting especially their sequence. While Paul does not craft an exact one-to-one configuration, such that each vice is set against one command, his list nevertheless

31. Guthrie, *Pastoral Epistles*, 70.

32. Brox, *Die Pastoralbriefe*, 105; Hanson, *Pastoral Letters*, 22; Knight, *Pastoral Epistles*, 415–16, 443–44; Spicq, *Les Épîtres Pastorales*, 356–57, 375–76.

does represent a rather elegant negative reflection of the Decalogue.[33] For instance, one could understand ἄνομος, ἀνυπότακτος, ἀσεβής, ἁμαρτωλός, ἀνοσίος, and βέβηλος as a complex of traits or person types that stand in violation of the proper posture to be accorded to God, and thus set themselves against the first four commandments collectively.[34] The next eight person types in Paul's list reflect radical infractions of the fifth through ninth commandments. Thus, πατρολῴας and μητρολῴας correspond to honoring one's father and mother, ἀνδροφόνος corresponds to the prohibition against murder, πόρνος and ἀρσενοκοίτης correspond to the prohibition against adultery, ἀνδραποδιστής corresponds to the prohibition against stealing, and ψεύστης and ἐπίορκος correspond to the prohibition against bearing false witness.[35] In the final clause of 1:10, καὶ εἴ τι ἕτερον τῇ ὑγιαινούσῃ διδασκαλίᾳ ἀντίκειται, Paul appears to gather together all outstanding negative traits or person types, along with the vices associated with them, so as to set them collectively against the tenth commandment, the prohibition against coveting.[36]

While the plausible correspondence between the Decalogue and the list of person types need not mean anything in itself, the *order* in which the various elements appear is suggestive. The arrangement of person types and vices corresponding to the sixth, seventh, and eighth commandments appear in the same sequence as that occurring in Exodus 20 and Deuteronomy 5 in the MT, as opposed to the sequence found in either passage as it appears in any extant *Vorlage* of the Greek translation of the OT.[37] The texts of Exod 20:13–15 and Deut 5:17–20 as they appear in the revised fifth edition of the BHS, are translated, "You shall not murder; you shall not commit adultery; you shall not steal," and they

33. Or as Quinn and Wacker put it, a "dramatic decalogue" (Quinn and Wacker, *Letters to Timothy*, 97). Johnson, on the other hand, refers to πατρολῴας and μητρολῴας as "extreme violations" of the commandment not to kill (Johnson, *Letters to Timothy*, 170).

34. Regarding this, Oberlinner offers a variant of this assessment, writing, "In these four expressions is given a complete summary of the violations of the first three commandments of the first table of the Decalogue" (Oberlinner, *Erster Timotheusbrief*, 27).

35. Collins, *Timothy and Titus*, 31–34; Johnson, *Letters to Timothy*, 168–71. Oberlinner also reflects part of this analysis (Oberlinner, *Erster Timotheusbrief*, 27).

36. Towner observes, "It is noticeable that [Paul] omitted any counterpart to the command about coveting . . . It would surely be implied (along with other sins) in the broad catchall category that concludes the list: 'and whatever else is contrary to the sound teaching'" (Towner, *Letters to Timothy and Titus*, 129).

37. Johnson, *Letters to Timothy*, 169, 176; Witherington, *Letters and Homilies*, 196.

are presented in that sequence: murder, adultery, stealing.[38] On the other
hand, the text of the LXX arranges the same prohibitions in the order,
"adultery, stealing, murder" in Exod 20:13–15, while the sequence is
"adultery, murder, stealing" in Deut 5:17–19.[39] These details would seem
to indicate that the writer does not depend upon a Greek translation of
the OT. Indeed, regarding this, Quinn and Wacker note, "The catechesis
here presumes a Palestinian tradition of the Hebrew text of the Decalogue that the MT adopted."[40] The critical feature at this point lies in the
indication that, in the conspicuous lack of direct literary dependence
here, the writer *alludes* to the Decalogue instead of *citing* it, and that,
by virtue of his allusion to the Hebrew version of Exod 20 (and Deut 5),
he may be seen to have come from a Jewish background, having gained
such familiarity with the Hebrew text that he thought of the Decalogue
in Hebrew rather than in Greek terms. Beyond this positive attestation
of a Hebrew version of the Torah standing behind 1 Tim 1:9–10, there
lies also the negative testimony of the absence of lexical common ground
between 1 Tim 1:9–10 and Exod 20:1–17 or Deut 5:6–21 in an extant
Greek translation of the Law, Prophets, and Writings. These details would
surprise no one in the case of Pauline authorship.

Other likely examples of OT allusions in 1 Timothy occur in 2:13–
15 and 5:19. In 2:13–15, on the one hand, while Paul clearly alludes to
(but does not cite) several spots in Genesis, such as 2:7, 3:13, and 3:16,
the BHS and the LXX texts show no remarkable differences in their respective versions of these passages, which results in neither confirmation nor correction of the hypothesis suggested here. On the other hand,
the situation may be more instructive in the case of 1 Tim 5:19, for here
Paul most likely alludes to (but again does not cite) Deut 19:15 in writing, ἐπὶ δύο ἢ τριῶν μαρτύρων. The LXX text from Deut 19:15 reads, ἐπὶ

38. In each instance, the Hebrew text reads, לא תרצח ס לא תנאף ס לא תגנב ס.

39. Exod 20:13–15 reads, οὐ μοιχεύσεις οὐ κλέψεις οὐ φονεύσεις. Deut 5:17–19
reads, οὐ μοιχεύσεις οὐ φονεύσεις οὐ κλέψεις. At the same time, it is worth noting that in
the variant reading found in A, with respect to both passages mentioned, the sequence
matches that of the BHS (LXX, 120, 296). In accordance with this observation, Sidney
Jellicoe suggests regarding A, "[The compiler's] object seems to have been to arrive at
a continuous text that would combine and integrate the fruits of the critical labours
of Palestine and Syria as well as those of his native Egypt" (Jellicoe, *Septuagint and
Modern Study*, 188). Harl, Dorival, and Munnich reflect a similar position, offering,
"The codex doubtless was drafted in Alexandria, but integrates textual data reflecting
Palestine and Syria" (Harl, Dorival, and Munnich, *La Bible Grecque des Septante*, 134).

40. Quinn and Wacker, *Letters to Timothy*, 99.

στόματος δύο μαρτύρων καὶ ἐπὶ στόματος τριῶν μαρτύρων, while the BHS text reads, עַל־פִּי שְׁנֵי עֵדִים אוֹ עַל־פִּי שְׁלֹשָׁה־עֵדִים. Here, the LXX uses καὶ instead ἤ between ἐπὶ στόματος δύο and ἐπὶ στόματος τριῶν μαρτύρων, which would indicate an intensifying function ("even") rather than an alternative ("or"), as would be more compatible with the alternative conjunction אוֹ.[41] In addition, even though the expression in 1 Timothy lacks the word στόματος, as well as the first occurrence of μαρτύρων that would correspond to Deut 19:15 in the Hebrew text, the numerical adjectives still occur in the genitive case, perhaps suggesting an elliptical noun, and indicating that Paul may have recalled the form and intent of the Hebrew version correctly, even if he did not cite or translate exactly.[42]

By contrast, in the one instance in 1 Timothy in which Paul explicitly cites the Law, Prophets, and Writings, the text reflects the lexis of the LXX exactly. Specifically, in 5:18, in which Paul cites Deut 25:4, he writes, βοῦν ἀλοῶντα οὐ φιμώσεις, while the LXX version reads, οὐ φιμώσεις βοῦν ἀλοῶντα. The only distinction between these two instances lies in the placement of βοῦς. It heads the citation in 1 Tim 5:18, as if to draw emphatic attention to the elders of whom he is writing.

Similar indications are observable in 2 Timothy that Paul, in his references to the Law, Prophets, and Writings, may have preferred to work from the Hebrew version rather than draw upon the LXX when he supported an assertion by allusion. In 2:19, Paul offers the reassuring comment, ὁ μέντοι στερεὸς θεμέλιος τοῦ θεοῦ ἕστηκεν, supported in part by an apparent allusion, the latter part of which likely derives from Joel 2:32 (3:5 in the BHS and LXX), πᾶς ὁ ὀνομάζων τὸ ὄνομα κυρίου. In this instance, the LXX translates the Hebrew קרא with ἐπικαλέω, while Paul uses ὀνομάζω, again seeming to translate appropriately, though per his own discretion.[43] At the same time, this is preceded by an apparent

41. BDB, 14–15; *TWOT*, 1:36.

42. Towner sees this example as a conflation of Deut 17:6 and 19:15, but otherwise marks most of the same observations noted here, writing, "The conjunction 'or' (*ē*) and the omission of the word 'mouth' (*stomatos*) reflect the wording of Deut 17:6, but the genitive object of the preposition (*dyo ē triōn martyrōn*) corresponds to Deut 19:15. On the assumption that it is the presence of the word 'mouth' in the Greek of Deut 19:15 that determines the genitives that complete the object (also present in the Hebrew of 17:6 but absent in the Greek translation at that point), Paul's genitive construction in 5:19 may correspond more closely to the more general application of the multiple witness principle in Deut 19:15" (Towner, "1–2 Timothy and Titus," 900b).

43. BDB, 894–96; *TWOT*, 2:810.

citation from Num 16:5, as Paul writes, ἔγνω κύριος τοὺς ὄντας αὐτοῦ.[44] In the LXX, Num 16:5 reads, ἔγνω ὁ θεὸς τοὺς ὄντας αὐτοῦ, with the only deviation in 2 Timothy from the LXX text lying in Paul's use of κύριος in place of ὁ θεός. This modification may reflect either his direct translation of the Hebrew יהוה or a desire to pull together the two sources that he adduces by utilizing κύριος as a common reference.[45]

These observations and the ensuing hypotheses must be offered with some reservation, since it is not possible to draw absolute conclusions on so little data. However, if the foregoing presentation provides any indication, one generally may argue that Paul demonstrates a preference for the expressions of ideas as they occur in the Hebrew texts when he *alludes* to passages from the OT, while he seems to follow the Greek translation in the instances in which he appears to *cite* OT passages.[46] In other words, the apparent tendencies observed in the examples adduced would make the greatest sense if the writer were more comfortable with the Hebrew in which he was first schooled when he wanted to make a general reference to a familiar teaching, but when directly citing Scripture familiar to his reader, he consciously adapted his writing for a reader (in this case, Timothy) more comfortable with the Greek translation of the OT. While it is possible that a hypothetical first- or second-century Paulinist may have had such familiarity with the Hebrew text, it seems more likely that this detail reflects a habit of thought typical of one schooled in Judaism and trained in the Hebrew texts of the Law, Prophets, and Writings. This, coupled with the writer's transparent concern to vindicate the Law of Moses while opposing its misuse against the church, serves to provide two points of otherwise incidental data testifying in favor of genuine Pauline authorship.[47]

44. While this also could be an allusion, in the absence of an unambiguous citation formula, such as that occurring in 1 Tim 5:18, the prefacing remark ἔχων τὴν σφραγῖδα also may indicate that a citation follows.

45. Knight, *Pastoral Epistles*, 415–16.

46. While Christopher Stanley does not address this particular phenomenon directly, he does observe "places where Paul follows a version of the Old Greek text that has been systematically revised in pre-Christian times toward a different (usually 'proto-Masoretic') Hebrew text" (Stanley, *Language of Scripture*, 255). Later, Stanley writes, "Had Paul relied on a version of the Greek text that he had (presumably) memorized in childhood, one would expect to see at least a measure of consistency in the textual affinities of his various quotations" (ibid.). One of the possibilities raised in this chapter is that, in fact, Paul may not have used an earlier or Hebraized Greek text at all, but may instead have drawn upon a Hebrew text.

47. Guthrie, *Pastoral Epistles*, 70.

One more point must be addressed. Among those who advocate an essentially Pauline authorship, Witherington proposes that, while Paul determined the content of the PE, Luke served as Paul's secretary.[48] His hypothesis rests largely upon the relatively high frequency of lexical common ground between the PE and Luke-Acts.[49] However, while Witherington's proposal does warrant consideration, he seems to fixate upon only one explanation for the shared lexis between Luke-Acts and the PE: namely, that the terms shared by Luke and Paul are distinctly Luke's terms, and that Paul therefore must have relied upon Luke. He does not address the possibility that Luke, as Paul's understudy, may have acquired some of his expressions from Paul.[50] After all, it is possible that Paul was the first one to proclaim the gospel to Luke at some point; certainly, there is ample testimony indicating that Luke was a frequent companion of Paul's. Furthermore, while it has already been shown that Paul occasionally seems to assume familiarity with a Hebrew text of the OT, Luke typically registers a thorough dependence upon the LXX in his writings, as Witherington himself notes.[51] Consequently, an acute sensitivity to the Hebrew text (such as that observed in 1 Tim 1:9–10 and 2 Tim 2:19) would seem inconsistent with a predominantly Lukan style or composition.

An alternative to Witherington's proposal lies in the notion that Paul and Luke, as frequent companions over the course of gospel ministry, may have exerted a mutual influence upon each other's expressions or idioms, so that it would be difficult to determine in such a limited survey sample what aspects actually emerge as "Lukan," and what aspects are "Pauline." In addition to these points, a survey of the remaining Pauline

48. See Witherington in note 2. See also Moule, "Problem of the Pastoral Epistles," 430–52. Knight considers this possibility, but then eliminates it (Knight, *Pastoral Epistles*, 50–51).

49. Witherington, *Letters and Homilies*, 57–61.

50. Prominent among his examples witnessing to a "Lukan hand," Witherington appeals to comparisons with Paul's speeches in Pidisian Antioch (Acts 13) and Miletus (Acts, 20), and to the use of ὑγιαίνω in Luke and Acts as compared to the PE. However, in the case of the speech material, both speeches are Paul's, which begs the question as to whether these are reported speeches or speeches composed by Luke. With respect to usages of ὑγιαίνω, even though this is not a commonly occurring verb in the NT, Paul's usage in 1 and 2 Timothy differs significantly from Luke's usage. Only in 1 and 2 Timothy is ὑγιαίνω used metaphorically, and only in these letters is it paired with either διδασκαλία or λόγος (Witherington, *Letters and Homilies*, 59–61). See also Johnson, *Letters to Timothy*, 68–69.

51. Witherington, *Letters and Homilies*, 56.

epistles indicates that, at least on several occasions when he relied upon assistance in the composition of his writings, Paul exhibited no reluctance to acknowledge the co-writer or coworker associated with the letter. Such an acknowledgment is conspicuously absent from either 1 or 2 Timothy.[52]

In view of the preceding observations and summations, along with the more extensive studies provided elsewhere, it is most reasonable and judicious to work with Paul's letters to Timothy as they present themselves, at least until such time as substantive evidence may emerge that either suggests another author or clearly testifies to the writer's non-Pauline identity.[53]

The Unity of the Letters to Timothy

Due to the "grouping" that often governs treatments of the PE, the conceptual and compositional unity of 1 and 2 Timothy frequently seems a foregone conclusion.[54] However, in keeping with how these letters present themselves, each one will be treated as an independent and self-contained composition in its own right. At the same time, since the aim of this study involves proposing one consistent and prevailing sense of

---

52. See, for instance, Rom 16:22, 1 Cor 1:1, 16:21; 2 Cor 1:1, Gal 6:11, Phil 1:1, Col 1:1, 1 Thess 1:1, 2 Thess 1:1, and 2 Thess 3:17. Witherington himself also acknowledges, "Something else is different about these letters: None of them have the final greetings in the hand of Paul as was customary in his earlier letters, and none of them mention a scribe or amanuensis or coauthor" (ibid., 54).

53. This reflects precisely the position recommended by Guthrie, for he writes, "In the case of writings like the Pastoral Epistles which at least claim to be written by Paul and which were clearly accepted as Pauline by the overwhelming testimony of external attestation, the only scientific procedure would seem to be to accept them as Pauline until such time as they are conclusively proved otherwise" (Guthrie, *Mind of Paul*, 5). Fee exhibits a similar temperance, suggesting, "It seems fair to observe that PE scholarship is sometimes overimpressed with its own judgments about what Paul could, or (especially) could not, have said or done. When one has as little evidence as is available from Paul—and what evidence we do have is occasional, not systematic, in nature—a much larger measure of caution than one usually finds in the literature would seem appropriate" (Fee, *Timothy and Titus*, 14). See also Edwards, "Genuineness of the Pastoral Epistles," 131–39; Metzger, "Reconsideration of Certain Arguments," 91–94.

54. The term "grouping" comes from Johnson, and refers to the tendency by many to treat all three PE as if they were composed by the same non-Pauline author, and at about the same time, and as if all of the traits marking one letter may be presumed to adhere to the other two (Johnson, *Letters to Timothy*, 63–64). On the other hand, Murphy-O'Connor finds it "improbable" for these two letters to have been written by the same person (Murphy-O'Connor, "2 Timothy Contrasted," 401–18).

γραφή—a sense derived from Paul's apparent understanding and use of γραφή in both letters—some explicit and plausible case must be made for the unity of these documents. Also, as indicated at the beginning of the chapter, the case for the unity of 1 and 2 Timothy does not amount to an apologetic for interpreting the occurrence of γραφή in one letter in terms of its usage in the other. Rather, when the interpretations of the two occurrences are considered side-by-side, the point of interest lies in the composite effect of these interpretations. Thus, if two consistent and compatible usages of γραφή emerge from the independent interpretation of each letter, then it may be said with confidence that when Paul uses γραφή, he conveys one uniform sense in both letters to Timothy.

"Unity," as it appears here, refers to a complexity of factors under consideration: the shared authorship and destination of the letters, the similarity of agenda reflected by the letters, and the consecutive relationship between the letters. With regard to this latter point, it is maintained here that 1 Timothy is the earlier work, having been written sometime after Paul's first imprisonment and trial in Rome (Acts 28:16–31), while 2 Timothy serves as Paul's last official correspondence of record: a kind of final charge and testament preceding his eventual martyrdom under Nero.[55] The following presentation of evidence for the unity of these letters is representative, not exhaustive, and will highlight only some of the more conspicuous details.

The most significant and most obvious first case for the unity of 1 and 2 Timothy lies in the designation of one author and one addressee shared by both letters. Both letters purport to be written by Paul and addressed to Timothy, a ministry associate with whom Paul enjoys an

55. The earliest explicit attestation for this sequential relationship between the two letters may be found in some of the superscriptions for each letter, in conjunction with testimony from Eusebius. Among the superscriptions for 1 Timothy, contained in A, P, 241, and cop[bo], occurs the testimony, πρὸς Τιμόθεον ά ἐγράφη ἀπὸ Λαοδικείας ["(The) First To Timothy, written from Laodicea"] (NA[27], 550; Metzger, *A Textual Commentary on the Greek New Testament*, 577–78). Similarly, one may find among the superscriptions for 2 Timothy, in A, 6, 1739*, and 1881, the phrase, πρὸς Τιμόθεον β'ἐγράφη ἀπὸ Ῥώμης ["(The Second) to Timothy written from Rome"] (NA[27], 556; Metzger, *A Textual Commentary on the Greek New Testament*, 583). Eusebius bears witness to the necessary period for such correspondence, outside the events recorded in Acts, writing, "Tradition has it that after defending himself the Apostle was again sent on the ministry of preaching, and coming a second time to the city suffered martyrdom under Nero. During this imprisonment he wrote the second Epistle to Timothy, indicating at the same time that his first defense had taken place and that his martyrdom was at hand" (Eusebius, *Ecclesiastical History*, 2:22.1–5).

affectionate partnership.[56] Furthermore, since this represents the explicit self-attestation of these documents, and since there exists no indication within the manuscript record of any other author or addressee for these documents,[57] there is good reason to take this information at face value in the case of both letters.

The second most conspicuous feature shared by these letters, which also sets them apart from all other NT writings except for Titus, entails the elliptical clause πιστὸς ὁ λόγος. This clause occurs three times in 1 Timothy and once in 2 Timothy.[58] In addition to the shared occurrences of the clause, each instance appears in both letters in the midst of discourse that pertains specifically to the apostolic proclamation of the gospel, either by citation (1 Tim 1:15) or by allusion (1 Tim 3:1, 4:9; 2 Tim 2:11).[59] Thus, the function of the clause—and not merely its occurrence and referent—is consistent in both documents, while it also reflects Paul's prevailing interest in the apostolic gospel message as a major motif of both letters.

A third feature common to these letters, which is indicative not only a shared authorship, but also a shared agenda, lies in the pairing of participial forms of ὑγιαίνω with either διδασκαλία or λόγος. While ὑγιαίνω appears on its own in other NT writings, it is used to modify διδασκαλία and λόγος only in these letters. 1 Tim 1:10 reads, καὶ εἴ τι ἕτερον τῇ ὑγιαινούσῃ διδασκαλίᾳ ἀντίκειται, while 6:3 reads, εἴ τις ἑτεροδιδασκαλεῖ καὶ μὴ προσέρχεται ὑγιαίνουσιν λόγοις τοῖς τοῦ κυρίου ἡμῶν Ἰησοῦ Χριστοῦ καὶ τῇ κατ' εὐσέβειαν διδασκαλίᾳ. 2 Timothy also contains one example of each pairing: Ὑποτύπωσιν ἔχε ὑγιανόντων λόγων ὧν παρ' ἐμοῦ ἤκουσας in 1:13, and Ἔσται γὰρ καιρὸς ὅτε τῆς ὑγιαινούσης διδασκαλίας οὐκ ἀνέξονται in 4:3.

Paul also exhibits a unique use of στρατεία and ἀγών in these letters, even by comparison with his other writings. In the first place, the

56. The *prooemium* of 1 Timothy reads, Παῦλος ἀπόστολος Χριστοῦ Ἰησοῦ κατ' ἐπιταγὴν θεοῦ σωτῆρος ἡμῶν καὶ Χριστοῦ Ἰησοῦ τῆς ἐλπίδος ἡμῶν Τιμοθέῳ γνησίῳ τέκνῳ ἐν πίστει, while that of 2 Timothy reads, Παῦλος ἀπόστολος Χριστοῦ Ἰησοῦ διὰ θελήματος θεοῦ κατ' ἐπαγγελίαν ζωῆς τῆς ἐν Χριστῷ Ἰησοῦ Τιμοθέῳ ἀγαπητῷ τέκνῳ. See also Knight, *Pastoral Epistles*, 3.

57. See note 29.

58. 1 Tim 1:15, 3:1, 4:9, and 2 Tim 2:11. A fifth occurrence may be found in Titus 3:8.

59. This is argued more thoroughly in chapters 3 and 5 below and in Swinson, "Πιστὸς ὁ λόγος: An Alternative Analysis." See also Rendall, "Faithful Is the Word," 314–20, Van Bruggen, "Vaste grond onder de voeten," 38–45.

appearance of these words at all lends further credence to the argument for the Pauline authorship of the PE, for only in Paul's writings does one find NT occurrences of στρατεία.[60] Furthermore, apart from an instance in Heb 12:1, only Paul among the NT writers uses ἀγών.[61] At the same time, none of these occurs in a context that could suggest literary dependence between the various documents. In the second place, in 1 and 2 Timothy alone στρατεία and ἀγών are paired with καλός. In each case, the resulting expressions (καλὴ στρατεία in 1 Tim 1:18 and καλὸν ἀγών in 1 Tim 6:12 and 2 Tim 4:7) serve as synonymous references to the struggle to commend and uphold the one apostolic gospel teaching, the "faithful" word and proclamation that this study identifies as the center of Paul's concern regarding the Ephesian church, as expressed through these letters.[62]

Once in each letter, Paul uses παρακολουθέω in order to commend his own apostolic teaching to Timothy, writing in 1 Tim 4:6, Ταῦτα ὑποτιθέμενος τοῖς ἀδελφοῖς καλὸς ἔσῃ διάκονος Χριστοῦ Ἰησοῦ, ἐντρεφόμενος τοῖς λόγοις τῆς πίστεως καὶ τῆς καλῆς διδασκαλίας ᾗ παρηκολούθηκας, while in 2 Tim 3:10 he writes, Σὺ δὲ παρακολούθησάς μου τῇ διδασκαλίᾳ. In both instances, references to "that which you have followed" serve to designate the material and message in which Timothy has been instructed and with which he stands entrusted.[63] In all of the NT, forms of παρακολουθέω appear in only two other texts, Mark 16:17 and Luke 1:3, marking the two shared occurrences in the letters to Timothy as even more significant.

Continuing with the consideration of uniquely shared or similar expressions, one may observe that in each letter Paul offers a similar statement indicating the gospel business with which he has been entrusted, writing in 1 Tim 2:7, εἰς ὃ ἐτέθην ἐγὼ κῆρυξ καὶ ἀπόστολος, ἀλήθειαν λέγω οὐ ψεύδομαι, διδάσκαλος ἐθνῶν ἐν πίστει καὶ ἀληθείᾳ, and in 2 Tim 1:11, εἰς ὃ ἐτέθην ἐγὼ κῆρυξ καὶ ἀπόστολος καὶ διδάσκαλος. At the same time, in each letter he also makes reference to Timothy's commissioning, urging in 1 Tim 4:14, μὴ ἀμέλει τοῦ ἐν σοὶ χαρίσματος, ὃ ἐδόθη σοι διὰ

---

60. 2 Cor 10:4 and 1 Tim 1:18.

61. Phil 1:30; Col 2:1; 1 Thess 2:2; 1 Tim 6:12; 2 Tim 4:7.

62. Collins, *Timothy and Titus*, 47–48; Fee, *Timothy and Titus*, 57–58; Johnson, *Letters to Timothy*, 306, 431–32; Knight, *Pastoral Epistles*, 107–8, 260, 262–63, 459–60; Spicq, *Les Épîtres Pastorales*, 49, 388.

63. Bassler, *1 Timothy, 2 Timothy*, 83–84, 163–64; Johnson, *Letters to Timothy*, 243, 416; Witherington, *Letters and Homilies*, 259, 313–14.

προφητείας μετὰ ἐπιθέσεως τῶν χειρῶν τοῦ πρεσβυτερίου, while he again exhorts Timothy in 2 Tim 1:6, ἀναμιμνῄσκω σε ἀναζωπυρεῖν τὸ χάρισμα τοῦ θεοῦ, ὅ ἐστιν ἐν σοὶ διὰ τῆς ἐπιθέσεως τῶν χειρῶν μου.[64]

When it comes to the use and content of τὸ εὐαγγέλιον, Paul shows notable consistency between the two letters, again without exhibiting indications of literary dependence. As may be seen in the surveys of the third and fifth chapters, the semantic thread traced through each letter clearly reveals a close correspondence between τὸ εὐαγγέλιον and the apostolic gospel proclamation for which Paul was commissioned, and which entails the heart of his apostolic mission.[65]

Outside of the content of the texts of these letters, a survey of the available Greek manuscripts will show that all of the manuscripts that contain 2 Timothy also contain 1 Timothy. While the opposite circumstance is virtually the case as well, there are six manuscripts that contain portions of 1 Timothy alone. However, against the fact that this takes into consideration more than twelve hundred majuscules and miniscules combined that contain all or part of 1 and 2 Timothy, and that come from the fourth to sixteenth centuries, this hardly represents a serious deviation.[66] Thus, while the manuscript survey does not prove the actual unity of these letters, it does suggest that they have been perceived and preserved as closely related pieces of correspondence since as far back as the manuscript record may be traced.

Reflecting back upon the overall argument proposed in this section, it is clear that the effect of the various points of literary similarity (though not exact literary dependence) presented above entails more than simply noting similarities or points of contact between the two letters. It also lies in observing that such points of contact display similarity of usage and reflect parallel agendas running through both letters. These aspects,

---

64. Bassler, *1 Timothy, 2 Timothy*, 87–88, 130; Johnson, *Letters to Timothy*, 253, 344–45; Marshall, *Pastoral Epistles*, 566–67, 697; Spicq, *Les Épîtres Pastorales*, 148–49, 311–12.

65. Regarding this latter point, Fee acknowledges, "One cannot read much of Paul without recognizing that at the heart of everything else is the gospel, the good news of God's gracious acceptance and forgiveness of sinners" (Fee, *Timothy and Titus*, 14).

66. NA[27], 690–714. At this point in time, there are no extant MSS from prior to the fourth century that contain either 1 or 2 Timothy, though p[32] (ca. 200) does contain Titus 1:11–15, 2:3–8 (NA[27], 685). See also Johnson, *Letters to Timothy*, 16; Marshall, *Pastoral Epistles*, 10. The six MSS that contain portions of 1 Timothy while lacking all of 2 Timothy are 061, 0259, 0262, 0278, 0285 (NA[27], 695, 702–3). See also Aland and Aland, *Text of the New Testament*, 103–42; Metzger, *Text of the New Testament*, 42–65.

coupled with shared terminology and self-attestation with regard to orig-ination and destination, along with the manuscript evidence, all support the premise that these letters stand as authentic and consecutive docu-ments of correspondence from Paul to Timothy.

Finally, it also must be said that, unlike attempting to argue for the pseudonymity of the letters to Timothy on the basis of how they differ lexically from the rest of the Pauline corpus, arguing for their unity on the basis of the traits shared between them is a less complicated endeavor. The reason for this is twofold. First, assessment of their unity or otherwise begins by respecting the *prima facie* testimony of the documents them-selves. Accordingly, the obstacle of corroborating the self-attestation of these letters is much less difficult to overcome than that for contesting such self-attestation. Second, it is a matter of some significance that argu-ments for the authenticity of these documents derive from positive data drawn from analyses that are conducted along several different axes—analyses that actually make a positive claim. By contrast, arguments for their inauthenticity ultimately rest upon negative and hypothetical data and suppositions. In other words, the case for non-Pauline authorship depends entirely upon projections of what Paul would not or could not say (or write), instead of relying upon a weighing of actual evidence that might attest positively to one author or another.

CHAPTER 3

1 Timothy: Tracing Discourse and Semantics Relative to γραφή

THE OBJECTIVE OF THIS chapter lies in mapping the predominant semantic stream or discourse flow of 1 Timothy, so as to demonstrate how γραφή functions as an integral component of the letter's discourse, and how it relates to and is affected by the primary concern that drives the letter's composition. Thus, while this chapter does not feature direct commentary on γραφή or the primary research question, it does assess the literary and rhetorical framework of the letter: the framework in which γραφή is used and of which it forms a part. More importantly, it also traces the development and emergence of successive terms or chains of terms that correspond to one another by virtue of usage and that may lie behind all that is expressed in γραφή. Since the ultimate interpretive decision is based upon usage, an assessment of the rhetorical scheme that develops through the letter as a whole is determinative for the interpretation and construal of γραφή.

At the outset, one first may observe that the likely overarching agenda of 1 Timothy is marked by the *inclusio* framing the body of the document formed by two instances of ἑτεροδιδασκαλέω.[1] These appear in 1:3 and 6:3, and stand as the only occurrences of this verb in the entire NT. In

---

1. Regarding this, Van Neste writes, "This abandonment of the faith is perceived as primarily a doctrinal problem. In 1.3 and 6.3 the opponents are introduced as 'certain ones' who 'teach wrongly' (τις ἑτεροδιδασκαλεῖ). This doctrinal problem is seen as well in the basis of the opponents' teaching" (Van Neste, *Cohesion and Structure*, 117). See ibid., 136–37. See also Collins, *Timothy and Titus*, 27, 155; Roloff, *Der erste Brief an Timotheus*, 63; Spicq, *Les Épîtres Pastorales*, 19–20.

addition to this, the directive to remain in Ephesus, ἵνα παραγγείλῃς τισὶν μὴ ἑτεροδιδασκαλεῖν μηδὲ προσέχειν μύθοις καὶ γενεαλογίαις ἀπεράντοις, dominates the first chapter.[2] The command that Timothy is to deliver emerges again as the primary point of reference in 1:5 and 1:18.[3] In 1:5, Paul discloses the goal or purpose of the command not to teach other teachings. In 1:18, Paul indicates that entrusting this command to Timothy effectively enlists him so that he might fight τὴν καλὴν στρατείαν, or, as he writes later in 6:12, τὸν καλὸν ἀγῶνα τῆς πίστεως.[4] Additionally, judging from Paul's reference in 1:10 to τῇ ὑγιαινούσῃ διδασκαλίᾳ, which "lawless and rebellious men" oppose, the "sound teaching" authorizes one specific teaching that is set over against any "other teaching." Furthermore, this teaching stands κατὰ τὸ εὐαγγέλιον τῆς δόξης τοῦ μακαρίου θεοῦ, which corresponds to the gospel message to which Paul refers as that ὃ ἐπιστεύθην ἐγώ.[5] Thus, on the basis of an initial survey of both the first and sixth chapters, the reader may observe that the prevailing concern of this letter consists in retrieving and reinforcing in Ephesus the "sound teaching" of the gospel, and correcting those who teach falsely, a corrective labor that constitutes the most critical aspect of "the good fight" to which Timothy is summoned.[6]

2. Bernard writes, "The purpose of Timothy's continued residence in Ephesus was that he might check the progress of heretical doctrine" (Bernard, *Pastoral Epistles*, 23). Van Neste offers a similar appraisal, writing, "The concern is with the content of this group's teaching (myths, genealogies, and law), and with the results of the teaching—speculation (v. 4), and verbal disputes (v. 6)—especially as contrasted with the result of Pauline teaching (vv. 4b–5)" (Van Neste, *Cohesion and Structure*, 19). See also Holtz, *Die Pastoralbriefe*, 33.

3. Regarding the correspondence between παραγγέλλω in 1:3 and παραγγελία in 1:5, Spicq writes, "The complement τῆς παραγγελίας suggests a recollection of this word in ἵνα παραγγείλῃς in verse 3" (Spicq, *Les Épîtres Pastorales*, 22).

4. Bernard, *Pastoral Epistles*, 34–35; Collins, *Timothy and Titus*, 48; Marshall, *Pastoral Epistles*, 369, 410; Oberlinner, *Erster Timotheusbrief*, 50–51.

5. Bernard, *Pastoral Epistles*, 29; Collins, *Timothy and Titus*, 34; Fee, *Timothy and Titus*, 46; Roloff, *Der erste Brief an Timotheus*, 63, note 44.

6. Robert Karris writes of the author's need to "ensure the apostolic teaching" (Karris, *Pastoral Epistles*, 47). Roloff as well states, "The word ἑτεροδιδάσκαλειν, appearing only here and in 6:3 in the NT, presumes the existence of a stock of 'more correct' teaching, against which as a normative instance, all teaching must be measured" (Roloff, *Der erste Brief an Timotheus*, 63). Van Neste writes, "The letter opens with a reminder that Timothy's role is to 'command' (παραγγέλλω) and the 'command' (παραγγελία), or basic message, is summarized. A chain of related words then runs through the letter, signifying the message which Timothy is to proclaim in contradistinction to the opponents" (Van Neste, *Cohesion and Structure*, 109). Wolfe also

These observations and their implications will be tested over the course of the following exegetical analysis. Bearing in mind that the primary goal of this study lies in determining the sense of γραφή as Paul uses it in 1 and 2 Timothy, this chapter will offer a survey of the whole of 1 Timothy, which will establish the exegetical parameters of Paul's argument and discourse. In turn, this analysis will enable the identification of the prevailing stream of ideas and terms that Paul uses to shape his letter (recurring and interchangeable expressions that Ray Van Neste calls "semantic chains"), giving special attention to those that relate to his chief concern and apostolic mission, and observing how they may cue Paul's understanding of γραφή.[7]

1:1–2—The Prooemium

The opening words of the epistle, Παῦλος, ἀπόστολος Χριστοῦ Ἰησοῦ, stake a claim on behalf of the writer, to the effect that he represents Χριστός Ἰησοῦς himself, and that he does so κατ᾽ ἐπιταγὴν θεοῦ σωτῆρος ἡμῶν καὶ Χριστοῦ Ἰησοῦ τῆς ἐλπίδος ἡμῶν.[8] The idea of being dispatched or commissioned so as to represent another person lies chiefly in the use of ἀπόστολος. Lexically, the word typically expresses the sense of

---

maintains, "[The PE] frequently call attention to 'sound doctrine,' and explicitly assert the wrongness (both doctrinally and ultimately ethically) of anyone in disagreement with the author's concept of correct doctrine" (Wolfe, *Place and Use of Scripture*, 1). See also Ramsay, *Historical Commentary*, 17.

7. According to Van Neste, recurring terms, whether individual words or whole expressions, can serve as "one of the most common and multifaceted means of creating cohesion . . . the subsequent occurrence of a word naturally connects back to the previous occurrence(s) thus creating cohesion" (Van Neste, *Cohesion and Structure*, 11–12).

8. The consensus on this point is relatively strong. For instance, Guthrie maintains, "Paul commences with a declaration of his own authority in order to make unmistakable the authority of the message he teaches . . . This idea of authority is intensified by the use of the expression *by the command of God*. Paul is more fond of saying 'by the will of God' (as in 2 Tim 1:1), but he uses the present expression (*kat' epitagen*) in Romans 16:26 to bring out the compulsion of the divine commission (see also 1 Cor 7:6 and 2 Cor 8:8)" (Guthrie, *Pastoral Epistles*, 65). Spicq also writes, "'According to the command of God' is linked directly to 'apostle' which it qualifies: apostle by the command, and defines the origin and firm foundation of that charge . . . Ἐπιταγή frequently in the Koine and inscriptions, is used above all of royal mandates that must be executed (cf. *Esth* I,8). The word derives from τάσσω: to put in a fixed place where appropriate; to arrange someone in a class, a category, to assign a place, notably as leader" (Spicq, *Les Épîtres Pastorales*, 2). See also Scott, *Pastoral Epistles*, 5.

"envoy," "messenger," "delegate," or "one sent by another."[9] Syntactically, this impression is reinforced by the genitival Χριστοῦ Ἰησοῦ, likely expressing origin, source, or possession. Together with the subsequent prepositional phrase, it serves to indicate whom the apostolic agent represents and under whose auspices he carries out his appointed tasks.[10] The importance of these details lies in the attending implication that Paul, the explicit writer of record of this letter, writes as a representative of—and under the superintendence of—Christ Jesus, and that he does so by the authority of God. Therefore, his message stands as nothing less than God's message to Timothy.[11]

1:3-11—Other Teaching Versus Sound Teaching

Upon the conclusion of his opening greetings, Paul urges Timothy to remain in Ephesus so as to continue in his service of the churches there, adding, ἵνα παραγγείλῃς τισὶν μὴ ἑτεροδιδασκαλεῖν μηδὲ προσέχειν μύθοις καὶ γενεαλογίαις ἀπεράντοις. As suggested above, the charge to "command certain men" certainly constitutes the initial task appointed

9. In defining the term, Francis H. Agnew writes of "one sent to act authoritatively in the name of another" (Agnew, "Origin of the Term *Apostolos*," 53). See also BDAG, 122; Louw and Nida, *Greek-English Lexicon of the New Testament*, 33.194, 53.74. Knight observes, "ἀπόστολος designates one who is sent with the authority of and on behalf of the one sending. With only a few exceptions, the NT uses ἀπόστολος to refer to the inner circle of leaders appointed by Christ and usually referred to as 'apostles of Jesus Christ' or known to be such, even without the addition of 'of Jesus Christ.'" (Knight, *Pastoral Epistles*, 58). Spicq also affirms, "It thus has a full and technical signification; it is an official title: the ambassador, more than a messenger, represents with authority the person who sends one (cf. Luke 6:13; Mic 3:14). Paul has an official mission that consists of announcing the good news, to witness authentically of the teaching and the resurrection of the Christ" (Spicq, *Les Épîtres Pastorales*, 1–2).

10. Towner writes, "His status is therefore that of an authoritative leader, one to whom a divine commission has been given . . . The genitive relationship indicates the source of his commission and authority (Gal 1:12) and the fact that he is sent to proclaim the gospel (= 'Christ Jesus'; cf. 1 Cor 1:23)" (Towner, *Letters to Timothy and Titus*, 95–96). Similarly, Wolfe states, "It is Paul's ministry which has given the church a handle on what the gospel is and what it means for them. Furthermore, his ministry can be trusted because it has its origin in God, and thereby is clothed with his authority . . . The picture which emerges here is one in which Paul is the standard in many ways for the church. His teaching and leadership are invested with divine authority, sanctioned, as it were, by God himself" (Wolfe, *Place and Use of Scripture*, 89, 91).

11. Aageson, "Pastoral Epistles, Apostolic Authority," 11; Bassler, *1 Timothy, 2 Timothy*, 35–36; Van Neste, *Cohesion and Structure*, 121.

to Timothy in this letter, and likely represents the essential task detailed through the remainder of the document.[12] As for the substance of the command, Timothy is to direct these "certain men (τισὶν)" not to "teach other teaching (ἑτεροδιδασκαλεῖν)," or perhaps even to "cease teaching other teaching." Even before carrying the examination further, one must note that this initial command carries with it the implication of a body of acceptable teaching or doctrine, relative to which the teaching advanced by the "certain men" mentioned in 1:3 stands in opposition, or at least in contradistinction.[13] Considering as well the effect of Paul's claim to be an ἀπόστολος Χριστοῦ Ἰησοῦ, this also serves as an early indication that the acceptable teaching is authorized by or originates with God, while the "other teaching" does not enjoy such standing.[14]

In 1:4, this impression gains even more impetus as one notes that the substance of what "certain men" teach consists in, or at least stands in company with, μύθοις καὶ γενεαλογίαις ἀπεράντοις, all of which promote ἐκζητήσεις rather than promoting and proving compatible with οἰκονομίαν θεοῦ τὴν ἐν πίστει.[15] By contrast, it may be supposed that the acceptable teaching, authorized by God as it is, does serve to advance οἰκονομίαν θεοῦ, here understood as, "the business of God."[16]

12. Remarking upon the essential singularity of Timothy's task as outlined in this letter, Collins writes, "The order is given to Timothy (*se*, 'you' in the singular, v. 3) to exercise pastoral responsibility by assuring that 'some people' (*tisin*) within the Ephesian community not teach falsely and not engage in idle speculation. The Pastor does not tell his readers who those 'some people' are. Throughout the epistle the Pastor continues to refer to these in the same anonymous fashion" (Collins, *Timothy and Titus*, 24). Later, he adds, "Timothy's mandate is focused. He is charged with giving the word (*parangeiles*) to some, obviously the teachers or would-be teachers of the community, that they are not 'to teach falsely'" (ibid., 27).

13. Fairbairn, *1 and 2 Timothy and Titus*, 77; Fee, *Timothy and Titus*, 40; Guthrie, *Pastoral Epistles*, 67; Knight, *Pastoral Epistles*, 72; Marcheselli-Casale, *Le Lettere Pastorali*, 95.

14. Fee, *Timothy and Titus*, 42; Mounce, *Pastoral Epistles*, 19.

15. Guthrie, *Pastoral Epistles*, 68; Knight, *Pastoral Epistles*, 72–73; Lenski, *St. Paul's Epistles*, 501.

16. While Knight prefers the NASB rendering, "God's purpose . . . revealed by . . . our Savior Christ Jesus . . . brought to light through the gospel" (Knight, *Pastoral Epistles*, 75–76), the idea of "purpose" is compatible with the construal offered here, "the business of God." Fee translates οἰκονομίαν θεοῦ in a compatible manner, construing it as "God's work," referring specifically to "the gospel as God's work, based on or known by faith, in contrast to the futility of the 'novelties'" (Fee, *Timothy and Titus*, 42). Regarding πίστις, Towner writes, "The point Paul makes, however, is polemical. It is genuine faith, namely that faith associated with his gospel, which has access to

According to Paul, these "certain men," characterized by their desire to be regarded as νομοδιδάσκαλοι, or "teachers of the law," effectively disqualify themselves by misunderstanding and misrepresenting the law altogether.[17] Observing that Paul has made reference to the law in his remarks about the would-be teachers, and that he previously had mentioned "myths and endless genealogies," it seems likely that, whatever else the unacceptable teaching may have entailed, it surely bore marks of Judaism, both in the fixation upon bloodlines and upon errant instruction deriving in some fashion from the Law.[18] By contrast, Paul explicitly upholds the law, affirming, οἴδαμεν . . . ὅτι καλὸς ὁ νόμος, ἐάν τις αὐτῷ νομίμως χρῆται. Paul further clarifies the "lawful" use of the law, noting that it is appointed for the correction of ἀνόμοις . . . καὶ ἀνυποτάκτοις, ἀσεβέσι καὶ ἁμαρτωλοῖς, ἀνοσίοις καὶ βεβήλοις, πατρολῴαις καὶ μητρολῴαις, ἀνδροφόνοις, πόρνοις, ἀρσενοκοίταις, ἀνδραποδισταῖς, ψεύσταις, ἐπιόρκοις, καὶ εἴ τι ἕτερον τῇ ὑγιαινούσῃ διδασκαλίᾳ ἀντίκειται.[19] Thus, in Paul's assessment, one may observe that those who stand in opposition to the law also resist ἡ ὑγιαίνουσα διδασκαλία.[20] Therefore, even as the use of ἑτεροδιδασκαλέω in 1:3 implicitly *suggested* the presence of a specific body of acceptable teaching, Paul confirms that point explicitly in 1:10, and he has implied as well that the "sound teaching" he commends is compatible with the Torah that he is also concerned to uphold.[21] It now remains to ascertain something of the content of that "sound teaching."

---

correct understanding of the will of God. The fundamental condition for understanding the way God has organized life (his *oikonomia*), and for carrying out the activities in the community and world that bring them into alignment, is adherence to genuine faith" (Towner, *Letters to Timothy and Titus*, 114).

17. Marcheselli-Casale, *Le Lettere Pastorali*, 102; Oberlinner, *Erster Timotheusbrief*, 19; Quinn and Wacker, *Letters to Timothy*, 81–82; Schlatter, *Die Kirche der Griechen*, 44; Spicq, *Les Épîtres Pastorales*, 24. Also, it is worth noting that νομοδιδάσκαλος, which Paul uses here, occurs elsewhere in the Greek text of the New Testament only in Luke 5:17 and Acts 5:34. Collins in fact observes, "The term *nomodidaskaloi*, 'teachers of the law,' was apparently first used by Christian writers. Luke used the expression to identify Gamaliel (Acts 5:34) and others among the Pharisees (Luke 5:17)" (Collins, *Timothy and Titus*, 29). See also Oberlinner, *Erster Timotheusbrief*, 19; Pirot and Clamer, *La Sainte Bible*, 207.

18. Guthrie, *Pastoral Epistles*, 68; Hanson, *Pastoral Letters*, 24; Karris, *Pastoral Epistles*, 57; Pirot and Clamer, *La Sainte Bible*, 207; Schlatter, *Die Kirche der Griechen*, 44.

19. Knight, *Pastoral Epistles*, 83; Towner, *Letters to Timothy and Titus*, 124.

20. Collins, *Timothy and Titus*, 34; Lock, *Pastoral Epistles*, 13; Oberlinner, *Erster Timotheusbrief*, 28; Quinn and Wacker, *Letters to Timothy*, 92, 94–95, 102–3.

21. Guthrie, *Pastoral Epistles*, 72; Mounce, *Pastoral Epistles*, 42; Spicq, *Les Épîtres*

In 1:11, Paul describes the "sound teaching" as something that stands κατὰ τὸ εὐαγγέλιον τῆς δόξης τοῦ μακαρίου θεοῦ, ὃ ἐπιστεύθην ἐγώ. The prepositional phrase is construed here as modifying the immediately preceding τῇ ὑγιαινούσῃ διδασκαλίᾳ.[22] This means that the "sound teaching" that Paul seems determined to uphold must concern or be in agreement with "the gospel," or perhaps it even serves to advance "the gospel," which itself reflects and derives from "the glory of the blessed God."[23] Furthermore, this gospel serves as the message with which Paul, ἀπόστολος Χριστοῦ Ἰησοῦ κατ᾽ ἐπιταγὴν θεοῦ σωτῆρος ἡμῶν καὶ Χριστοῦ Ἰησοῦ τῆς ἐλπίδος ἡμῶν, has been entrusted, with which he views the law as compatible, and which yet appears to serve as a body of teaching distinct from the law.[24] One may infer then that a primary function of Paul's apostolic commissioning entails his service as a messenger or representative of τὸ εὐαγγέλιον τῆς δόξης τοῦ μακαρίου θεοῦ.[25] In view of this,

---

Pastorales, 28–29. Contra Witherington, *Letters and Homilies*, 198.

22. Knight, *Pastoral Epistles*, 89–90; Mounce, *Pastoral Epistles*, 42.

23. Dibelius and Conzelmann write, "The Pastorals designate with 'sound teaching' (ὑγιαίνουσα διδασκαλία) or 'sound words' (ὑγιαίνοντες λόγοι) the loftiest and holiest things they know: the true faith, the true message about faith. According to the Pauline use of language one could (e.g., in 1 Tim 6:3) substitute a phrase containing the term 'gospel' (εὐαγγέλιον)" (Dibelius and Conzelmann, *Commentary on the Pastoral Epistles*, 24). Knight also suggests, "The phrase here in 1:11 qualifies ὑγιαινούσῃ διδασκαλίᾳ . . . κατὰ τὸ εὐαγγέλιον by its connection with ὑγιαινούσῃ διδασκαλίᾳ provides the norm for that teaching and for its soundness. The εὐαγγέλιον is the essence of the saving good news about the person and work of Jesus Christ, especially his death and resurrection, in relation to human sin" (Knight, *Pastoral Epistles*, 90). Towner states simply, "*Euangelion* is the message that was entrusted to Paul (1 Tim 1.11; 2 Tim 1.8, 11). The substance of this message, the Christ-event, can be seen in the traditional formulae laid down at each mention of the word (1 Tim 1.15; 2 Tim 1.9–10; 2.8–13)" (Towner, *Goal of Our Instruction*, 123).

24. Guthrie, *Pastoral Epistles*, 73; Hanson, *Pastoral Letters*, 25; Marcheselli-Casale, *Le Lettere Pastorali*, 114; Spicq, *Les Épîtres Pastorales*, 28.

25. Collins writes, "His reference to sound teaching and to the gospel provides a Christian focus for this otherwise Hellenistic Jewish list. According to the Pastor, the law has been established for those who oppose sound teaching (see Titus 1:9, 2:1). That teaching is qualified as being in accordance with the gospel of the blessed God. In effect, sound teaching is an explanation of that gospel . . . The gospel was entrusted to Paul (see 1 Thess 2:4). Ultimately, sound teaching is defined by the Pauline gospel of God" (Collins, *Timothy and Titus*, 34). Karris, in his discussions, often refers to "Paul's gospel" (Karris, *Pastoral Epistles*, 53), while Quinn and Wacker remark upon "the apostolic concern for faith" that "appears at every turn" of the first chapter (Quinn and Wacker, *Letters to Timothy*, 72). Also, Witherington assumes a strong position relative to the relationship between ἡ ὑγιαίνουσα and τὸ εὐαγγέλιον τῆς δόξης τοῦ μακαρίου

and for all of its apparent fundamental importance and its relationship to the "sound teaching," it is remarkable that Paul does not take the time to explain τὸ εὐαγγέλιον. In other words, while he does link it directly to "the sound teaching," and while he does specify that it serves as the essential substance of his apostolic trust, Paul yet refers to it in a manner that suggests Timothy's prior familiarity with it; the term τὸ εὐαγγέλιον already holds meaning for him.[26]

Thus far, the specific content of the "gospel" or the "sound teaching" remains opaque in 1 Timothy. However, through the first eleven verses, Paul has established significant footing upon which he will build throughout the remainder of the letter. He clearly marks a specific body of teaching as "sound" in contradistinction to any other teaching. Furthermore, he explicitly associates this "sound teaching" with "the gospel of the glory of the blessed God," thereby signaling the familiar and technical status of τὸ εὐαγγέλιον even in Paul's day, and anchoring its origin in God himself; it is God's gospel message. Also, with his assertion that he has been entrusted with the "gospel," and his claim to serve as an "apostle of Christ Jesus, by the command of God our savior and Christ Jesus our hope," Paul presents himself as an agent on behalf of God, entrusted with God's gospel message and the sound teaching associated with it.[27] Consequently, from this point on in the letter, Paul's own words are vested with

---

θεοῦ, averring, "Paul emphatically reminds Timothy that he was entrusted with this gospel about the glory of 'the glory of the blessed God' (only here and at 1 Tim 6:15). In short, the gospel comes from the blessed God, who once gave the Mosaic law" (Witherington, *Letters and Homilies*, 198).

26. Concerning the expression, τὸ εὐαγγέλιον, Marshall writes, "By this time, τὸ εὐαγγέλιον 'good news, gospel,' had become the stereotyped term for the Christian message in its broadest sense as the good news of salvation" (Marshall, *Pastoral Epistles*, 382). Mounce states, "Because of its use to describe the message of Jesus, it eventually became a technical term in Christian teaching for the good news of Christ" (Mounce, *Pastoral Epistles*, 42). Wolfe also writes, "The gospel of Paul has become a fixed tradition, and the PE are perhaps the clearest expression of this" (Wolfe, *Place and Use of Scripture*, 4; cf. Spicq, *Les Épitres Pastorales*, cxlii). If such is the case, it seems counterintuitive to maintain that such a firm and meaning-laden usage of τὸ εὐαγγέλιον could not have been in circulation during the lifetime of Paul. Furthermore, that would seem to serve as circumstantial evidence for the existence of a possible gospel genre that disclosed not only the effect of Jesus' work on the cross, but the details of the life that led up to his crucifixion and resurrection.

27. Norbert Brox maintains that the clause ὃ ἐπιστεύθην ἐγώ is not autobiographical, as the "guarantor" of the gospel message (Brox, *Die Pastoralbriefe*, 108). See also Roloff, *Der erste Brief an Timotheus*, 80; Wolter, *Die Pastoralbriefe als Paulustradition*, 27.

the authority that derives from speaking or writing on behalf of God, an authority that compares with that attributed to the Torah.[28] Thus, even though the ultimate objective of determining how one should construe γραφή as it is used in 1 and 2 Timothy still remains to be addressed directly, these early details begin to mark vital literary and conceptual boundaries for the discussion.

1:12-20—Sound Teaching and the Faithful Word

Paul's reflection upon his trust and calling as expressed in 1:11 carries over into the initial clauses of the next literary unit, as he gives thanks to Christ Jesus because, as he writes, πιστόν με ἡγήσατο θέμενος εἰς διακονίαν. By virtue of these remarks, Paul more sharply defines his concept of ἀπόστολος Χριστοῦ Ἰησοῦ, as he speaks of Christ's having established him in διακονία, or ministry.[29] Based upon preceding material, this "ministry," or "service," must concern "the gospel" with which Paul has been entrusted (ὃ ἐπιστεύθην ἐγώ): That is, God's gospel message, which also is commensurate with "the sound teaching."[30]

In 1:15, Paul writes of the "faithful" word (πιστὸς ὁ λόγος). Upon an initial reading, this reference seems to appear suddenly, as it represents the first instance of any use of λόγος in the epistle. However, since Paul has already indicated his determination to guard a particular message or teaching, designated "the gospel" and "the sound teaching" in previous material, one may reasonably suppose that the "faithful" word at least stands as a message or word compatible with the body of instruction already mentioned. Indeed, this study maintains that πιστὸς ὁ λόγος in these letters serves as an affirmation of the worth and merits of the gospel message and teaching mentioned previously, meaning that this message also stands as *God's* faithful word.[31] Thus, the "faithful" word, which

28. Fee, *Timothy and Titus*, 47; Johnson, *Letters to Timothy*, 178; Schlatter, *Die Kirche der Griechen*, 51–52, 54; Witherington, *Letters and Homilies*, 199.

29. Hentschel, *Diakonia im Neuen Testament*, 156–57; Knight, *Pastoral Epistles*, 94–95; Spicq, *Les Épîtres Pastorales*, 39.

30. Marshall, *Pastoral Epistles*, 384; Mounce, *Pastoral Epistles*, 47, 51; Spicq, *Les Épîtres Pastorales*, 40; Towner, *Letters to Timothy and Titus*, 134.

31. This construal, as argued with each subsequent occurrence, certainly yields a coherent and plausible treatment of πιστὸς ὁ λόγος as it occurs repeatedly in the literary context of the letter. It is defended in Rendall ("Faithful Is the Word," 314–20), Van Bruggen ("Vaste grond onder de voeten," 38–45), and Swinson ("Πιστὸς ὁ λόγος: An

testifies that Χριστὸς Ἰησοῦς ἦλθεν εἰς τὸν κόσμον ἁμαρτωλοὺς σῶσαι, provides the first explicit indication of the content of the "sound teaching" and "the gospel" of which Paul speaks in 1:10–11 and which he so jealously guards.[32] However, by reflecting as well upon the personal remarks that lead into and derive from the affirmation, πιστὸς ὁ λόγος, one may observe that this "faithful" word also bears witness to ἡ χάρις τοῦ κυρίου ἡμῶν (1:14) and to the fact that the sinners whom Christ Jesus came to save include οἱ μέλλοντες πιστεύειν ἐπ᾽ αὐτῷ εἰς ζωὴν αἰώνιον (1:16). Therefore, λόγος most likely cues not the exact citation of a fixed expression, but the report of a basic truth; Χριστὸς Ἰησοῦς ἦλθεν εἰς τὸν κόσμον ἁμαρτωλοὺς σῶσαι stands as one formulation of this essential word or proclamation.[33] Following Paul's personal reflection upon his status as a beneficiary of "the grace of God" in 1:14, the formula "the word is faithful and worthy of all acceptance" thus functions as an emphatic confirmation, as if he were saying, "God's grace saves even me, indeed, the word regarding this grace is faithful!"

In the affirmation of 1:18, Ταύτην τὴν παραγγελίαν παρατίθεμαί σοι, τέκνον Τιμόθεε, Paul revisits the notion of the παραγγελία that first appeared in 1:3–5.[34] Viewed against the whole of 1:3–17, "this command" which Paul entrusts to Timothy can refer only to Paul's directive to Timothy to "command" certain men not to "teach other teachings," a task he now represents as ἡ καλὴ στρατεία.[35] Moreover, this "good fight" directly concerns ἡ πίστις, regarding which τινες . . . ἐναυάγησαν. In view of the stream of terms employed by Paul to this point, it seems reasonable to construe ἡ πίστις as a metonym for "the gospel," "the sound teaching," or the "faithful" word. In other words, "the faith" refers to that set of convictions and conduct that rest upon the teaching expressed in "the gospel," and perhaps even the gospel proclamation itself.[36]

Alternative Analysis").

32. Towner states simply, "*Pistos* in v. 15 denotes the trustworthiness of the apostolic traditions" (Towner, *Goal of Our Instruction*, 79).

33. Or as Collins writes, "In 1 Tim 1:15 the long formula precedes a common affirmation of the early church's faith" (Collins, *Timothy and Titus*, 41).

34. Fee, *Timothy and Titus*, 57; Oberlinner, *Erster Timotheusbrief*, 8, 51; Quinn and Wacker, *Letters to Timothy*, 147; Spicq, *Les Épîtres Pastorales*, 47; Towner, *Letters to Timothy and Titus*, 114, 155.

35. Roloff observes of this fight, "Such a struggle is not the exception, but the rule. Wherever the gospel is heard, opposition arises, hostility is elevated" (Roloff, *Der erste Brief an Timotheus*, 104).

36. Collins, *Timothy and Titus*, 48–49; Knight, *Pastoral Epistles*, 110; Witherington,

Based upon the analysis thus far, the original premise concerning the chief agenda of the letter—on the one hand, to reinforce the "sound teaching" concerning "the gospel" or "faithful word," while on the other hand, to correct those who commend any other teaching in its place—is sustained, at least through the first chapter.[37] Of perhaps equal importance however, is Paul's obvious fixation upon one essential apostolic message. In other words, Paul has given no indication that he serves as a bearer of multiple, though compatible, messages; he is an apostle for the sake of the gospel message only, whatever form it may assume.[38] At the same time, adjectival expressions such as "sound" (participial ὑγιαίνω) and "faithful" (πιστός) convey the added force of excluding anything but the single message or "gospel" from God.[39] Finally, it must be remembered that this message is the very one "entrusted" to Paul as Christ's own apostolic servant or representative, one who speaks on Christ's behalf by virtue of the commissioning and authority of God.[40] As indicated by the details gathered to this point, Paul views his apostolic teaching as nothing less than God's own gospel message: a message as authoritative and as God-given as the Torah. It has been entrusted to Paul so that he might guard the truth and purity of its content and disperse that content among the peoples.

2:1—3:1a—Suitable Conduct and the Faithful Word

In the midst of a unit in which Paul summons the believers to prayer as they work out godly and peaceable living, Paul affirms that such conduct is pleasing to God,[41] whom he then describes further with the clause, ὃς πάντας ἀνθρώπους θέλει σωθῆναι καὶ εἰς ἐπίγνωσιν ἀληθείας ἐλθεῖν.[42] This description then is supported by the subsequent assertion, εἰς γὰρ

Letters and Homilies, 209; Wolfe, *Place and Use of Scripture*, 92.

37. Fee, *Timothy and Titus*, 59; Lenski, *St. Paul's Epistles*, 528–29.

38. Wolfe, *Place and Use of Scripture*, 88–89, 94–95.

39. Towner, *Goal of Our Instruction*, 118, 121–23.

40. Bassler, *1 Timothy, 2 Timothy, Titus*, 48–49; Witherington, *Letters and Homilies*, 188.

41. Fee contends, "The concern here . . . is not that Christians should have a life free from trouble or distress (which hardly fits the point of view of 2 Tim 1:8 and 3:12) but that they should live in such a way that 'no one will speak evil of the name of God and of our teaching' (6:1)" (Fee, *Timothy and Titus*, 63).

42. Towner, *Letters to Timothy and Titus*, 177.

θεός, εἷς καὶ μεσίτης θεοῦ καὶ ἀνθρώπων, ἄνθρωπος Χριστὸς Ἰησοῦς, ὁ δοὺς ἑαυτὸν ἀντίλυτρον ὑπὲρ πάντων.[43] Paul next refers to the report contained in the concluding relative clause—that Christ Jesus gave himself as a ransom on behalf of all—as τὸ μαρτύριον καιροῖς ἰδίοις. This designation may even apply to the entire assertion of 2:5–6.[44]

Apart from the content of the statement itself, several details here warrant particular attention. The first entails Paul's reference to ἡ ἀλήθεια, which in this context specifies a body of reliable teaching, even "the sound teaching" or "the gospel" of which Paul has been writing.[45] The second lies in his designation of the message of redemption purchased by Christ Jesus as "the testimony" (τὸ μαρτύριον), a term that vests the record of Christ's work with particular significance.[46] The third detail concerns Paul's claim on his own behalf with respect to this report, for he follows the account with the remark in 2:7, εἰς ὃ ἐτέθην ἐγὼ κῆρυξ καὶ

43. Barrett, *Pastoral Epistles*, 51; Towner, *Letters to Timothy and Titus*, 179–80.

44. Roloff offers, as one explanation of τὸ μαρτύριον καιροῖς ἰδίοις, "Witness (μαρτύριον) in the deutero-Pauline literature (2 Thess 1:10; 2 Tim 1:8) is a *terminus technicus* for the apostolic proclamation, as also in Acts (4:33)." (Roloff, *Der erste Brief an Timotheus*, 123).

45. Collins affirms, "This expression is a household word within the Pastor's community. It designates the full message of the Christian gospel issuing forth into a life characterized by godliness" (Collins, *Timothy and Titus*, 60). Marshall likewise maintains, "'To come to a knowledge' views conversion from the standpoint of the rational decision about the divine message, 'truth', which it entails. In the PE ἀλήθεια refers to the authentic revelation of God bringing salvation. The background is Jewish, truth, a quality of God, is the criterion by which his saving message is determined . . . Throughout the PE its content and polemic thrust are evident as it contrasts the apostolic message as God's message with that of the false teachers" (Marshall, *Pastoral Epistles*, 428). Towner proposes, "The phrase used to describe the salvation process at the close of v. 4 [*eis epignosin aletheias elthein*; cf. 2 Tim 2.25; 3.7; Titus 1.1] also corresponds to the polemical thrust of the passage. It emphasizes the rational aspect of belief, in keeping with the close connection drawn in the Pastorals between 'belief' and apostolic doctrine" (Towner, *Goal of Our Instruction*, 84). Later, he also states, "Closely related to *pistis* is the term *aletheia*. It too signifies the content of 'the faith' in an inclusive sense, though from a slightly different perspective . . . In the earlier Paul and in the Pastorals *aletheia* is related closely to the gospel. When Paul makes this connection *aletheia* refers to an objective, knowable fact where the subject is the message about Christ" (ibid., 122). See also Oberlinner, *Erster Timotheusbrief*, 73; Quinn and Wacker, *Letters to Timothy*, 165, 180; Schlatter, *Die Kirche der Griechen*, 43; Witherington, *Letters and Homilies*, 215.

46. Fee, *Timothy and Titus*, 66; Marshall, *Pastoral Epistles*, 433; Witherington views the incarnation and death themselves as τὸ μαρτύριον, rather than the message regarding the incarnation and death (Witherington, *Letters and Homilies*, 216), while Knight declines to assume the either/or position (Knight, *Pastoral Epistles*, 124).

ἀπόστολος, ἀλήθειαν λέγω οὐ ψεύδομαι, διδάσκαλος ἐθνῶν ἐν πίστει καὶ ἀληθείᾳ.[47] Thus, on the one hand, Paul has previously stated that he was entrusted with "the gospel of the glory of the blessed God" (1:11), while on the other hand, he now claims that his apostolic appointment exists for the sake of advancing this most recent formulation (2:5).[48] Consequently, the only way to reconcile these two claims by Paul lies in construing the timely "testimony" as the substance of the basic apostolic gospel proclamation, which, in less than two full chapters, has assumed at least two different though compatible forms.[49] Accordingly, whether Paul writes, Χριστὸς Ἰησοῦς ἦλθεν εἰς τὸν κόσμον ἁμαρτωλοὺς σῶσαι, or εἷς . . . θεός, εἷς καὶ μεσίτης θεοῦ καὶ ἀνθρώπων, ἄνθρωπος Χριστὸς Ἰησοῦς, ὁ δοὺς ἑαυτὸν ἀντίλυτρον ὑπὲρ πάντων, either of which may serve as a reasonable expression of the apostolic gospel message, it remains the "sound teaching," the "faithful" word, "the truth," and God's gospel message entrusted to his apostolic agent.[50]

It already has been argued that πιστὸς ὁ λόγος as it appears in 1:15 serves as a commentary upon the essential apostolic gospel proclamation, and that the remainder of the verse offers one formulation of that "faithful" word. The same expression now appears for the second time in 3:1a. However, this occurrence of the affirmation, πιστὸς ὁ λόγος, is

47. Guthrie writes, "A question arises whether this assertion would not be better linked with the following rather than the preceding words. If so, veracity would be given to Paul's claim to be especially appointed *a teacher to the Gentiles* rather than to his claim to apostleship. But the two claims are inseparable . . . They embrace both the spirit of the teacher and the content of the message" (Guthrie, *Pastoral Epistles*, 83). Quinn and Wacker assert, "For the PE, Paul is the herald-apostle, or apostolic herald, entrusted with the *kerygma* for which he in turn commissions others" (Quinn and Wacker, *Letters to Timothy*, 189).

48. Spicq unequivocally equates the two assertions, for in his remarks on 2:7, he writes, "The central idea of the Gospel: salvation by means of Christ, always conveys in Saint Paul reference to his personal mission (cf. 2 Cor. 5:18—6:1; Eph 3:7, 8). It is that the whole reason for the existence of his vocation is to participate in the salvation work, to announce to all people and to apply to them the outcome of this ransom . . . εἰς ὅ . . . It is to continue this witness or to advance this salvation that I was appointed (the aorist passive ἐτέθην excludes human initiative, cf. 1:12) herald, apostle and teacher (cf. 2 Tim 2:11), three practically equivalent terms for 'preacher' that accentuate the affirmation" (Spicq, *Les Épîtres Pastorales*, 61).

49. Barrett, *Pastoral Epistles*, 52; Marshall, *Pastoral Epistles*, 433–34; Scott, *Pastoral Epistles*, 22; Witherington, *Letters and Homilies*, 216–17.

50. Fee, *Timothy and Titus*, 67; Towner, *Goal of Our Instruction*, 87; Witherington, *Letters and Homilies*, 217.

not accompanied by an explicit presentation of any gospel formulation.[51] Therefore, a sense of what Paul is doing in the second chapter of the letter can help one come to terms with his usage of πιστὸς ὁ λόγος in 3:1a.

In 1:15a, one may note that the expression πιστὸς ὁ λόγος occurred after Paul's reflections upon his own experience of God's grace. Thus, the affirmation likely functioned as a response to these reflections.[52] In a similar manner, from the beginning of chapter 2, Paul urges Timothy to call the believers in Ephesus to a renewed focus upon what they must be doing as a matter of course. To the general community, he issues a summons to prayer for "all peoples."[53] Paul then addresses two distinct segments of that community. First, the men are to pray with holy hands, as opposed to hands polluted by "anger or quarreling."[54] Next, the women are instructed to concentrate upon the faithfulness and holiness to which they are called instead of striving after prominence or attention.[55] They are assured that if they do so they will not lose the promised salvation brought to light in the gospel proclamation.[56] Here then, in the words of assurance to the women of Ephesus, lies the remark that triggers a second statement of confirmation, for indeed, the "sound teaching," the gospel word, is "faithful," and they may rely upon it.[57]

51. Indeed, the broad uncertainty regarding the referent of πιστὸς ὁ λόγος here is exhibited in the divergence of solutions proposed (see, for instance, Collins, *Timothy and Titus*, 42, 77–78; Johnson, *Letters to Timothy*, 203; Knight, *Faithful Sayings*, 54–57; Roloff, *Der erste Brief an Timotheus*, 90, 147, 153; Witherington, *Letters and Homilies*, 201–4).

52. Putting it somewhat differently, Knight asserts, "Since Paul wants to relate his own experience as a demonstration of the Christian truth, he quotes a saying that states what he had experienced as a general truth" (Knight, *Pastoral Epistles*, 100).

53. Guthrie, *Pastoral Epistles*, 80; Johnson, *Letters to Timothy*, 196–97; Knight, *Pastoral Epistles*, 115, 119; Quinn and Wacker, *Letters to Timothy*, 156–75.

54. Bassler, *1 Timothy, 2 Timothy, Titus*, 56–57; Knight, *Pastoral Epistles*, 129–30, 131; Johnson, *Letters to Timothy*, 199; Mounce, *Pastoral Epistles*, 105.

55. Collins, *Timothy and Titus*, 77; Knight, *Pastoral Epistles*, 131, 136–42; Mounce, *Pastoral Epistles*, 146–47; Towner, *Letters to Timothy and Titus*, 235.

56. Barrett, *Pastoral Epistles*, 56–57; Collins, *Timothy and Titus*, 77; Van Neste, *Cohesion and Structure*, 39. However, Knight sees the remarks on "childbearing" as a reference to the birth of the Messiah or Christ child (Knight, *Pastoral Epistles*, 145–47).

57. Bover writes, "Saint Paul not only praises or recommends this ideal, but he affirms that, trying to conform herself to him, the woman shall be saved, 'she will obtain salvation or the eternal life.' And with this, the faithful saying continues in text B and enters completely the order of things in texts A, C, D and E; it coincides substantially with them. And we have it then that the object or content of the five formulas is in definitely one and the same: That is to say, the reality or consistency of the divine

As has been noted previously, Paul remains fixed upon lifting up, vindicating, and holding forth the gospel message of God with which he stands entrusted as one of God's apostolic messengers of God's grace and salvation.[58] This established focus, along with Paul's apparently interchangeable usage of such terms as ἡ ἀλήθεια, διδασκαλία, εὐαγγέλιον, λόγος, μαρτύριον, and πίστις, will contribute significantly to the appraisal of his use of γραφή.[59]

3:1b–16—Would-be Leaders and the Mystery of the Faith

While many read this unit as a virtual manual for the appointment of individuals to church offices—namely, those of ἐπίσκοπος and διακόνος— such a reading does not give sufficient attention to the thrust of the immediately preceding material or to the innate impetus of the epistle.[60]

---

promises and the security and solidity of our hope in the eternal life" (Bover, "Fidelis Sermo," 77). See also Rendall, "Faithful Is the Word," 319; Van Bruggen, "Vaste grond onder de voeten." 44.

58. With regard to the entirety of 1 Tim 2:1—6:21, Barrett maintains, "The author's main concerns stand out clearly: The purity of the apostolic Gospel must be maintained" (Barrett, *Pastoral Epistles*, 48). Towner gathers together most of the terms already discussed and presents them accordingly: "In sum, we can specify that the proclamation denoted by *euangelion*, *martyrion*, and *kerygma* consists of the message of God's grace in Christ, the purpose of which is the dissemination of salvation in the world. *Didaskalia*, on the other hand, was directed to the believing community. The most evident common-denominator of the two 'proclamations' can be seen in their content, at the center of which in each case (in addition to the decided ethical orientation of *didaskalia*) was the tradition about the historical Christ-event and the salvation it produced" (Towner, *Goal of Our Instruction*, 124).

59. Van Neste observes a similar correlation of terms, proposing, "In addition to the semantic link running throughout, there are significant lexical repetitions as διδασκαλία occurs seven times and λόγος occurs five times. Both of these terms are described as 'sound,' and they are used in conjunction with each other twice (4.6; 5.17). The message is also connected with faith as it is 'the mystery of the faith' (3.9), 'the words of the faith' (4.6), and Paul teaches 'faith and truth' (2.7)" (Van Neste, *Cohesion and Structure*, 110).

60. Accordingly, Fee writes, "It is often suggested that what is being given in (chapters 2 and 3) is an early church manual, of the kind that would have been needed for setting a congregation in order . . . By and large, however, the 'church manual' view sees very little relationship between chapters 2 and 3 and the charge to Timothy in chapter 1. But since the new section begins with the conjunction 'therefore' (NIV, then), implying a result or inference from what has preceded, it seems much more likely that all of this material is a direct consequence of what was said in chapter 1" (Fee, *Timothy and Titus*, 61). Mounce likewise maintains that "the message of the

In the preceding unit, Paul began to directly address the character and conduct of the believers in Ephesus, beginning with a broad directive and then shifting to more particular instructions to men and then to women. He continues in a similar vein, focusing his attention this time upon those who already hold positions of responsibility in the churches as well as upon those who aspire to such positions.[61] In other words, this unit is not chiefly concerned with appointing individuals to office or with establishing new offices. Rather, it continues to develop the corrective teaching that has dominated the letter from 1:3. The various traits mentioned as appropriate to the offices of "overseer" and "minister," stand over against those with which Paul has found fault as they are manifested among "certain men."[62] Thus, those who exhibit the traits found in 3:2–7 are cast in opposition to men who ἀστοχήσαντες ἐξετράπησαν εἰς ματαιολογίαν θέλοντες εἶναι νομοδιδάσκαλοι, μὴ νοοῦντες μήτε ἃ λέγουσιν μήτε περὶ τίνων διαβεβαιοῦνται (1:6–7), who in their ambition have done more to advance αἱ ἐκζητήσεις rather than ἡ οἰκονομία θεοῦ τὴν ἐν πίστει (1:4), and who περὶ τὴν πίστιν ἐναυάγησαν (1:19).[63]

---

chapter is missed if the reader does not interpret it in light of the Ephesian situation. Almost every quality Paul specifies here has its negative counterpart in the Ephesian opponents" (Mounce, *Pastoral Epistles*, 153).

61. Witherington represents a similar position, acknowledging, "Gordon Fee probably is right that we should see this material as having been shaped by the need to respond to the false teachers and describe what real church leaders and teachers should be like" (Witherington, *Letters and Homilies*, 232).

62. Johnson hints at this when he writes, "To ask for a leader who has moral probity and is known by outsiders as having such virtue is to make a legitimate request at any time, but, above all, when the reputation of the community is threatened by leaders who lack such qualities" (Johnson, *Letters to Timothy*, 225). Witherington also seems to detect among the criteria listed in these verses a continued polemic against the "certain men" of 1 Timothy 1, as he observes, "The condemnation here of greediness is perhaps in part due to the fact that this seems to have been a trait of the false teachers" (Witherington, *Letters and Homilies*, 237).

63. To his earlier comments, Fee adds, "Why then *this* instruction? Again, the evidence points to the character and activities of the false teachers. In this regard two things must be noted: First, many of the items in the list stand in sharp contrast to what is said elsewhere in the letter about the false teachers. Second, the list itself has three notable features: (1) It gives qualifications, not duties; (2) most of the items reflect outward, observable behavior; and (3) none of the items is distinctively Christian . . . Rather, they reflect the highest ideals of Hellenistic moral philosophy" (Fee, *Timothy and Titus*, 78). Of particular significance to the observations offered in this study, Fee follows these remarks with, "Since the whole passage points toward and concludes with verse 7, that is, concern for the overseer's (and thus the church's) reputation with outsiders, this suggests that the false teachers were, by their behavior,

Within the framework of Paul's continuing admonitions, and viewed in terms of the prevailing concern of the letter thus far, the specific trait of διδακτικός that is required of ἐπίσκοποι (3:2) most likely pertains specifically to instruction that advances "the gospel," the "sound teaching," the "faithful" word, or "the faith."[64] In a similar way, and with the same concerns in mind, Paul insists that those who would be διακόνοι must hold τὸ μυστήριον τῆς πίστεως ἐν καθαρᾷ συνειδήσει.[65]

Based upon the literary context established thus far, the most coherent reading of τὸ μυστήριον τῆς πίστεως would construe this expression in a manner comparable with the interchangeable terms already noted. Clearly, the would-be minister (διάκονος) must adhere to some kind of teaching or principle. Also, based upon the preceding context, the most plausible construal of this teaching associates it with the same type of ideas that the overseers are competent to teach and which Paul is so anxious to protect.[66] In this instance, the genitive τῆς πίστεως functions epexegetically, conveying the sense, "the mystery that is the faith," while τὸ μυστήριον introduces into the letter a new element that consists in a "mystery" associated with the faith, or with the gospel proclamation.[67] Furthermore, while the use of τὸ μυστήριον suggests something not readily perceived or widely known, one also must recall Paul's early efforts to establish his apostolic role as one who proclaims τὸ εὐαγγέλιον τῆς δόξης τοῦ μακαρίου θεοῦ (1:11). Thus, in referring to τὸ μυστήριον τῆς πίστεως, Paul likely emphasizes the revelatory nature of the apostolic gospel with

---

bringing the gospel into disrepute" (ibid., emphasis mine).

64. Spicq is very clear on this, stating, "The bishop must be able to teach (διδακτικός; cf. 2 Tim 2:24; *hap. b.*) not because he necessarily is eloquent, nor even that he has position (Cajetan), but because he is studied in the knowledge of God and the gospel, and capable in addition of explaining and deciding doctrinal disputes (cf. Tit 1:9)" (Spicq, *Les Épîtres Pastorales*, 81).

65. Guthrie, *Pastoral Epistles*, 96; Knight, *Pastoral Epistles*, 169; Mounce, *Pastoral Epistles*, 199; Spicq, *Les Épîtres Pastorales*, 99.

66. Knight proposes that this designation refers to "'the revealed truth of the Christian faith' with πίστις referring here to that which is believed" (Knight, *Pastoral Epistles*, 169). Towner maintains, "'The faith' in this sense clearly denotes the sum total of orthodox doctrine" (Towner, *Goal of Our Instruction*, 122).

67. Regarding this point, Spicq writes, "We do not think that τῆς πίστεως is a subjective genitive; it is in apposition to τὸ μυστήριον, designating the collection of hidden truth, inaccessible to reason, and that one can know only by divine revelation. The object of the faith is a revealed mystery (cf. 3:15; Eph 3:4; Col 4:3)" (Spicq, *Les Épîtres Pastorales*, 99).

which he stands entrusted.[68] It is this that he has proclaimed among the Ephesian believers, and to which he now reminds the ministers to adhere. Further insight may be found in Paul's use of τὸ μυστήριον, as it appears a few verses later.

In 3:14–16, Paul offers a summation of the preceding material much like that which appeared in 1:18–20. When he writes, Ταῦτα σοι γράφω ἐλπίζων ἐλθεῖν πρὸς σὲ ἐν τάχει· ἐὰν δὲ βραδύνω, ἵνα εἰδῇς πῶς δεῖ ἐν οἴκῳ θεοῦ ἀναστρέφεσθαι, ταῦτα most likely refers to the instructions that one finds in 2:1—3:13, in which his focus has shifted from predominantly doctrinal matters to matters of ethics and conduct.[69] Nevertheless, even while addressing conduct, Paul offers in the midst of this summation yet another reminder of the heart of the "sound teaching" upon which "the faith" rests. Thus, he explicitly draws attention to the correspondence between his admonition on right conduct and to the believers' responsibility to stand as ἐκκλησία θεοῦ ζῶντος, στῦλος καὶ ἑδραίωμα τῆς ἀληθείας.[70] As in the case with its occurrence in 2:4, ἡ ἀλήθεια here in 3:15 is understood as a reference to the "sound teaching" and the gospel proclamation with which Paul stands entrusted.[71] Paul then follows this admonition with the curious affirmation, καὶ ὁμολογουμένως μέγα ἐστὶν τὸ τῆς εὐσεβείας μυστήριον· ὃς ἐφανερώθη ἐν σαρκί, ἐδικαιώθη ἐν πνεύματι, ὤφθη ἀγγέλοις, ἐκηρύχθη ἐν ἔθνεσιν, ἐπιστεύθη ἐν κόσμῳ, ἀνελήμφθη ἐν δόξῃ. Because of the paratactic syntactical relationship between 3:15b and 3:16, signaled by καί, the most plausible analysis entails construing 3:16 as standing in series with 3:15b.[72] Consequently, even though Paul has used ἡ εὐσέβεια

68. Indeed, Witherington seems to presume this very thing, observing, "The term *mysterion* in 1 Timothy 3:9 refers to something once obscure, unknown or hidden that has now been revealed . . . It seems to refer to the salvation available to us as revealed in and through Christ" (Witherington, *Letters and Homilies*, 241).

69. Collins, *Timothy and Titus*, 99; Fee, *Timothy and Titus*, 91; Knight, *Pastoral Epistles*, 178–79; Marshall, *Pastoral Epistles*, 498, 506–7.

70. Guthrie, *Pastoral Epistles*, 99–100; Spicq, *Les Épîtres Pastorales*, 103; Towner, *Letters to Timothy and Titus*, 274–75; Witherington, *Letters and Homilies*, 244–45.

71. Oberlinner maintains, "The appositional genitive τῆς ἀληθείας is not to be understood as a qualitative genitive, but as a genitive of origin. This also is supported by the fact that this 'truth' in the following verse is expounded as 'truth of the faith'" (Oberlinner, *Erster Timotheusbrief*, 160). Witherington also writes, "Paul calls the assembly the pillar and support or buttress of the truth. The point is that believers hold up and represent the truth to the world, and therefore their behavior is all the more crucial" (Witherington, *Letters and Homilies*, 245).

72. Following Spicq, Knight here construes καί as "indeed" (Knight, *Pastoral Epistles*, 182). Marshall, however, sees 3:16 as a further development of the idea

only in 2:2 prior to this point in the letter, the most natural treatment equates ἡ εὐσέβεια in the main clause with the traits appropriate to believers who commend the truth as they collectively serve as στῦλος καὶ ἑδραίωμα τῆς ἀληθείας. This also is consistent with the reading in 2:2, where Paul opens his admonitions regarding the churches with the summons to peaceable and quiet lives, ἐν πάσῃ εὐσεβείᾳ καὶ σεμνότητι.[73] However, in this instance Paul presents τὸ μυστήριον, not merely as a conceptual "mystery" now disclosed, but as a reference fundamentally associated with a person, expressed by the relative clauses ὃς ἐφανερώθη ἐν σαρκί, ἐδικαιώθη ἐν πνεύματι, ὤφθη ἀγγέλοις, ἐκηρύχθη ἐν ἔθνεσιν, ἐπιστεύθη ἐν κόσμῳ, ἀνελήμφθη ἐν δόξῃ.[74] Indeed, it would appear that the entire gospel message, the "mystery of the faith," relates chiefly to—and even is embodied and revealed in—this one person. Based upon the pieces of information that Paul has provided through the letter, particularly in those texts in which he has disclosed the contents of the "faithful" word, this person can only be Christ Jesus, whom that word concerns and on whose behalf Paul carries out his apostolic mission.[75]

If the preceding analysis is correct, it carries significant implications for the focal point of this study. Thus far, Paul has used several terms in parallel and virtually synonymous references to the apostolic gospel message with which he was entrusted and which comes from God. At the same time, each term makes its own unique and subtle contribution to the shaping of the general idea. Therefore, while one may use "the gospel," "the sound teaching," "the faith," the "faithful" word, "the truth," or "the mystery of the faith" to refer to essentially one and the same thing, each unique referent lays some emphasis upon one aspect or another relative to that essential message. In this latter instance, τὸ τῆς εὐσεβείας μυστήριον now incorporates a direct association between the message and Christ Jesus, whom it concerns.[76]

---

represented by ἀλήθεια (Marshall, *Pastoral Epistles*, 521–22).

73. Towner, *Letters to Timothy and Titus*, 270.

74. Knight, *Pastoral Epistles*, 183–84, 186; Marshall, *Pastoral Epistles*, 499, 523; Spicq, *Les Épîtres Pastorales*, 107–6; Witherington, *Letters and Homilies*, 246.

75. Barrett, *Pastoral Epistles*, 65; Mounce, *Pastoral Epistles*, 225–30; Spicq, *Les Épîtres Pastorales*, 106–7; Towner, *Letters to Timothy and Titus*, 277.

76. Fee, *Timothy and Titus*, 95; Knight, *Pastoral Epistles*, 186; Marshall, *Pastoral Epistles*, 499, 523; Towner, *Goal of Our Instruction*, 88; Witherington, *Letters and Homilies*, 246–48.

4:1–5—The Faith and the Word of God

Lending credence to the identification of the predominant agenda of the letter as argued so far in this study, Paul opens the next literary unit with the admonition, ἐν ὑστέροις καιροῖς ἀποστήσονταί τινες τῆς πίστεως. This abandonment of "the faith" carried out by "certain men" shall be accompanied by their preoccupation with πνεύματα πλάνοι and διδασκαλίαι δαιμονίων. With relentless consistency then, Paul continues to lift up and commend "the faith," which he identifies with "the sound teaching," as he also sets the truth in sharp opposition to "deceiving spirits" and "demonic teachings."[77] Thus, Paul once again knits "truth" together with "the sound teaching" that is associated with God's gospel message or "faithful" word.[78]

With respect to marriage and foods that are to be received without prejudice, Paul refers to them as those things ἃ ὁ θεὸς ἔκτισεν εἰς μετάλημψιν μετὰ εὐχαριστίας τοῖς πιστοῖς καὶ ἐπεγνωκόσι τὴν ἀλήθειαν. He then supports this assertion with the grounding argument, ὅτι πᾶν κτίσμα θεοῦ καλὸν καὶ οὐδὲν ἀπόβλητον μετὰ εὐχαριστίας λαμβανόμενον, a statement he further justifies by the claim, ἁγιάζεται γὰρ διὰ λόγου θεοῦ καὶ ἐντεύξεως.[79] In this series of remarks, one finds not only the administration of a corrective to an excessive and misplaced asceticism attended by a liberating and positive perspective upon marriage and the partaking of food, but also an implied semantic association between ἡ ἀλήθεια and λόγος θεοῦ.[80] It begins with the occurrence in 4:3 of ἐπεγνωκόσι τὴν

77. Fee, *Timothy and Titus*, 97; Johnson, *Letters to Timothy*, 238–39; Oberlinner, *Erster Timotheusbrief*, 175–76; Roloff, *Der erste Brief an Timotheus*, 220; Schlatter, *Die Kirche der Griechen*, 116–17.

78. This is especially likely in view of Paul's use of ἡ ἀλήθεια in both 2:4 and 3:15 (Collins, *Timothy and Titus*, 113; Fee, *Timothy and Titus*, 97; Johnson, *Letters to Timothy*, 241).

79. Knight, *Pastoral Epistles*, 191–92; Marshall, *Pastoral Epistles*, 545; Towner, *Letters to Timothy and Titus*, 297–99; Witherington, *Letters and Homilies*, 254–55.

80. Fee makes a similar observation, suggesting, "In the PE, *the word of God* invariably refers to the gospel message (2 Tim 2:19; Titus 1:3; 2:5; cf. 1 Tim 5:17; 2 Tim 2:15; 4:2). If that is the case here then it reflects the idea of believers' having come to *know the truth* (v. 3) that in Christ there are no food laws" (Fee, *Timothy and Titus*, 101, emphasis Fee's). Mounce, while ultimately rejecting this explanation in favor of an allusion to the creation narrative, nevertheless also offers as a possible accounting, "'Word of God' can be the gospel message, which includes the message that food laws are now passé. This interpretation has much to commend it. (a) It parallels the previous phrase, 'by those who are faithful and know the truth' (1 Tim 4:3b), which refers to those who believe the gospel. (b) The phrase means the gospel when it is used elsewhere in the PE (2 Tim 2:9; 4:2; Titus 2:5; cf. similar expression in 1 Tim 5:6; 2

ἀλήθειαν, which recalls ἐπίγνωσιν τὴν ἀλήθειαν from 2:4, construed as a reference to salvation.[81] As already argued, this earlier "knowledge of the truth" entails an apprehension of and adherence to God's "faithful" word that bears witness to his saving work in Christ Jesus. Consequently, these to whom Paul refers as οἱ πίστοι καὶ ἐπεγνωκότες τὴν ἀλήθειαν (4:3) also are εἰς ἐπίγνωσιν ἀληθείας ἐχόμενοι, a designation that tightens the semantic link between ἀλήθεια and God's "faithful" word. At the very least, those who understand ἀλήθεια also recognize that the λόγος θεοῦ authorizes marriages and all foods. Such an association is especially significant in light of the analysis of γραφή with which this study is ultimately concerned.

Consistent with the prevailing treatment of the phrase as it occurs here in 1 Timothy, λόγος θεοῦ is construed subjectively (or possessively), reflected in the translation, "God's word."[82] However, the precise referent of λόγος θεοῦ is difficult to determine. One possibility of a parallel OT passage is suggested by the notes found in the margin of the NA[27]: namely, the declaration of the writer of Genesis in 1:31, "And God saw everything that he had made and, behold, it was very good."[83] While impossible to prove, this suggestion certainly appears plausible upon an initial reading. It would reflect a perspective on the created order consistent with that commended by Paul, and it would indicate a high view of Torah, also a distinctly Pauline trait and a feature of this letter already noted with

---

Tim 2:15) and Paul" (Mounce, *Pastoral Epistles*, 241). Towner also offers, "This might refer to a specific divine logion (cf. Rom 3:4; 9:6), in which case Gen 1:31, or the entire early section of Genesis, or a word of Jesus (Mark 7:1–23) might come to mind. Or 'word of God' (see 1:15 note) might be understood in the sense of the gospel message. In this case, sanctification comes by way of proclamation and teaching of the Christian message that enlightens people concerning God's will" (Towner, *Letters to Timothy and Titus*, 299).

81. Regarding this, Johnson writes, "The combination of terms in effect identifies those who are likely to give thanks to God for marriage and food. They are *pistoi*— that is, those who perceive the *oikonomia theou* 'in faith' (*en pistei*, 1:4). And they are among 'the saved,' since they have 'come to the recognition of the truth' (2:4). Such as these are not the only ones whom God blesses or who partake in the goods of creation, but they are the only ones who recognize them as God's creation and give thanks for them to the creator" (Johnson, *Letters to Timothy*, 241). See also Spicq, *Les Épîtres Pastorales*, 138.

82. Knight, *Pastoral Epistles*, 192; Mounce, *Pastoral Epistles*, 241.

83. NA[27], 546. In the LXX, it reads, καὶ εἶδεν ὁ θεὸς τὰ πάντα ὅσα ἐποίησεν καὶ ἰδοὺ καλὰ λίαν. Similar notation occurs in the footnotes of the UBS[4] (718). As Towner points out, several of these very terms are reflected in Paul's words here, ὅτι πᾶν κτίσμα θεοῦ (Towner, *Letters to Timothy and Titus*, 300).

regard to 1:8–11.[84] The point is reinforced by God's words to the man and woman in Gen 1:29, "Behold, I give to you every seed-bearing plant that is upon the face of the earth and every seed-bearing fruit tree to you to be for food."

However, against limiting the solution to this suggestion alone, one must observe that while the writer of Genesis declares the creation "very good," and God implies such goodness and good purpose in the creation by his presentation of food-worthy flora to the man and the woman, the passage does not depict either God himself or the Torah as issuing any direct statements regarding the sanctioning of all food, nor does it use any language that would forge a direct and indisputable link to ἁγιάζεται . . . διὰ λόγου θεοῦ καὶ ἐντεύξεως. Furthermore, in Gen 1:31 there is no direct comment upon either food or marriage, the topics at issue in 1 Tim 4:3–4. Most importantly however, this solution for λόγος θεοῦ fails to take into account the immediate literary context of 1 Timothy and any prior usage of ὁ λόγος in the letter. Consequently, this suggestion may serve at best as an indirect equivalent for food and marriage having been "sanctified" by God's word, and as only part of the intended referent of λόγος θεοῦ.[85]

With respect to the literary context of the letter, it has already been observed that λόγος often serves as a technical reference to the gospel proclamation. That this is a plausible construal may also be seen in the lexical surveys of Gerhard Kittel, Walter Bauer and Frederick Danker, and Johannes Louw and Eugene Nida. For instance, Bauer and Danker include among their listings, in correspondence with Acts 6:7, 12:24, 19:20, and 2 Tim 2:9, "In these places and many others, ὁ λόγος τοῦ θεοῦ is simply the Christian message, the gospel."[86] In a similar fashion, Gerhard Kittel writes,

> For [Paul] the λόγος τοῦ θεοῦ (τοῦ θεοῦ or κυρίου) is the mes-
> sage proclaimed by him and accepted by his churches. That is

84. Contra Bassler, who construes Paul's view of the created order as ambivalent to indifferent (Bassler, *1 Timothy, 2 Timothy, Titus*, 81–82).

85. The same evaluation applies to marriage and Gen 2:18–25.

86. BDAG, 599b. Likewise, while Johnson first suggests, "Paul could mean by this God's word as expressed in Scripture (Rom 3:4; 9:6). In this case, 'the word of God' would refer to God's creative and approving word in Genesis" (Johnson, *Letters to Timothy*, 242). Johnson then adds, "Much more frequently, however, Paul uses *logos tou theou* with specific reference to the Christian message (1 Cor 14:36; 2 Cor 2:17; 4:2; Col 1:25; 1 Thess 2:13; 2 Tim 2:9)" (ibid.).

to say, it is simply the message about Christ . . . The content of the λόγος is given in 1 Tim 1:15; ὅτι Χριστὸς Ἰησοῦς ἦλθεν εἰς τὸν κόσμον ἁμαρτωλοὺς σῶσαι . . . This fact that the Word is effica-cious in individual lives is the content of the recurrent πιστὸς ὁ λόγος of the Pastorals.[87]

Louw and Nida concur, offering as one definition for λόγος "the con-tent of what is preached about Christ or about the good news—'what is preached, gospel,' ὁ λόγος τοῦ θεοῦ 'what is preached concerning Christ' or 'the good news about Christ.'"[88] Knight and Towner reflect a similar as-sessment.[89] While the preceding lexical survey cannot in itself determine meaning for λόγος in the specific context of 4:5, it does indicate that the construal of λόγος offered here falls well within a recognized semantic domain. This analysis is further advanced by the examination of recur-ring terms such as ἡ ὑγιαίνουσα διδασκαλία, τὸ εὐαγγέλιον τῆς δόξης τοῦ μακαρίου θεοῦ, ὁ λόγος, ὁ [πιστὸς] λόγος, ἡ πίστις, τὸ μαρτύριον, ἡ ἀλήθεια, τὸ μυστήριον τῆς πίστεως, and οἱ λόγοι τῆς πίστεως, all of which are con-strued in this study as functioning interchangeably with ὁ λόγος.[90]

In view of these factors, it may be significant that in the Gospel of Luke (along with the other Synoptics), among the teachings of Jesus, one finds statements that exhibit a striking correlation with both topics as they are addressed in 1 Timothy 4.[91] Indeed, the informal nature of

87. Kittel, "λέγω, λόγος, λαλέω, ῥῆμα, κ.τ.λ.," 115–19.

88. Louw and Nida, *Greek-English Lexicon of the New Testament*, 33.260.

89. Knight states, "When the New Testament writers speak of *the* word (ὁ λόγος), they have in view that special word, the truth of God, unless the context indicates otherwise. This is so obvious in the one place in the Pastoral Letters, excluding the πιστὸς ὁ λόγος passages, where ὁ λόγος appears simply with the definite article (κήρυξον τὸν λόγον). Likewise the five-fold reference to ὁ λόγος in πιστὸς ὁ λόγος fits in this same category. The word (ὁ λόγος) is πιστός because it is the word setting forth God's truth . . . Since teaching often and preaching especially is oral, and since ὁ λόγος is commonly understood as the Christian message, λόγος itself may designate procla-mation or instruction" (Knight, *Faithful Sayings*, 14–15). Similarly, Towner writes, "In several cases *logos* (modified by *tou theou*, 2 Tim 2.9; Titus 2.5; *autou*, Titus 1.3; independent, 2 Tim 4.2) denotes the gospel message. The balance of the occurrences indicates that the source of the message is God and that the purpose of its proclama-tion is salvation" (Towner, *Goal of Our Instruction*, 123–24). See also Karris, "Polemic of the Pastoral Epistles," 558–59.

90. See again Van Neste's remarks regarding "semantic chains" (Van Neste, *Co-hesion and Structure*, 11–12); Reed, "Cohesive Ties in 1 Timothy," 131–47; cf. Reed, "Discourse Features," 228–52.

91. The instruction concerning foods is found in Luke 11:37–41, Matt 15:1–20, and Mark 7:1–23. Instruction concerning marriage appears in Luke 16:18, Matt 5:31–32;

the allusions to food and marriage in 4:3–4, their explicit association with λόγος θεοῦ, and the coincidence of their interpretation with the Lukan tradition, along with the absence of any direct literary dependence, would seem to favor something more complex than a simple Logion source lying behind Paul's words in this passage, or even another allusion to the Torah. Also, if that correspondence is placed alongside the established observation that in 1 Timothy Paul utilizes several virtually synonymous expressions to designate the apostolic message concerning Jesus that God entrusted to Paul, then implications of a more substantive nature begin to emerge.

Naturally, this line of analysis touches upon the issues of the authorship and the date of composition of Luke, which shall be addressed briefly in the next chapter. Even so, prevailing opinions regarding the Lukan writings must not be permitted to rule out *a priori* a judicious consideration of data that may point to a plausible correspondence between Luke's gospel and 1 Timothy.[92] Indeed, it is worth noting that if Paul actually draws upon material that now appears in any of the canonical gospels, and if he also designates it λόγος θεοῦ, then the implications are far-reaching, especially with respect to construals of γραφή.

4:6–16—The Good Minister of Christ Jesus

In view of the situation assessment found in 4:1–3, along with the corrective provided in 4:4–5, in 4:6 Paul gathers all of the teaching contained in 2:1—4:5 into the pronoun ταῦτα, and encourages Timothy to remind the believers of "these things."[93] If Timothy carries through with this reminder, Paul writes that he shall show himself to be καλὸς . . . διάκονος Χριστοῦ

19:1–2, and Mark 10:11–12. These passages and their pertinence to the topic will be discussed in the next chapter.

92. Collins also notes this correspondence between 1 Timothy and the Synoptic Gospels (Collins, *Timothy and Titus*, 117). Johnson's previously cited remarks seem to indicate just such an *a priori* judgment, for on the one hand, he acknowledges that this "word of God" could indeed denote Jesus' teaching on such matters, while on the other hand, he seems to presume that if Paul is referring to "Scripture," he must have in mind the Gen 1:31 decree (Johnson, *Letters to Timothy*, 241).

93. Fee, *Timothy and Titus*, 102. Ταῦτα possibly may reach back only as far as Paul's instructions in 3:1–16. This is the position taken by Bassler (Bassler, *1 Timothy, 2 Timothy, Titus*, 83) and Collins (Collins, *Timothy and Titus*, 120–21), while Bernard limits the range to 4:1–5 (Bernard, *Pastoral Epistles*, 68). Spicq, on the other hand, traces the referent all the way back to 1:18, by way of 3:15–16 (Spicq, *Les Épîtres Pastorales*, 140).

Ἰησοῦ, ἐντρεφόμενος τοῖς λόγοις τῆς πίστεως καὶ τῆς καλῆς διδασκαλίας ᾗ παρηκολούθηκας. According to the analysis behind this study, the second genitival expression of 4:6c, τῆς καλῆς διδασκαλίας, functions epexegetically with τῆς πίστεως and further qualifies τοῖς λόγοις.[94] In addition to this, Paul also reprises his use of "the faith" as a reference to the beliefs and corresponding conduct that rest upon "the good teaching." Thus, in the statement of 4:6c, Paul explicitly associates "the words of the faith" with "the good teaching," which corresponds to the "sound teaching" that stands in accordance with τὸ εὐαγγέλιον τῆς δόξης τοῦ μακαρίου θεοῦ of 1:11. Consequently, one may surmise that "the words of the faith" also correspond to this same gospel with which Paul was entrusted and which he proclaimed.[95] Furthermore, with this first occurrence of the dative plural, τοῖς λόγοις, it is proposed here that Paul seeks to draw attention not merely to the "faithful" word of God's gospel message, but also to the very expressions that he has used as one designated a κῆρυξ καὶ ἀπόστολος . . . διδάσκαλος of that word: possibly expressions with which Timothy is familiar and by which he already stands instructed, since the teaching he is to sustain is also that ᾗ παρηκολούθηκας.[96] If this were the case, it would signal not only that Paul jealously guards the gospel word

94. Marshall argues that τοῖς λόγοις τῆς πίστεως, 'the words of the faith' is equivalent to "other phrases that sum up the truth expressed in the gospel" (Marshall, *Pastoral Epistles*, 549). He writes, "It is almost synonymous with the next phrase: καὶ τῆς καλῆς διδασκαλίας: 'and [the words] of the good teaching'" (ibid.). Quinn and Wacker also contend that "it is almost certain here that *the words* are equivalent to 'my words,' i.e., Paul's way of articulating the realities in which Christians put their faith . . . The *kales didaskalias* is further qualified here as *hei parekolouthekas*, 'with which you are quite familiar' . . . The relationship here certainly involves receiving a teaching that, because of its origin as well as the immediacy of the witness to it, has considerable authority" (Quinn and Wacker, *Letters to Timothy*, 372–73). On the other hand, Mounce writes, "The primary source of Timothy's support is the gospel, but to make the point clear Paul distinguishes between the gospel itself (τοῖς λόγοις τῆς πίστεως) and the doctrine contained in that gospel (τοῖς λόγοις . . . τῆς καλῆς διδασκαλίας) . . . The grammar does not allow λόγοις, 'words,' and διδασκαλία, 'teaching,' to be a hendiadys" (Mounce, *Pastoral Epistles*, 249). Mounce's analysis, however, seems arbitrary, as no grammatical (or other) criteria are offered by which one is to differentiate between "the gospel itself" and "the doctrine contained in that gospel."

95. Hanson, *Pastoral Letters*, 51; Johnson, *Letters to Timothy*, 243; Marcheselli-Casale, *Le Lettere Pastorali*, 311; Oberlinner, *Erster Timotheusbrief*, 189–90; Roloff, *Der erste Brief an Timotheus*, 242; Schlatter, *Die Kirche der Griechen*, 122.

96. Johnson, *Letters to Timothy*, 243; Witherington, *Letters and Homilies*, 255. This emphasis would be similar to Paul's remarks in 1 Cor 2:12–13 regarding the very expressions by which he (and the rest of his apostolic brethren) convey the truths of God (Swinson, "Words Taught by the Spirit"; Kaiser, "A Neglected Text").

received from God with which he stands entrusted, but also that he puts great stock in his own or other apostolic expressions of it as authoritative representations of God's word as well.[97]

In 4:7, Paul then admonishes Timothy to keep himself clear of "profane and silly myths" and instead to γύμναζε . . . σεαυτὸν πρὸς εὐσέβειαν. The justification for this admonition lies in the principle, ἡ σωματικὴ γυμνασία πρὸς ὀλίγον ἐστὶν ὠφέλιμος, ἡ δὲ εὐσέβεια πρὸς πάντα ὠφέλιμός ἐστιν ἐπαγγελίαν ἔχουσα ζωῆς τῆς νῦν καὶ τῆς μελλούσης.[98] Subsequently, in 4:9, one may find the third occurrence of πιστὸς ὁ λόγος in 1 Timothy. Consistent with what has been observed in previous instances of πιστὸς ὁ λόγος in 1 Timothy, the formula materializes here as if to confirm the assertion regarding the timeless worth and promise of godliness.[99] Consequently, as with the previous occurrences, ὁ λόγος here most likely does not refer back or forward to something cited; rather, it probably refers to the apostolic gospel proclamation generally. At the same time, that proclamation, and thus the affirmation πιστὸς ὁ λόγος, surely does *pertain to* adjacent material. In this case, the promises that attend godliness are also witnessed in the apostolic message, namely "the life to come (4:8)," or "eternal life (1:16)."[100] Once again, God's word concerning Jesus is deemed "faithful" and πάσης ἀποδοχῆς ἄξιος. More importantly, this "faithful" word remains the most prominent object of Paul's urgent concern in the letter, while both the content and implications of that word—essentially

97. Note also that Paul writes of τῆς καλῆς διδασκαλίας ᾗ παρηκολούθηκας, suggesting that Timothy recognizes the authority that stands behind the instruction that he gained from Paul (see Guthrie, *Pastoral Epistles*, 106; Quinn and Wacker, *Letters to Timothy*, 373).

98. Collins writes, "The reason why godliness is so advantageous is that it carries with it the promise of life (*epangelian echousa zōēs*) in the present age (*tēs nyn*) and in the age to come (*kai tēs mellousēs*)" (Collins, *Timothy and Titus*, 122). Furthermore, Witherington asserts, "But being a good servant means not only nourishing and guiding others, but also nourishing oneself on the words of faith and true teachings that Timothy was already familiar with and following" (Witherington, *Letters and Homilies*, 255).

99. While he views the summons to godliness as the faithful saying itself (against the proposal in this study), Towner concurs with the analysis here that the formula and subsequent paranaesis serves to "motivate Timothy to pursue real *eusebeia*" (Towner, *Goal of Our Instruction*, 238).

100. Indeed, Van Neste writes, "4.8 provides a ground for 4.7b, a reason for exerting oneself in training for godliness, namely that εὐσέβεια brings with it the promise of eternal life" (Van Neste, *Cohesion and Structure*, 49). See also, Knight, *Pastoral Epistles*, 200–201; Rendall, "Faithful Is the Word," 319.

all of the paranaesis that appears in 2:1—4:5 and that qualifies as compatible with οἱ λόγοι τῆς πίστεως—serve as the direct object (ταῦτα) of παράγγελλε . . . καὶ δίδασκε (4:11).[101] The very fact of such a charge may emphasize the authoritative and normative quality that Paul attaches to his own apostolic teaching or word.[102]

In 4:13 one reads, ἕως ἔρχομαι πρόσεχε τῇ ἀναγνώσει, τῇ παρακλήσει, τῇ διδασκαλίᾳ. While this is the second time in the letter that Paul has indicated his intent to come to Ephesus and see Timothy again, the more critical details here lie in his admonition to "attend to the reading, to the exhortation, and to the teaching." On the one hand, Paul does not provide explicit data with respect to what Timothy is to read, apparently assuming that the object of the commended reading is understood. On the other hand, Paul does convey the direct association of ἀνάγνωσις with both παράκλησις and διδασκαλία.[103] Here, Paul's use of multiple terms to designate the one apostolic trust that is the faithful word again comes into play, particularly his designations "the sound teaching" and "the gospel."

101. Van Bruggen writes, "Once again Paul gives the exclamation in 4:9. He has just said that godliness holds promise of life for today and the future. Godliness endures. Why? Because Christ endures. Faithful and completely reliable is the word of the gospel!" (Van Bruggen, "Vaste grond onder de voeten," 44). See also Collins, *Timothy and Titus*, 128; Rendall, "Faithful Is the Word," 318–19; Spicq, *Les Épîtres Pastorales*, 146.

102. See Marcheselli-Casale, *Le Lettere Pastorali*, 311; Quinn and Wacker, *Letters to Timothy*, 372–73.

103. Quinn and Wacker observe, "There is a clear line from the *anagnosis* (the public reading of the OT) to the *paraklesis* (an exhortation or summons to Christian faith and then to Christian conduct in a way that is recognizably linked to the faith, worship and conduct of Israel as evidence by the OT)" (Quinn and Wacker, *Letters to Timothy*, 385). Later, Quinn and Wacker add, "The three articular nouns in asyndeton that are the object of *proseche* give the impression that the functions so crisply listed need no further definition, that the terms are virtually technical in this context. The order is not accidental, for each function described seems to presume the previous. The final and climactic *didaskalia* (the explanation and application of the OT according to Pauline hermeneutics) to which the Pauline coworker is to dedicate himself presupposes that he has first read publicly in an assembly the OT Scriptures" (ibid., 390). Ramsay also comments directly upon this point, contending, "Reading of the Scriptures of course implies much in the way of explanation and interpretation and comment. Exhortation and reproval are often referred to, for example in 3:15, 4:1–2, 6:17, and clearly Timothy was intended to keep an attentive eye on the conduct, the life, and the development of all members of the congregation so far as possible. Teaching is closely related both to reading and exhortation. The three kinds of work go naturally together, and each helps the other: Exhortation and teaching must be based on the Scriptures" (Ramsay, *Historical Commentary*, 122).

The last of the three terms that Paul groups together here, "the teaching (ἡ διδασκαλία)," is by now the most familiar to the reader. Paul has used it twice in the letter so far, in the expressions "the sound teaching" (1:10) and "the good teaching," (4:6) both of which, it has been argued, serve as references that are synonymous with "the gospel" and the "faithful" word, all of which denote God's apostolic gospel proclamation entrusted to Paul. For Paul now to urge Timothy to "attend to" (προσέχω) this teaching, thereby summoning him to constancy in carrying out the task of instructing the church in "the teaching," follows naturally from his previous comments to "command and teach these things," even as it stands in keeping with the agenda and chief concern of the letter.[104]

In conjunction with that, the notion conveyed by παράκλησις is coordinate with διδασκαλία, reflecting its content and also following reasonably from what Paul has written.[105] Thus, in the case of διδασκαλία and παράκλησις here, Paul uses one expression with which Timothy is already familiar and that has existing currency with respect to the literary fabric of the letter, and another that fits logically within that fabric. The most critical implication of this evaluation of ἡ παράκλησις and ἡ διδασκαλία is that both terms function as signifiers of some expression of Paul's apostolic gospel message and indicate some phase in its proclamation.[106] This in turn provides guidance in the effort to determine what Paul may mean when he writes of ἡ ἀνάγνωσις.

In an initial appraisal of ἡ ἀνάγνωσις, one may observe that this word appears in only two other passages in the Greek New Testament, Acts 13:15 and 2 Cor 3:14. In each of these instances, it functions as part of a statement concerning the reading of the Law, Prophets, and Writings. Furthermore, it already stands established that Paul holds the Torah in high esteem. Thus, it might seem reasonable to limit the semantic range

104. Collins, *Timothy and Titus*, 129–30; Knight, *Pastoral Epistles*, 207–8.

105. Marcheselli-Casale proposes a close conceptual integration of these terms (Marcheselli-Casale, *Le Lettere Pastorali*, 326–29), while Roloff also notes the correspondence between these two terms, writing, "With παράκλησις, preaching in the context of worship is intended ... παράκλησις occurs only in this one place in the Pastorals, while διδασκαλία is one of its central key concepts (1:10; 4:1–6; 5:17; 6:1–3; 2 Tim 3:10, etc.). We are dealing here with the whole of what the church received from its apostle as binding instruction and teaching (See 1:10)" (Roloff, *Der erste Brief an Timotheus*, 254–55).

106. Guthrie, *Pastoral Epistles*, 109; Kelly, *Pastoral Epistles*, 105; Knight, *Pastoral Epistles*, 207–8; Quinn and Wacker, *Letters to Timothy*, 384–85, 390.

of ἡ ἀνάγνωσις to this material.[107] However, throughout 1 Timothy to this point, the primary entity or source with which Paul has exhibited an abiding interest consists in the faithful word that is God's gospel message. It constitutes his apostolic trust, the "good teaching" and "sound teaching" expressed in "the words of the faith." By contrast, while Paul's instruction indicates a fundamental compatibility between the gospel message and the Law, Prophets, and Writings, he never charges Timothy to instruct the church in this latter collection of material.[108] In addition to this, since ἡ ἀνάγνωσις appears in a cluster of three terms in this letter, the remaining two of which denote some phase of the gospel message, it would seem to be an arbitrary shift in subject matter if ἡ ἀνάγνωσις were to serve as a designation of the OT only. On the other hand, Paul's citations of and allusions to the Torah suggest that ἡ ἀνάγνωσις must include at least the writings of the OT. Consequently, based upon internal literary criteria, the most likely referent of "the reading" entails some written form of the apostolic gospel message in conjunction with the OT,[109] thus marking

107. This is the solution offered by Witherington, though there is no discussion regarding any other possibility (Witherington, *Letters and Homilies*, 258). Johnson also hints at this when he speaks of the similarities between the practices of the *ekklesia* and the synagogue (Johnson, *Letters to Timothy*, 252).

108. His remarks concerning the synagogue and *ekklesia* notwithstanding, Johnson also seems to entertain the possibility that Paul may have included the idea of his own letters and teaching under the three-fold reference ἀνάγνωσις, παρακλήσις and διδασκαλία, for he writes, "It was in the context of such public reading, in fact, that Paul's own letters were undoubtedly first read" (Johnson, *Letters to Timothy*, 252). See also Nielsen, "Scripture in the Pastoral Epistles," 20.

109. Bernard maintains that ἀνάγνωσις, while certainly referring to the OT, also could denote the apostolic letters as well (Bernard, *Pastoral Epistles*, 71–72). Conybeare and Howson allow, "The books so read were (at this period) probably those of the Old Testament, and perhaps the earlier gospels" (Conybeare and Howson, *Life and Epistles of Saint Paul*, 817). Knight, by means of several distinct statements, also links the three terms in a very similar manner. He writes, "The 'reading,' like that of the other two NT occurrences, would be of those writings that were regarded as authoritative, and, in addition to the OT, would include extant NT writings [cf. the admonitions of Paul to the congregation to read the letter he write to them and to others with the related verb ἀναγινώσκω: 1 Thess 5:27; Col 4:16; cf. also Acts 15:31; Rev 1:3; cr. further 1 Tim 5:18, where a statement of Jesus found in Matt 10:10 and Luke 10:7 may be quoted under the rubric of 'Scripture says' λέγει ἡ γραφή . . . παράκλησις is used in correlation with ἀναγνώσις here as in Acts 13:15. There the content of the παράκλησις is that Jesus is the promised Messiah of the OT and that those who believe in him receive forgiveness of sins . . . διδασκαλία . . . is the teaching of the Scripture read, analogous to the use of παράκλησις" (Knight, *Pastoral Epistles*, 207–8). Lock also states, "This would, with the OT, include Apostolic letters [1 Thess 5:27, Eph 34, Col

this instance of ἡ ἀνάγνωσις as one indication that the gospel message probably assumed a written form as early as A.D. 65, if not earlier.[110] This particular line of analysis will receive more focused attention over the course of the next chapter.

In view of the preceding observations, it seems reasonable to suppose that the content of ἡ ἀνάγνωσις, ἡ παράκλησις, and ἡ διδασκαλία concerns or addresses the matters expressed in the recurring pronoun ταῦτα. In other words, with each occurrence of ταῦτα, it has been suggested that the actual content represented lies in the accumulated instructions as they appear in the letter, all of which either reside in or stem from ἡ καλὴ διδασκαλία or ἡ ὑγιαίνουσα διδασκαλία of the apostolic proclamation.[111] Considering that Paul has previously advised Timothy regarding the worth of "setting these things before the brethren," and that he then urged Timothy, παράγγελλε ταῦτα καὶ δίδασκε, his admonition, πρόσεχε τῇ ἀναγνώσει, τῇ παρακλήσει, τῇ διδασκαλίᾳ reiterates the same concern and mission.[112] Thus, not only is Timothy charged with instructing the believers in Ephesus with regard to "these things" (ταῦτα), his own attention to such matters plays a crucial role in his ministry among them, for Paul writes in 4:15–16, ταῦτα μελέτα, ἐν τούτοις ἴσθι, ἵνα σου ἡ προκοπὴ φανερὰ ᾖ πᾶσιν. ἔπεχε σεαυτῷ καὶ τῇ διδασκαλίᾳ, ἐπίμενε αὐτοῖς· τοῦτο γὰρ ποιῶν καὶ σεαυτὸν σώσεις καὶ τοὺς ἀκούοντάς σου. Once again, one may note the explicit link that Paul forges between ταῦτα (which in this study is construed as summarizing all of the paranetic material up to this point) and ἡ διδασκαλία.[113] Consequently, for Timothy to "practice

---

4:16, Euseb. *H.E.* 4.23], apocalypses . . . the memoirs of the Apostles or the writings of the prophets" (Lock, *Pastoral Epistles*, 53). While conditioned by his assumption of the pseudepigraphy of the PE, Marcheselli-Casale allows, "That he may employ an already written gospel, that of Luke, for example, or another such as Matthew or Mark, cannot be ruled out, here having already preceded it in the narration of the words and deeds of Jesus [cf. Luke 1:1–4]" (Marcheselli-Casale, *Le Lettere Pastorali*, 409). Similarly, Spicq writes, "Ἀνάγνωσις is the public reading of Holy Scripture based upon the practice in the Jewish gathering at the synagogue . . . but it included in addition the reading of the apostolic writings" (Spicq, *Les Épîtres Pastorales*, 148;). See also Cothenet, "Directives pastorales dan les Épîtres a Timothée," 19.

110. Collins remarks that this reading must have been the basis of Timothy's teaching and admonition (Collins, *Timothy and Titus*, 129–30).

111. Quinn and Wacker write, "ταῦτα takes one back again to 3:14 and 4:6, 11 above and seems to be a generic reference to the Pauline teaching" (Quinn and Wacker, *Letters to Timothy*, 406).

112. Fee, *Timothy and Titus*, 106–7.

113. Knight proposes, "Plural αὐτοῖς probably refers to the nearest possible

these things" and to "be in them" is for him also to fulfill the admonition, "attend to yourself and the teaching."

5:1-16—Old, Young, and Widows

While the material found in 5:1-16 does not offer a great deal in terms of advancing or building upon an understanding of Paul's use of terms, particularly those that pertain to God's gospel message, it does continue to give some indication of the authority Paul conferred upon Timothy and of Paul's determination to commend the faith that rests upon the gospel message.[114] In a sweeping commentary, Paul instructs Timothy to exhort older men rather than rebuking them, treating them as he would fathers, and to treat younger men as brothers, older women as mothers, and younger women as sisters. In each case, while Timothy has the authority to teach, command, and correct, he nevertheless must adopt an unassuming, gentle, and honorable posture before those in his care.[115] These instructions supplement and provide guidance for the more forceful directives that typified the previous unit. Next, Paul counsels Timothy on how best to handle issues pertaining to the care and provision for widows who make up part of the church community.[116] This counsel occupies the remainder of the unit. In the midst of these instructions (5:7), Paul again employs the expression, ταῦτα παράγγελλε. Unlike previous instances of ταῦτα with either παράγγελλε or δίδασκε (or both), this instance is most likely confined to the immediate context of 5:1-16 and Paul's instructions regarding widows.[117] In part, this is clear by virtue of its appearance in the midst of very specifically targeted instruction. Also, the purpose behind the admonition, ταῦτα παράγγελλε, is ἵνα ἀνεπίλημπτοι ὦσιν, in which the

---

antecedents, σεαυτῷ καὶ τῇ διδασκαλίᾳ . . . Ἐπιμένω with reference to διδασκαλίᾳ refers to persistent fidelity to the teaching and a constant urging of it upon his hearers . . . Paul is reminding Timothy that he must embrace and personally persevere in that which he teaches" (Knight, *Pastoral Epistles*, 210–11).

114. Fee, *Timothy and Titus*, 118.

115. Knight points out, "The keynote of this passage is the responsibility and authority of a minister of God to give such instruction, albeit to give it with respect" (Knight, *Pastoral Epistles*, 215).

116. Bassler, *1 Timothy, 2 Timothy, Titus*, 92–94; Johnson, *Letters to Timothy*, 261–63; Knight, *Pastoral Epistles*, 215.

117. Johnson, *Letters to Timothy*, 263; Knight, *Pastoral Epistles*, 220; Mounce, *Pastoral Epistles*, 283–84; Witherington, *Letters and Homilies*, 268.

implied subject of ὦσιν could be only the widows about whom Paul has just been writing.[118] Nevertheless, even in this eminently practical unit, Paul exhibits flashes of his primary concern to uphold and commend "the faith" and its message in warning that one who fails to care for those of his own household τὴν πίστιν ἤρνηται καὶ ἔστιν ἀπίστου χείρων.[119]

5:17–25—Elders: Reward and Discipline

For all of its prominence as it relates to the primary research question of the present study, this unit does not differ markedly from any other in the letter in its overall emphasis. It reflects a continuation of Paul's specific instructions to Timothy, and whereas the previous section gave much attention to the ministerial care of widows, this unit offers instructions governing Timothy's supervision of the elders (πρεσβύτεροι) of Ephesus.[120] In 5:17–18, Paul's first comments speak to the compensation due to those elders οἱ καλῶς προεστῶτες. Such elders, Paul declares, διπλῆς τιμῆς ἀξιούσθωσαν.[121] He then narrows the field of those elders οἱ καλῶς προεστῶτες, emphasizing the special worth of οἱ κοπιῶντες ἐν λόγῳ καὶ διδασκαλίᾳ. Based upon the investigation of 1 Timothy thus far, Paul's mention of those "laboring in word and teaching" refers to those who work on behalf of the church to spread God's apostolic gospel message, referred to in the letter variously as "the gospel," the "faithful" word, "the sound teaching," "the truth," "the mystery of the faith," the "word of God," or the "words of the faith."[122] Paul justifies his assertion that such fine

118. Witherington observes the same persistent concern, noting, "Paul insists because the world is watching, and so such widows who draw support must be irreproachable in character. There is a constant concern in the Pastoral Epistles about the church having a good public image" (Witherington, *Letters and Homilies*, 268).

119. Fee, *Timothy and Titus*, 118; Johnson, *Letters to Timothy*, 263; Knight, *Pastoral Epistles*, 220–21; Mounce, *Pastoral Epistles*, 285.

120. Bassler, *1 Timothy, 2 Timothy, Titus*, 99; Knight, *Pastoral Epistles*, 231; Towner, *Letters to Timothy and Titus*, 360–61; Witherington, *Letters and Homilies*, 273.

121. Typically understood as remuneration or honoraria (Bassler, *1 Timothy, 2 Timothy, Titus*, 99; Fee, *Timothy and Titus*, 128–29; Guthrie, *Pastoral Epistles*, 117; Knight, *Pastoral Epistles*, 232; Spicq, *Les Épîtres Pastorales*, 175).

122. Marcheselli-Casale affirms this, writing, "One can maintain with good basis that the author-redactor refers here to a type of 'senior elder' particularly dedicated to the ministry of the preaching and teaching of the word: the true 'teaching' in force within the Christian community for the study and discussion of questions pertaining to men before the gospel" (Marcheselli-Casale, *Le Lettere Pastorali*, 380).

leaders warrant fair compensation by appealing to material that he designates ἡ γραφή, introduced by the formula λέγει γὰρ ἡ γραφή, presumably so as to lend the weight of God's written word to his admonition.[123] This reference is then followed by two apparent biblical citations. The first citation, βοῦν ἀλοῶντα οὐ φιμώσεις, features a nearly exact rendering of Deut 25:4. The second, ἄξιος ὁ ἐργάτης τοῦ μισθοῦ αὐτοῦ, mirrors precisely a part of Luke 10:7 and offers yet another possible indication that ἡ ἀνάγνωσις in 4:13, as well as ἡ γραφή here, may refer to a written form of that Gospel.[124] The focal point of the next chapter entails evaluating the source of the second citation.

6:1-2—Servants

From his discussion of elders, Paul shifts his attention to those whom he describes as ὑπὸ ζυγὸν δοῦλοι, urging that such individuals exhibit due honor toward their masters. This admonition applies whether the master is a believer or unbeliever, and, considering Paul's explanation, ἵνα μὴ τὸ ὄνομα τοῦ θεοῦ καὶ ἡ διδασκαλία βλασφημῆται, it is given so as to ensure that even the slaves and servants among the people commend the apostolic gospel message at all times.[125] With this, Paul once again recalls his expression, ἡ διδασκαλία, this time distinguishing it only with the definite article, and associating it with τὸ ὄνομα τοῦ θεοῦ, whose message it is and from whom it derives.[126]

123. Guthrie, *Pastoral Epistles*, 117; Knight, *Pastoral Epistles*, 233; Schnabel, *Inspiration und Offenbarung*, 125–26; Scott, *Pastoral Epistles*, 65; Spicq, *Les Épîtres Pastorales*, 175–76.

124. While asserting that that second citation must come from a Logion source associated with Q, Collins nevertheless acknowledges that "the Pastoral Epistles provide no evidence that the Q collection was available to the Pastor's circles" (Collins, *Timothy and Titus*, 146). Hanson, in his discussion of the second citation, allows, "The author may be quoting Luke's gospel as Scripture; but it is more likely that he is quoting Jesus' saying as part of his oral tradition and loosely equating it with Scripture" (Hanson, *Pastoral Letters*, 62). On the other hand, Fee points out, "This is a saying of Jesus, exactly as it appears in Luke 10:7 . . . It should be noted that in the only other instance where Paul actually cites the words of Jesus (1 Cor 11:24–25), he also cites a version he shares with Luke, in contrast to Mark and Matthew" (Fee, *Timothy and Titus*, 129).

125. Collins, *Timothy and Titus*, 153; Spicq, *Les Épîtres Pastorales*, 183; Towner, *Letters to Timothy and Titus*, 382; Witherington, *Letters and Homilies*, 278–79.

126. Johnson writes, "As everywhere in ancient moral discourse, we find here the assumption that bad behavior discredits the *didaskalia* represented by the teacher—and, in this case, the God of whom the teaching speaks" (Johnson, *Letters to Timothy*,

6:3–10—ἑτεροδιδασκαλέω Revisted

With the recurrence of ἑτεροδιδασκαλέω in 6:3 near the conclusion of 1 Timothy, Paul launches a final invective upon the "certain men" against whom he has been writing through the letter. More importantly, he recapitulates several essential ideas found in 1:3–10, verifying in the process that his prevailing concern over the course of the letter is the defense and promotion of the exclusive apostolic gospel teaching.[127] In 6:3–5, by means of a lengthy conditional construction, Paul describes those whom he views as false teachers and the source of trouble in Ephesus, writing in the *protasis* of 6:3, εἴ τις ἑτεροδιδασκαλεῖ καὶ μὴ προσέρχεται ὑγιαίνουσιν λόγοις τοῖς τοῦ κυρίου ἡμῶν Ἰησοῦ Χριστοῦ καὶ τῇ κατ' εὐσέβειαν διδασκαλίᾳ.[128] Within the clauses that comprise this *protasis*, and in conjunction with the recurrence of ἑτεροδιδασκαλέω, one may observe a reprise from the first chapter of the idea of the soundness of the message (ὑγιαίνουσιν λόγοις), the use of λόγος to designate a specific message, the reference once again to a particular teaching—this time teaching associated with godliness (τῇ κατ' εὐσέβειαν διδασκαλίᾳ)—and the implication that the message, words, and teaching all concern the Lord Jesus Christ

---

283). Towner likewise states, "First, insubordination, especially in the case of a Christian slave under a pagan master, puts 'God's name' at risk of being 'slandered' or 'maligned' . . . Also at risk, secondly, is the 'teaching,' which again refers widely to the Christian message or doctrine by which the church is known (Titus 2:10; see on 1 Tim 1:10; 4:6, 13)" (Towner, *Letters to Timothy and Titus*, 382).

127. Fee writes, "In this section [Paul] presents the final exposure and indictment of the false teachers. Much that is said in the first paragraph (vv. 3–5) is reminiscent of the language of chapter 1" (Fee, *Timothy and Titus*, 140). Marshall shows the clearest affinity with structural analysis proposed at the beginning of this chapter, writing, "The use of ἑτεροδιδασκαλέω (1:3) is a deliberate contrast with διδάσκῃ in the previous verse, and the word may have been chosen to strengthen the *inclusio* with ch. 1" (Marshall, *Pastoral Epistles*, 638). Oberlinner also observes this correspondence, stating simply with regard to 6:3–10, "The passage recalls 1:3–7" (Oberlinner, *Erster Timotheusbrief*, 271). Van Neste is equally definitive, stating, "The argument that parallels between 1:3–20 and 6:3–21 suggest an inclusio was first put forth by Thurén in 1970 . . . There are also similarities in the discussion of the opponents. For example, both sections open with reference to ἑτεροδιδασκαλέω (1:3; 6:3) . . . Little has been made of the fact that both 1:3–20 and 6:3–21 both open and close with a discussion of the opponents, forming parallel inclusios around these sections, as was argued above" (Van Neste, *Cohesion and Structure*, 136–37).

128. Fee, *Timothy and Titus*, 140–41; Knight, *Pastoral Epistles*, 249–50; Marshall, *Pastoral Epistles*, 638; Mounce, *Pastoral Epistles*, 336–37; Witherington, *Letters and Homilies*, 283.

(ὑγιαίνουσιν λόγοις τοῖς τοῦ κυρίου ἡμῶν Ἰησοῦ Χριστοῦ).[129] Similarly, in the *apodosis* of 6:4–5, Paul's descriptions of those who promote "other teachings" reflect traits comparable to the "certain men" as described in 1:3–7. He writes that anyone commending "other teaching" τετύφωται, μηδὲν ἐπιστάμενος, ἀλλὰ νοσῶν περὶ ζητήσεις καὶ λογομαχίας.[130] Here, an allegation of delusion and lack of understanding similar to that found in 1:7 is apparent, leading to the further charge of producing "debates and disputes about words" (ζητήσεις καὶ λογομαχίας), which recalls Paul's use of ἐκζητήσις in 1:4.[131] However, Paul elaborates further, declaring that such men, whose obsession for disputes and arguments results in φθόνος ἔρις βλασφημίαι, ὑπόνοιαι πονηραί, διαπαρατριβαὶ διεφθαρμένων ἀνθρώπων τὸν νοῦν καὶ ἀπεστερημένων τῆς ἀληθείας, also have an unhealthy longing for money, and because of that longing (which indeed may lie at the root of their errant teaching and misdeeds), they ἀπεπλανήθησαν ἀπὸ τῆς πίστεως.[132]

Such a conceptual and lexical correspondence between this unit and 1:3–10 strongly suggests that whatever other concerns and instructions occupy various portions of the letter, they stand as derivative and subordinate matters relative to the overarching issue, which lies in securing the "sound teaching" or "sound words" while suppressing any "other teaching" that violates or competes with it. Thus, at all points, Paul seeks to vindicate "the faith" or "the truth" of God's apostolic gospel message proclaiming Christ Jesus the Lord and the "faithful" word of salvation, a word which implies an ethic of godliness in upholding the Law.[133] Not only does this support the hypothesis regarding 1 Timothy articulated at the beginning of this chapter, it also establishes the rhetorical boundaries of the letter and the primary intent behind its composition. This, in turn, must be taken into consideration when assessing γραφή and its sense and place within the rhetorical scheme.

---

129. Wolfe writes, "There can by no denying that the reference in chapter 1 to the 'sound doctrine' is to the gospel in a general sense. This then lends a great deal of probability to the same understanding in 6.3" (Wolfe, *Place and Use of Scripture*, 85).

130. Barrett, *Pastoral Epistles*, 83; Knight, *Pastoral Epistles*, 251; Marshall, *Pastoral Epistles*, 638–40; Towner, *Letters to Timothy and Titus*, 394–95; Witherington, *Letters and Homilies*, 283.

131. Knight, *Pastoral Epistles*, 251; Marshall, *Pastoral Epistles*, 640; Mounce, *Pastoral Epistles*, 338.

132. Bassler, *1 Timothy, 2 Timothy, Titus*, 109; Johnson, *Letters to Timothy*, 297; Knight, *Pastoral Epistles*, 252–53; Witherington, *Letters and Homilies*, 284, 289.

133. Knight, *Pastoral Epistles*, 276; Scott, *Pastoral Epistles*, 73.

6:11–21—Final Charge

While the literary unit that occupies 6:3–10 contains Paul's final remarks concerning the "certain men" who oppose the "sound teaching," Paul uses the closing unit to underscore the stark contrast between these men and the life and ministry to which he summons Timothy one last time, marking the unit by the emphatic use of a second-person personal pronoun in construct with an adversative conjunction, Σὺ δέ.[134] Paul completes the idea begun by this address by advising Timothy, ταῦτα φεῦγε, in which the clause ταῦτα refers to the traits and behaviors that typify the false teachers in Ephesus as described in 6:3–10, much like previous occurrences of ταῦτα in 5:7, 5:21, and 6:2.[135] In contrast to "fleeing" such things, Paul then admonishes Timothy, δίωκε δὲ δικαιοσύνην εὐσέβειαν πίστιν, ἀγάπην ὑπομονὴν πραϋπαθίαν. Following hard upon his admonition, Paul then restates his charge in other words, urging ἀγωνίζου τὸν καλὸν ἀγῶνα τῆς πίστεως. In the process of expressing this command, he brings to resolution the notion of ἡ καλὴ στρατεία (1:18) introduced in the early stages of the letter, and explicitly ties the struggle that has carried the entire letter with "the faith," although his modified form likely includes a reference to Timothy's own battle to retain integrity in the faith in his own life.[136] Thus, over the final two units Paul reiterates his initial charge—which authorized Timothy to censure τίνες and to command them μὴ ἑτεροδιδασκαλεῖν, compliance with which formed the substance of τὴν παραγγελίαν and ἡ καλὴ στρατεία—by describing the traits and behaviors that typify anyone who ἑτεροδιδασκαλεῖ and reminding him, ἀγωνίζου τὸν καλὸν ἀγῶνα τῆς πίστεως.[137]

Meanwhile, ὁ καλὸς ἀγών τῆς πίστεως also entails the positive labor of confessing τὴν καλὴν ὁμολογίαν, in imitation of Christ Jesus himself, ὁ μαρτυρήσας ἐπὶ Ποντίου Πιλάτου τὴν καλὴν ὁμολογίαν.[138] It is all but cer-

---

134. Guthrie, *Pastoral Epistles*, 126; Knight, *Pastoral Epistles*, 260; Marshall, *Pastoral Epistles*, 656; Mounce, *Pastoral Epistles*, 353; Towner, *Letters to Timothy and Titus*, 407.

135. Fee, *Timothy and Titus*, 149; Knight, *Pastoral Epistles*, 260–61; Mounce, *Pastoral Epistles*, 353; Witherington, *Letters and Homilies*, 292.

136. Bassler, *1 Timothy, 2 Timothy, Titus*, 113; Lock, *Pastoral Epistles*, 70; Mounce, *Pastoral Epistles*, 355; Towner, *Letters to Timothy and Titus*, 410.

137. Johnson, *Letters to Timothy*, 308; Knight, *Pastoral Epistles*, 263; Quinn and Wacker, *Letters to Timothy*, 528–29.

138. Johnson, *Letters to Timothy*, 307–8; Knight, *Pastoral Epistles*, 265–66; Mounce, *Pastoral Epistles*, 357.

tain that ἡ καλὴ ὁμολογία in these two instances and in such close proximity must share the same referent. This is further reinforced by the implicit comparative function that attends Paul's allusion to Jesus' testimony, such that, even as Jesus bore witness to "the good confession," so Timothy also must continue to profess "the good confession."[139] Timothy's confession most likely lay in his recognition of Jesus as Lord or Christ, even as Jesus acknowledged to Pilate his own status as "King of the Jews," which led to his crucifixion and ultimate witness.[140] Thus, it is in the presence of this Jesus who did so testify that Paul solemnly enjoins Timothy, τηρῆσαί σε τὴν ἐντολὴν ἄσπιλον ἀνεπίλημπτον μέχρι τῆς ἐπιφανείας τοῦ κυρίου ἡμῶν Ἰησοῦ Χριστοῦ. Here ἡ ἐντολή probably refers to Paul's directive to "fight the good fight of the faith," which entails more broadly the struggle to uphold and vindicate the apostolic teaching.[141] Finally, on one last occasion, Paul reiterates his solemn charge to Timothy, τὴν παραθήκην φύλαξον. Since in this final imperative, ἡ παραθήκη serves as the nominal cognate of παρατίθημι found in 1:18, it probably designates the same cause for which Timothy stands called to battle and the same overriding concern that has driven Paul's writing, specifically the apostolic gospel message that must be upheld against all opposition, human or ideological.[142] In

139. Johnson writes, "Timothy finds his own model in the behavior of Jesus (compare 2 Tim 2:8). Timothy's pronouncing 'the noble profession before many witnesses' (6:12) has as its exemplar Jesus' own witnessing to the noble profession before Pontius Pilate (6:13)" (Johnson, *Letters to Timothy*, 313).

140. Lock, *Pastoral Epistles*, 72; Marshall, *Pastoral Epistles*, 661, 663; Towner, *Letters to Timothy and Titus*, 412; Witherington, *Letters and Homilies*, 294.

141. Regarding this, Marshall writes, "Probably the reference is to what Timothy is commissioned to do, including the specific instructions given to him, especially in view of the way in which this chapter tends to repeat the themes of ch. 1" (Marshall, *Pastoral Epistles*, 665). Towner also states, "The reference is surely to what Paul has charged Timothy to do in Ephesus, introduced in 1:3–5 and filled out in the course of the letter" (Towner, *Letters to Timothy and Titus*, 414). See also Collins, *Timothy and Titus*, 165; Quinn and Wacker, *Letters to Timothy*, 533.

142. Towner's assessment is perhaps the strongest, for he writes, "The concept of a fixed body of teaching or tradition reflected in terms such as *hē hygiainousa didaskalia* comes most clearly to expression in the term *parathēkē* . . . This new thought of guarding and transmitting 'the deposit' (*parathēkē*), though in the NT limited to the Pastorals, has parallels in Greek, Roman, and Jewish practices . . . A *parathēkē*-institution existed in each of these contexts, through which some commodity could be passed securely from one party to another, by entrusting it to an authorized agent. The fact that the configuration *phylattein parathēkēn*, which occurs three times in the Pastorals (*ten parathēkēn phylaxon*, 1 Tim 6.20; *tēn parathēkēn*, 2 Tim 1:12; *tēn kalēn parathēkēn phylaxon* 1.14), was the *terminus technicus* for this process strongly suggests that the

the process of taking up his charge, Timothy indeed shall correct those who commend other teachings and who set themselves against the "sound teaching" of the apostolic gospel proclamation. At the same time, he shall uphold the proclamation Paul has entrusted to him, even as God entrusted the message itself to Paul.[143]

1 Timothy Discourse
and Semantic Overview—Concluding Remarks

While the preceding does not pretend to offer a complete commentary upon 1 Timothy, it has provided a survey of semantically related terms and expressions that Paul uses to designate the gospel message entrusted to him by God and the substance of his apostolic mission. More importantly, it has mapped in detail the predominant discourse flow that runs through the letter and that supplies the structural and thematic core of the letter's discourse. All of this discourse falls within the framework established by the two conspicuous occurrences of ἑτεροδιδασκαλέω in 1:3 and 6:3, which also signal the primary concern and purpose of the letter.

In the process of tracing the discourse and rhetorical structure, this chapter has argued that among those terms or expressions that refer to the apostolic gospel message concerning Jesus Christ, one must include ἡ ὑγιαίνουσα διδασκαλία, τὸ εὐαγγέλιον τῆς δόξης τοῦ μακαρίου θεοῦ, ὁ λόγος, ὁ [πιστὸς] λόγος, λόγος θεοῦ, ἡ πίστις, τὸ μαρτύριον, ἡ ἀλήθεια, τὸ μυστήριον τῆς πίστεως, τοῖς λόγοις τῆς πίστεως, ἡ καλὴ διδασκαλία, ἀνάγνωσις (in company with both παράκλησις and διδασκαλία), ἡ διδασκαλία, ὑγιαίνοντες

---

author had adopted the *parathēkē*-concept from a well-known 'deposit'-institution. The content of the *parathēkē* can be determined by an examination of the term's use in the Pastorals. In two of is three occurrences (1 Tim 6.20; 2 Tim 1.14) the term clearly denotes the gospel message in one form or another" (Towner, *Goal of Our Instruction*, 124–25).

143. Barrett writes, "Like Paul, the Pastorals emphasize the primary importance of the content of the Gospel. The Church's life depends upon the purity and faithfulness of its doctrine" (Barrett, *Pastoral Epistles*, 89). Hanson's remarks are especially suggestive, for he maintains, "[the deposit] means no doubt 'the deposit of faith,' the body of teaching which by the author's time had come to be regarded as constituting Christianity . . . Because we live in an age which is inclined to challenge and reject every form of tradition, we should be particularly careful not to ignore what is valuable in the idea of a deposit of faith. There is a tradition of Christian belief, thought, and practice which has to be handed on from generation to generation if Christianity is to survive" (Hanson, *Pastoral Letters*, 73).

λόγοι οἱ τοῦ κυρίου ἡμῶν Ἰησοῦ Χριστοῦ, and ἡ παραθήκη. Cumulatively, this stream of interchangeable expressions elevates the apostolic proclamation as the single most vital issue for Paul in the letter. This proposal, as presented thus far, finds broad agreement among the sources cited, even though they represent considerable variances in their assumptions regarding the authorship, date of composition, and perlocutionary intent of the letters to Timothy. Additionally, since both λόγος θεοῦ (4:5) and ἀνάγνωσις (4:13) lie embedded within the semantic stream observed, these expressions may indicate the presence and circulation of a written form of this same apostolic message, also designated ἡ γραφή.[144]

As yet, the main thesis of this study remains to be addressed directly, though it shall serve as the focal point of the next chapter. However, alongside the consideration of the various terms listed above and the interweaving of their usage and meaning, and in view of the prevailing concern dominating the letter, it should be apparent that ἡ γραφή may well share some correspondence with λόγος θεοῦ and ἡ ἀνάγνωσις, particularly in light of its apparent and explicit association with Luke 10:7. Indeed, it shall be argued that ἡ γραφή, while functioning most obviously as a reference to the Law, Prophets, and Writings, also includes as its referent the very apostolic proclamation that Paul upholds throughout the letter. By implication, therefore, one must consider the further possibility that ἡ γραφή also may refer to Paul's own teachings and writings, along with those of the rest of the apostolic company, and perhaps early forms of the gospel writings themselves.

144. Van Neste, *Cohesion and Structure*, 109–10.

CHAPTER 4

Γραφη With Reference
to the Immediate Literary Context of 1 Timothy

AS ARGUED AT THE conclusion of the previous chapter, Paul employs several interchangeable expressions over the course of 1 Timothy to denote the apostolic gospel proclamation entrusted to him. When one considers the pattern of these terms and their usage as established, combined with the obvious esteem with which Paul viewed both the material of the Law, Prophets, and Writings and his own revelatory proclamation of Jesus Christ, little distinction may be seen between Paul's treatments of either of these two bodies of teaching. In other words, Paul views his own apostolic gospel proclamation as originating with God, as surely as the Law, Prophets, and Writings originate with God.[1] It has also been shown that scholars exhibit a great deal of agreement on this point, even while they take a wide range of positions concerning the authorship, date of composition, and epistolary intent of the letters to Timothy. In addition, the prevailing concern of the letter lies in upholding and preserving that gospel. Occurrences of multiple expressions that refer to the gospel message form the most persistent semantic thread running through 1 Timothy. The overall trajectory of this predominant motif, as proposed in chapter 3, also finds agreement across the broad witness of the sources consulted. At the same time, in the great majority of these cases, that same widely recognized trajectory seems to have little effect upon the manner according to which ἡ γραφή is construed as it forms part of the

1. Guthrie, *Pastoral Epistles*, 73; Johnson, *Letters to Timothy*, 172–74; Lenski, *St. Paul's Epistles*, 514; Quinn and Wacker, *Letters to Timothy*, 103–4; Witherington, *Letters and Homilies*, 198.

citation formula, λέγει γὰρ ἡ γραφή, in 1 Tim 5:18. Specifically, for most scholars seeking to account for the referent of ἡ γραφή in the citation formula, the difficulty occurs when they reflect upon ἡ γραφή relative to the second citation following the formula: namely, ἄξιος ὁ ἐργάτης τοῦ μισθοῦ αὐτοῦ. Accordingly, while there exists a virtual consensus among scholars regarding the source of the first citation, βοῦν ἀλοῶντα οὐ φιμώσεις, explanations for the second vary considerably. It is at this juncture that the present study departs most significantly from conventional treatments of 1 Tim 5:18.

On one end of the continuum, while a few scholars insist that the formula applies only to the first citation, most posit the existence of a relatively well-known Logion source, possibly related to Q, or the use of a widely familiar proverbial tradition.[2] Either of these latter explanations, proffered so as to account for the correlation between 1 Tim 5:18 and Luke 10:7 without requiring the existence of any written document now contained in the NT, would imply some later collation by Luke as he integrated the saying into his own gospel. However, even among adherents of these positions, one finds the occasional qualifying comment to the effect that the occurrence of ἄξιος ὁ ἐργάτης τοῦ μισθοῦ αὐτοῦ here in 1 Tim 5:18, coupled with its "conspicuous correspondence with Luke 10:7,"[3] could reflect an actual written source, perhaps even indicating the use of Christian writings alongside Jewish Scriptures.[4] On the other end of the continuum, others argue that the most coherent explanation of the available data lies in the existence of a written form of Luke's gospel, available to the writer of 1 Timothy and known to his recipient.[5] Between

2. Bassler, *1 Timothy, 2 Timothy, Titus*, 100; Belleville, "Canon of the New Testament," 378; Collins, *Timothy and Titus*, 145–46; Fiore, *Pastoral Epistles*, 111; Oberlinner, *Erster Timotheusbrief*, 254–55; Roloff, *Der erste Brief an Timotheus*, 306.

3. Oberlinner, *Erster Timotheusbrief*, 254.

4. Towner remarks only, "If a written source is required by the exact verbal correspondence, surely it is sufficient to posit that by this time various written collections of the sayings of Jesus had begun to circulate, and that Paul had access to the version that Luke eventually consulted . . . The saying of Jesus provides supplementary authoritative support for the command to recompense the community's hardworking faithful elders" (Towner, *Letters to Timothy and Titus*, 366–67). See also Roloff, *Der erste Brief an Timotheus*, 309.

5. Knight, for example, maintains, "Since, however, γραφή usually refers to what is written and recognized as scripture, and since the words quoted are found verbatim in Luke's gospel, Paul's dependence on that Gospel is the only alternative that fits all the data" (Knight, *Pastoral Epistles*, 234). Meier also observes, "Some claim that the Pastor is not using Luke's gospel but only *oral* tradition; that hardly fits the designation

these two positions lie various other possibilities tending toward one or the other of the two poles.

Among the multitude of factors at play in this discussion, prior assumptions regarding the Synoptic Gospels (especially the Lukan writings) as well as the authorship and dating of the PE significantly influence scholarly opinion, and often set the dispute beyond the reach of the primary data, even before an evaluation of the actual text of 1 Timothy may be conducted.[6] Not only does this complicate the effort to engage in meaningful discourse, it also has the troubling effect of ruling out *a priori* some plausible explanations for the appearance of ἄξιος ὁ ἐργάτης τοῦ μισθοῦ αὐτοῦ in 1 Tim 5:18 before they can receive due consideration. This chapter is presented, in part, as an attempt to remedy that situation to some extent, since pride of place in this study is reserved for the data and implications deriving directly from the text of 1 Timothy, even though other factors—such as word studies or composition hypotheses relative to the Lukan writings—might be integrated into the analysis.

In this chapter, the data gathered over the course of the preceding exegetical survey of 1 Timothy establish the framework within which a close analysis of 5:17–18 will determine the most likely interpretation of the passage as it lies amidst the prevailing literary stream of the letter. Accordingly, this assessment shall proceed along four converging axes. First, ἡ γραφή shall be examined in view of the apparent citation of Deut 25:4, the first probable referent of the clause, λέγει γὰρ ἡ γραφή. This will include some discussion of a similar citation as it appears in 1 Cor 9:9. Second, this shall be followed by a reflection upon Paul's perspective and treatment of the Old Testament writings generally, as inferred from 1 Timothy. Third, there will be an assessment of Paul's apparent attitude regarding his own apostolic teachings and writings, along with some reflection upon that disposition in comparison with his view of the

---

of *graphe*. Normative or not, Scripture or not, the saying is said to be written" (Meier, "What Counts as Scripture?" 77). Spicq is even more bold, asserting, "Therefore it seems clear that the apostle cites a particular text that is before his eyes (Padovani, Belser, doubtless Jeremias), or that surely is memorized and already known by the church of Ephesus. This is the oldest citation of a gospel word as 'Scripture'" (Spicq, *Les Épîtres Pastorales*, 177).

6. Guthrie remarks on this in passing, as he notes, "Scholars who maintain the non-Pauline authorship of the Pastorals claim that their position presents less difficulty, for the later writer might actually be using Luke's gospel, which could not be said of Paul if the prevailing estimate of the date of Luke's gospel is correct (i.e., A.D. 80–85)" (Guthrie, *Pastoral Epistles*, 117–18).

OT. Finally, the correlation of ἡ γραφή with the apparent citation of Luke 10:7, the second likely referent of λέγει γὰρ ἡ γραφή, shall be taken under consideration, particularly in light of Paul's usage of citations and allusions from the Law, Prophets, and Writings. This latter discussion shall be somewhat more extensive than the three preceding it, since, in addition to taking stock of the literary cues in 1 Timothy, it will also require coming to terms with the plausible dating of Luke's gospel.

Over the course of this analysis, it will be argued, among other things, that Paul's view of the authority and binding nature of the OT is indistinguishable from the authority he ascribes to his own apostolic teachings and perhaps to the teachings of his apostolic coworkers. Consequently, he treats both bodies of teaching as if they stand on an equal footing with respect to their authority and their origination in God. At the same time, Paul's chief concern lies with the apostolic gospel proclamation, not with the Law, Prophets, and Writings.[7] These details address two criteria that must be satisfied in order to conclude that Paul refers to both citations as "Scripture." However, most importantly, it is proposed further here that Paul not only refers to both citations as "Scripture," but also that he intentionally cites a written version of Luke's gospel.

Γραφή and the First Citation

As indicated in the literature review of chapter 1, there exists neither doubt nor dispute that the first citation in 1 Tim 5:18, βοῦν ἀλοῶντα οὐ φιμώσεις, comes from Deut 25:4, and that it stands as a nearly exact citation from the LXX.[8] In the first place, the equivalence with which both

7. Or as Nielsen states, "The Pastorals do not stress the Old Testament. In these writings Paul has eclipsed the Old Testament" (Nielsen, "Scripture in the Pastoral Epistles," 20). If, by "eclipsed," Nielsen means something on the order of "replaced," or "displaced," then he clearly overstates. It has already been established that the PE reflect a high view of the OT. On the other hand, Barton also testifies to the predominance in the first two centuries of citations from NT sources as opposed to those from the OT, indicating that the NT quickly became more important to the early church (Barton, *Holy Writings, Sacred Text*, 18). In either case, it is clear that Paul's concern in the PE entails vindicating and elevating the gospel message, not the Law, Prophets, and Writings. Birger Gerhardsson indicates as much when he affirms, "As we have already pointed out, the gospel tradition is not one section among many in the Pauline tradition. It forms a foundation and a focus: From one point of view, it has an even more central position than the Scriptures" (Gerhardsson, *Memory and Manuscript*, 301).

8. A comparison of 1 Tim 5:18 (βοῦν ἀλοῶντα οὐ φιμώσεις) with Deut 25:4 (οὐ φιμώσεις βοῦν ἀλοῶντα) shows that the subject and predicate are reversed in the later

texts share lexis and grammar virtually ensures this conclusion. However, it also is a matter of some significance that this is not the only instance in which Paul either has cited or alluded to Deut 25:4 to support the claim that the church must fairly compensate and provide for the gospel laborers.[9]

In 1 Cor 9:1–14, Paul defends his freedom as an apostle to enjoy several amenities,[10] among them the right to be married and to secure a living from his apostolic labors (ἢ μόνος ἐγὼ καὶ Βαρναβᾶς οὐκ ἔχομεν ἐξουσίαν μὴ ἐργάζεσθαι; τίς στρατεύεται ἰδίοις ὀψωνίοις ποτέ; τίς φυτεύει ἀμπελῶνα καὶ τὸν καρπὸν αὐτοῦ οὐκ ἐσθίει; ἢ τίς ποιμαίνει ποίμνην καὶ ἐκ τοῦ γάλακτος τῆς ποίμνης οὐκ ἐσθίει). In his justification of the latter point, occurring in 9:9, he refers to Moses and the Law, citing Deut 25:4, οὐ κημώσεις βοῦν ἀλοῶντα. Two specific issues arise in this example. First, one may observe that, according to the eclectic texts of the NA[27] and UBS[4], the 1 Corinthians citation of Deut 25:4 features the verb κημόω, rather than φιμόω, the latter of which appears in both the LXX and 1 Tim 5:18. Second, not only does the 1 Corinthians passage employ Deut 25:4 in a manner similar to its function in 1 Tim 5:18, but by submitting the rhetorical questions, μὴ τῶν βοῶν μέλει τῷ θεῷ ἢ δι' ἡμᾶς πάντως λέγει, Paul also explicitly indicates that the meaning he draws from it is consistent with its original intent, even though the primary sense he draws from it has nothing to do with oxen.[11] In the case of the first observation concerning the appearance of κημόω instead of φιμόω in the standard Greek New Testament texts, the text-critical data lead to somewhat conflicting conclusions. On the one hand, the external evidence found in the number, breadth, and quality of manuscripts containing 1 Corinthians 9 actually suggests rather strongly that Paul used φιμόω in his citation of

---

document. This could reflect little more than a point of emphasis upon the "ox," in this case representing the elder who governs well, as opposed to a slight emphasis upon the individual Israelite whose community obligations were at issue in Deuteronomy 25.

9. Bassler, 1 Timothy, 2 Timothy, Titus, 99; Johnson, Letters to Timothy, 278; Knight, Pastoral Epistles, 233; Spicq, Les Épîtres Pastorales, 175–76.

10. He does this, however, so as to present more starkly his own practice of declining such prerogatives, which likely has the rhetorical effect of calling the Corinthians to a similar standard (Collins, First Corinthians, 327–43; Lenski, Epistle to the Corinthians, 350–68; Morris, Paul to the Corinthians, 129–34; Thrall, Paul to the Corinthians, 65–70).

11. Fee, First Epistle to the Corinthians, 406–8; Lindemann, Der erste Korintherbrief, 204; Morris, Paul to the Corinthians, 132; Thiselton, First Epistle to the Corinthians, 686–88; Thrall, Paul to the Corinthians, 67.

Deut 25:4, just as it appears in the LXX.[12] On the other hand, apart from
its usage in the original autograph of 1 Corinthians, it proves difficult to
account for the occurrence of κημόω in other manuscripts, even though
they stand in a marked minority and comprise a collection of somewhat
less highly regarded witnesses. On the balance, most commentators
yield to the principle of choosing the harder reading as the original (or
in this case, the most difficult to account for), and conclude that κημόω
was the verb originally used by Paul.[13] However, even assuming such
circumstances, it need not necessarily be problematic to explain Paul's
choice of κημόω instead of φιμόω. It was argued in chapter 2 that Paul
exhibits a tendency to employ septuagintal expressions when he is citing
directly from a Greek translation of the OT, while he appears to translate
by means of other words when he is working from memory or from a
Hebrew text.[14] Thus, the appearance of κημόω in 1 Corinthians could signify an instance of one of the latter possibilities. Either way, apart from
the indications that φιμόω may express the additional idea of silencing
someone or something, both terms appear to be semantically equivalent
with the Hebrew, חסם, and thus seem equally suited to serve in its place.[15]

With regard to the second observation, a strong similarity is dis-
cernable between the Deut 25:4 citation's usages in both 1 Cor 9:9 and 1
Tim 5:18. In both cases, at first glance Paul appears to disregard the most
transparent point of the comment from Deuteronomy 25 as it pertains
to oxen, and instead draws from it a principle that has primary bearing
upon the just treatment of human workers.[16] However, while an isolated

12. φιμόω–p46 ℵ A B² C D¹ Y 33. 1881 M; Or Epiph | *txt* B* D* F G 1739 (NA²⁷,
454). See this discussion also in Collins, *First Corinthians*, 339; Thiselton, *First Epistle
to the Corinthians*, 685.

13. Collins, *First Corinthians*, 339, Fee, *First Epistle to the Corinthians*, 398; Thiselton, *First Epistle to the Corinthians*, 685.

14. See discussion in chapter 2, pages 33–39.

15. BDB, 340; BDAG, 542b, 1060a; *TWOT*, 1:308; Louw and Nida, *Greek-English
Lexicon of the New Testament*, 44.6. One other distinction occasionally proposed is
that, while φιμόω may be a more "literary" term, κημόω reflects a more common idiom
(Collins, *First Corinthians*, 339; Metzger, *Textual Commentary*, 492; Thiselton, *First
Epistle to the Corinthians*, 685).

16. As Collins observes, "Deuteronomy 25:4 is quoted with similar purpose in 1
Tim 5:18, where the biblical text is cited with the words used in the LXX (cf. *Did.*
13:1). The appearance of Deut 25:4 in this deutero-Pauline text may be a indication
of its author's familiarity with 1 Corinthians" (Collins, *First Corinthians*, 339). While
this latter remark depends as much upon Collin's presumption of the non-Pauline
authorship of 1 Tim—along with his assumption of a relatively late composition—as it

assessment of Deut 25:4 may lead one to determine that Paul has set aside the fundamental sense of the decree, offering an interpretation that outstrips its original meaning,[17] an evaluation of the more extensive context in which Deut 25:4 is found indicates otherwise. For instance, when the statement οὐ φιμώσεις βοῦν ἀλοῶντα appears in Deut 25:4,[18] it falls in the midst of decrees that concern one's proper conduct relative to fellow Israelites under a multitude of circumstances. This series of decrees arguably runs from 23:15—25:19.[19] In no other directive appearing in this body of material is there any mention of the proper treatment of animals, the most apparent significance of לא־תחסם שור בדישו in its original occurrence.[20] Such a singular type of law embedded in the otherwise seamless fabric of decrees concerning community obligations suggests that more than oxen are at issue here—indeed, that this command to permit the oxen to feed even as they labor conveyed, from its initial utterance, the more significant lesson of ensuring that human workers receive the benefits of their labor.[21] If that is the case, the placement of לא־תחסם שור בדישו

---

does any formal features in the text, it nevertheless is striking that he would find such literary correspondence so significant.

17. While he does not hold to the conventional wisdom on the matter, Kaiser lists several who maintain that Paul employs either allegory or some variety of rabbinic interpretive approach, among them Conzelmann, Deissmann, Hanson, Longenecker, and Orr and Walther (Kaiser, "Current Crisis in Exegesis," 12–13). Later, Kaiser insists, "Paul did *not* (1) allegorize (Hanson, Longenecker), (2) establish typico-allegorical counterparts for the OT (H. A. W. Meyer), (3) contend only for what loosely belonged to the whole of Scripture as his inerrant grounds (Lohfink), (4) try to draw on the entire theological corpus of Scripture as 'witness' (Sanders, Lohfink), or (5) claim that he had God's meaning (a *sensus plenior* or new hermeneutic) that was over and above or in addition to whatever the original meaning might have been" (ibid., 17). Lee writes more typically of Paul's treatment: "He feels his way carefully towards his bold allegorical interpretation" (Lee, "Studies in Texts," 123). See also Hanson, *Paul's Technique and Theology*, 161–66; Lenski, *Epistle to the Corinthians*, 361; Longenecker, *Biblical Exegesis*, 109–10.

18. In the LXX. It reads לא־תחסם שור בדישו in the BHS.

19. Kalland, "Deuteronomy," 142; Tigay, *Deuteronomy*, 213, 448–49. See also Driver, *Commentary on Deuteronomy*, 280.

20. Kalland marks this fact as well, observing, "This law concerning threshing animals occurs only here in the OT" (Kalland, "Deuteronomy," 149). Tigay, on the other hand, states, "This rule is of the same humanitarian character as 22:10, reflecting the maxim that 'a righteous man knows the needs of his beast'" (Tigay, *Deuteronomy*, 231). See also Prov 12:10.

21. Kaiser, reflecting upon Godet's remarks, writes, "It will be our contention here that Paul has neither abandoned the literal meaning nor taken liberties with the Mosaic legislation in order to obtain divine authorization for ministerial honoraria . . . The

(οὐ φιμώσεις βοῦν ἀλοῶντα) in the midst of Deut 23:15—25:19 not only makes sense, but it also authorizes the manner in which Paul uses it in both 1 Cor 9:9 and 1 Tim 5:18. Consequently, Paul not only cites this text from the Law, but as surely as he follows its most obvious original intent, he also demonstrates his regard for it as authoritative Scripture that governs both conscience and conduct.

1 Timothy and the Law, Prophets, and Writings

Paul's high regard for the Law, Prophets, and Writings emerges at several points throughout 1 Timothy. As argued in chapters 2 and 3, when Paul allusively appeals to the legal standards of the Decalogue (1 Tim 1:8–11) in order to mark those for whom the Law was appointed, he exhibits a high view of the Law even as he censures those who misuse the Law in support of their own agendas. In 2:9–15, while making his case against the placement of women in positions of authority over men, Paul alludes to and grounds his argument upon the lessons found in Gen 2:7, 3:13, and 3:16, again seeming to draw upon the intrinsic authority that he ascribes to this material. In 5:18, as discussed above, he states his case

---

whole Deuteronomic context, [Godet] argued, showed that Moses' concern was not for oxen alone but to develop gentleness and gratitude in their owners. 'It was the duties of *moral beings* on one another that God wished to impress' on mankind" (Kaiser, "Current Crisis in Exegesis," 13). By contrast, on the one hand, Merrill writes, "The very lowest creatures on the 'social' scale, the animals themselves, fell under the protection of the Lord and the covenant" (Merrill, *Deuteronomy*, 325). On the other hand, Merrill then proposes, "The purpose clearly was not only to provide for the ox itself but to make the point by *a fortiori* argument that if a mere animal was worthy of humane treatment, how much more so was a human being created as the image of God" (ibid.). Merrill further explains, "To abuse animal life is to fail to discharge that stewardship (entrusted to the human), to fail to show mercy to God's lowest creatures is to open the door to disregard human life as well" (ibid., 326). While Tigay exhibits some compatibility with the position proposed here, asserting that this section of Deuteronomy "deals primarily with private matters concerning individuals, their families, and their neighbors" (Tigay, *Deuteronomy*, 455), and while he also concedes that "a degree of subjectivity enters into such explanations" (ibid., 451), he yet prefers to account for this particular regulation as related to those around it by the inference that refusing the oxen would require striking, like beating an olive tree, or like the flogging of a criminal (ibid., 458). Looking to the Mishnah, Wolfe observes, "Especially relevant are the examples from tractates *Baba Metzi'a* and *Gittin*. In both of these, Deut 25:4 is used to support a worker's right to eat of the food that falls while the work is being done" (Wolfe, "Sagacious Use of Scripture," 201). See also Craigie, *Book of Deuteronomy*, 313; Kaiser, "Current Crisis in Exegesis," 14–15; Morris, *Paul to the Corinthians*, 132.

for making due provision for those overseers who carry out their tasks well based upon Deut 25:4, and in 5:19, he cautions against receiving too readily any word of accusation against one of the church's leaders. Justifying his admonition with ἐκτὸς εἰ μὴ ἐπὶ δύο ἢ τριῶν μαρτύρων, he again references a biblical text as the basis for his counsel, likely appealing to Deut 19:15.[22]

In each of these instances in which Paul draws upon the Law, either by allusion or citation, he would appear to locate the authoritative element in the most transparent illocutionary intent of the passage, notwithstanding claims that he relies upon certain rabbinic interpretive approaches with respect to the use of Deut 25:4 in 1 Cor 9:9.[23] This means that Paul confines himself in these examples to the primary meaning of these texts as their initial audience may have discerned them, which further validates their usage as corroborative witnesses that support his own teaching. In employing such an apparently conservative interpretive approach, he treats with great respect and seriousness the material as it appears in its original context, thereby displaying a high view of the OT as Scripture.[24] At the same time, he also appears to expect Timothy

22. Johnson, *Letters to Timothy*, 279; Knight, *Pastoral Epistles*, 235. Also, see chapter 2, where it is suggested that this is probably an allusion to Deut 19:15 as it appears in the BHS, closely though not exactly reflecting how it would be translated into Greek. This inexact duplication of Greek or Hebrew forms may also indicate a conflation of Deut 17:6 with 19:15, though this seems unlikely, since ἵνα καὶ οἱ λοιποὶ φόβον ἔχωσιν in 1 Tim 5:20 suggests the influence of Deut 19:20 (Johnson, *Letters to Timothy*, 280; Towner, *Letters to Timothy and Titus*, 367–70; Witherington, *Letters and Homilies*, 276).

23. Collins, *First Corinthians*, 330, 339; Lee, "Studies in Texts," 123; Lenski, *Epistle to the Corinthians*, 361; Thiselton, *First Epistle to the Corinthians*, 686–88.

24. Indeed, Edwin Blum makes this case forcefully, arguing, "Constant throughout all New Testament books is the view that the Old Testament is authoritative . . . To the apostles, the Old Testament Scripture was clearly their supreme authority! It is an absolute, not a relative, authority. They do not attempt to correct it, nor do they seek to put one Old Testament book or saying against another" (Blum, "Apostles' View of Scripture," 41). See also ibid., 43–47. Brian Rosner likewise observes in Paul a strong and sustained attitude of reverence toward Scripture. At various points, he observes, "Many of the introductory formulae do reveal Paul's high regard for Scripture . . . One thing that is abundantly clear about Paul's and the Jewish view of Scripture is the undoubted relevance of Scripture . . . Thus we have some basis here for the dictum 'what Scripture says, God says' . . . There are traces of evidence to indicate that Paul regarded Scripture as the very words of God" (Rosner, "'Written for Us,'" 88–89, 92). As he summarizes his findings, Rosner affirms, "Paul's view of Scripture is thus in large measure the standard Jewish view. With regard to its nature, like other Jews he regards Scripture as God's holy Word, as oracles of God. He sees it as both sacred and

likewise to regard these texts so highly that he too will recognize and respond appropriately to the weight of their testimony. It now remains to be seen just how Paul viewed his own writings and those of his apostolic colleagues, several of which now comprise the NT.

Γραφή and the Second Citation

As far as the second citation in 1 Tim 5:18 is concerned, while there exists some dispute as to the original source, no one denies that it reflects remarkably the words of Jesus as found in Luke 10:7, ἄξιος γὰρ ὁ ἐργάτης τοῦ μισθοῦ αὐτοῦ, with the exception of the conjunction γὰρ, which appears in Luke but not in 1 Timothy.[25] Indeed, the concord between this citation and the admonition of 5:17 is even more exact than that between that same admonition and the excerpt from Deut 25:4.[26] This presents the scholar with a curious set of circumstances, which shall be evaluated by beginning with the most apparent literary cues in the text of 1 Timothy itself, followed by a discussion of the plausibility of the availability of Lukan material as the source of the second citation.

Cues in 1 Timothy

Without distinguishing between the two citations, Paul has simply written, λέγει γὰρ ἡ γραφή, a citation formula that is followed by two excerpts joined together by καί. One might suggest that since Paul uses the singular noun and verb in his citation formula, it refers only to one of the excerpts presented, and the reader must determine which one is actually the indicated citation, in which case, the Deuteronomy text likely would garner near-universal acceptance.[27] However, this is not the only

---

central. Like all Jews, he expects Scripture to speak to the questions of daily conduct in the present. Like those at Qumran, he looks to Scripture to testify to God's decisive eschatological and revelatory act" (ibid., 103). These remarks stand in sharp opposition to McDonald's claim that Paul and others had no sense of the "inviolability" of the OT (McDonald, *Biblical Canon*, 198, 244–45).

25. Knight, *Pastoral Epistles*, 233; Mounce, *Pastoral Epistles*, 311; Nielsen, "Scripture in the Pastoral Epistles," 17.

26. Meier, "What Counts as Scripture?" 77.

27. For instance, Mounce suggests, "The problem of calling the citation 'Scripture' is accounted for by recognizing that 'Scripture' need only apply to Paul's first citation from the OT" (Mounce, *Pastoral Epistles*, 311).

place in the NT where a singular citation formula may indicate more than one citation. In Acts 1:20, Luke writes, γέγραπται γὰρ ἐν βίβλῳ ψαλμῶν, which is then followed by γενηθήτω ἡ ἔπαυλις αὐτοῦ ἔρημος καὶ μὴ ἔστω ὁ κατοικῶν ἐν αὐτῇ, καί· τὴν ἐπισκοπὴν αὐτοῦ λαβέτω ἕτερος: two citations from the OT joined by καί. Also, one may observe in 1 Pet 2:6–8 the introductory formula περιέχει ἐν γραφῇ, which is then followed by a series of three citations drawn from Isaiah and Psalms. These occur in verses 6–8 and read,

> "Behold, I lay in Zion a stone, a cornerstone, chosen and precious, and he who trusts in him shall not be put to shame" (Isa 28:16), therefore, the honor [is] for you who believe, but for those who disbelieve, "The stone which the builders rejected, this has become the chief cornerstone" (Ps 118:22), and, "a stone of stumbling and a rock of offense" (Isa 8:14), and the ones disobeying the word stumble, to which they also were appointed.[28]

In view of these examples, one cannot rule out, simply on the basis of singular γραφή, the possibility that the citation formula in 1 Tim 5:18 in fact is intended to indicate both excerpts. More importantly, however, by virtue of the lexical concord between 5:17 and 5:18c, the literary context strongly suggests that both citations are in view. Specifically, when one sets the final clause of 5:18 (ἄξιος ὁ ἐργάτης τοῦ μισθοῦ αὐτοῦ) against the main clause of 5:17 (Οἱ καλῶς προεστῶτες πρεσβύτεροι διπλῆς τιμῆς ἀξιούσθωσαν), it is clear that the second citation—not the first, drawn from Deuteronomy—reflects more transparently and more immediately both the concern and lexis (ἄξιος, ἀξιόω) of the primary clause.[29] Consequently, with both citations traceable to specific written documents, the most obvious assessment of this passage in its own literary context is that Paul indeed cites both texts as "Scripture."[30]

28. Knight, *Pastoral Epistles*, 234. Knight makes a similar point with respect to multiple citations.

29. Meier, "What Counts as Scripture?" 77. See also, Wolfe, "Sagacious Use of Scripture," 212.

30. As Blum writes, "In 1 Timothy 5:18 Paul writes, 'For the Scripture says, "Do not muzzle the ox while it is treading out the grain," and "The worker deserves his wages."' The first quotation comes from Deuteronomy 25:4 and the second from Luke 10:7. The most normal inference is that Paul considers both Deuteronomy and Luke to be Scripture" (Blum, "Apostles' View of Scripture," 53). Marshall also observes, "For the author the second citation had equal authority with the OT" (Marshall, *Pastoral Epistles*, 615). See also Knight, *Pastoral Epistles*, 233–34; Meier, "What Counts as Scripture?" 77–79; Nielsen, "Scripture in the Pastoral Epistles," 17.

At least two additional factors weigh in favor of the argument proposed here. First, it is important to acknowledge that Paul does not discriminate in the manner according to which he uses the two citations. As already argued, each one provides a warrant for the primary clause of 5:17, and both are offered in sequence and without qualification as authoritative texts that apparently retain their original illocutionary force. In other words, Paul has not cast either one in a sense alien to its original utterance or inscription.

Second, within the literary context of 1 Timothy, the care with which Paul expects his own apostolic teaching to be received and followed indicates that he ascribes a great deal of authority to that teaching, enough at least to refer to it as ἡ ὑγιαίνουσα διδασκαλία, ὁ λόγος, ὁ [πιστὸς] λόγος, λόγος θεοῦ, ἡ ἀλήθεια, ἡ διδασκαλία, ὑγιαίνοντες λόγοι ὅι τοῦ κυρίου ἡμῶν Ἰησοῦ Χριστοῦ, ἡ παραθήκη, and ἡ παράκλησις, among other designations. Consider the following summary of points raised over the course of the analysis of 1 Timothy in the previous chapter.

1. In the opening two verses of the letter, Paul indicates that, as ἀπόστολος Χριστοῦ Ἰησοῦ, he writes as a representative of—and under the superintendence of—Christ Jesus, and that he does so by the authority of God.[31]

2. The "sound teaching" that Paul determines to uphold concerns "the gospel," a term for which Paul offers no explanation, and which itself reflects and derives from "the glory of the blessed God."[32] Furthermore, this gospel serves as the message with which Paul, ἀπόστολος Χριστοῦ Ἰησοῦ κατ' ἐπιταγὴν θεοῦ σωτῆρος ἡμῶν καὶ Χριστοῦ Ἰησοῦ τῆς ἐλπίδος ἡμῶν, has been entrusted by God.

3. The preceding point signals the familiar and technical status of τὸ εὐαγγέλιον even in Paul's day, and anchors the origin of τὸ εὐαγγέλιον in God himself; it is *God's* gospel message. Consequently, Paul presents himself as an agent on behalf of God entrusted with God's gospel message and the sound teaching associated with it.[33] Fur-

31. Aageson, "Pastoral Epistles, Apostolic Authority," 11; Bassler, *1 Timothy, 2 Timothy, Titus*, 35–36; Fiore, *Pastoral Epistles*, 31–32; Johnson, *Letters to Timothy*, 159; Knight, *Pastoral Epistles*, 58, 61.

32. Barrett, *Pastoral Epistles*, 43–44; Collins, *Timothy and Titus*, 34; Dibelius and Conzelmann, *Commentary on the Pastoral Epistles*, 24; Johnson, *Letters to Timothy*, 171–72, 174.

33. Brox, *Die Pastoralbriefe*, 108; Roloff, *Der erste Brief an Timotheus*, 80.

thermore, Paul's own words are vested with authority comparable with that attributed to the Torah.[34]

4. By virtue of the fact that those who embrace τὸ εὐαγγέλιον also are those who εἰς ἐπίγνωσιν ἀληθείας ἦλθον, Paul apparently equates ἡ ἀλήθεια with τὸ εὐαγγέλιον. Furthermore, it already stands established that ἡ ὑγιαίνουσα διδασκαλία serves as another Pauline designation of this same gospel proclamation.[35]

5. Those who understand ἡ ἀλήθεια also recognize that λόγος θεοῦ witnesses to the acceptability of marriage and all foods. Also, while most commentators rush to discussions of the OT alone relative to the one occurrence of λόγος θεοῦ in 4:5, there yet remains a considerable consensus that, throughout the letter, λόγος typically stands as yet another designation of τὸ εὐαγγέλιον.[36]

6. Paul urges Timothy, ἕως ἔρχομαι πρόσεχε τῇ ἀναγνώσει, τῇ παρακλήσει, τῇ διδασκαλίᾳ. Since ἡ ὑγιαίνουσα διδασκαλία and ἡ καλὴ διδασκαλία have served as references that are synonymous with τὸ εὐαγγέλιον, it may be supposed that unmodified ἡ διδασκαλία retains this meaning. Furthermore, because of the close association between ἡ παράκλησις and ἡ διδασκαλία, one may conclude that both terms function as signifiers of some phase of the gospel proclamation.[37]

Following this summary, it is clear that Paul's gospel proclamation not only constitutes "sound teaching," it also comprises "the word of God." The cumulative effect of these data suggests that Paul puts his own instruction on a level commensurate with God's OT Scriptures,[38]

34. Schlatter suggests as much in his remarks, "First, that the law and the gospel are two different words of God . . . Second, that God's will in the law and the gospel is the same . . . But, in that Paul is contested, the gospel is contested. For God has entrusted the message to him" (Schlatter, *Die Kirche der Griechen*, 52, 54).

35. Collins, *Timothy and Titus*, 34, 60; Oberlinner, *Erster Timotheusbrief*, 73; Wolter, *Die Pastoralbriefe als Paulustradition*, 70–71.

36. BDAG, 599b; Johnson, *Letters to Timothy*, 242; Kittel, "λέγω, λόγος, λαλέω, ῥῆμα, κ.τ.λ.," 115–19; Karris, "Polemic of the Pastoral Epistles," 558–59; Louw and Nida, *Greek-English Lexicon of the New Testament*, 33.260; Mounce, *Pastoral Epistles*, 241; Towner, *Goal of Our Instruction*, 123–24.

37. Kelly, *Pastoral Epistles*, 105; Knight, *Pastoral Epistles*, 207–8; Marshall, *Pastoral Epistles*, 563; Towner, *Letters to Timothy and Titus*, 320–21.

38. Aageson proposes, "To the extent that [the recipients] accept the apostolic authority of Paul as divinely given and submit to the authority of the texts as representing

which in turn raises the same possibility for the writings of others of the apostolic company, a company of which Luke, the frequent companion of Paul, was a member. At the same time, again as noted in chapter 3, Paul clearly views his own teaching and apostolic proclamation as the standard of truth and right belief by which any other teaching is shown to be false.[39] Nevertheless, it remains to be shown that λόγος θεοῦ in 4:5 and ἡ ἀνάγνωσις in 4:13 more plausibly function as references to apostolic writings alongside the Law, Prophets, and Writings than as references to the OT alone.

Lukan Connections

Since each of Luke's and Matthew's gospels contain a version of Jesus' assertion as found in 1 Tim 5:18, it is often suggested that Paul draws upon a common Jesus tradition, preserved in various forms in the Synoptic literature, without necessarily intending to cite the form found distinctly in Luke.[40] In reply, it also might be asked why, if such a well-known and influential collection of Jesus sayings existed (so as to justify citation with an attending expectation of its recognition), no manuscripts have yet appeared that might bear witness to such a collection. It also would be fair to ask, if the gospel tradition were so fluid in its early days, why no significantly differing (or developing) versions of Luke's or Matthew's gospels appear anywhere in the manuscript tradi-

---

correct teaching, these epistles will come to be heard as sacred address" (Aageson, "Pastoral Epistles, Apostolic Authority," 11). With regard to Paul's teaching on Jesus, Peter Balla argues more pointedly, "We may argue with probability, that [Paul's] own reports, when put in writing, share the authority of the prophetic writings that foretold the same events" (Balla, "Evidence for an Early Christian Canon," 373). Also pertaining to this point, John Barton observes, "In asking whether or not a Christian book is cited as *graphe*—that is, in the same manner as the Old Testament—one is discovering whether or not the Church attributed to it the same status as the Old Testament" (Barton, *Holy Writings, Sacred Text*, 5). See also Belleville, "Canon of the New Testament," 379; Dunbar, "Biblical Canon," 320–21, 328; Nielsen, "Scripture in the Pastoral Epistles," 20. Perhaps even more suggestive are Paul's remarks concerning ἡ καινὴ διαθήκη and ἡ παλαιὰ διαθήκη, as found in 2 Cor 3:6 and 14. Here there seems to be an explicit correlation drawn between the Law, Prophets, and Writings, on the one hand, and the apostolic preaching, on the other (Carmignac, "2 Corinthiens 3. 6,14 et le Début de la Formation du Nouveau Testament," 386).

39. Dunbar, "Biblical Canon," 322–23.

40. Bassler, *1 Timothy, 2 Timothy, Titus*, 100; Collins, *Timothy and Titus*, 145; Oberlinner, *Erster Timotheusbrief*, 254; Roloff, *Der erste Brief an Timotheus*, 306.

tion. However, rather than relying upon arguments from silence, it is possible to draw upon some positive text-critical data that do speak to these points, at least in part.

First, Matt 10:10 incorporates τῆς τροφῆς instead of τοῦ μισθοῦ in its version of the saying cited,[41] an alternative reading that also appears in three of the manuscripts containing 1 Timothy, though this variant is not well-attested.[42] At the same time, while some of the manuscripts containing Matthew feature the variant τοῦ μισθοῦ as found in Luke, rather than τῆς τροφῆς,[43] no corresponding variant appears in *any* manuscript containing Luke's gospel. The fact that the available text-critical data indicate no variance of forms associated with Luke's gospel bears testimony to the stability of that text at this point. It would also seem to tell against a diffused or broad Logion source, or even proverbial tradition that Luke may have worked into his first volume, even though at least one other version of the saying was known to some of the later copyists who worked with 1 Timothy.[44] However, and more importantly, this apparent textual stability also indicates that Paul did not cite loosely, but that he intentionally selected this particular form of Jesus' commentary respecting the worthy worker.

Second, a survey of all of the variant readings on record for Luke's gospel shows that, while some words, and even occasionally lengthy phrases and clauses, may differ from manuscript to manuscript, none of the pericopae differ in content or sequence, nor is there any indication that a prior, provisional, or developing form or edition of Luke's gospel ever existed.[45]

---

41. Matt 10:10 reads, ἄξιος γὰρ ὁ ἐργάτης τῆς τροφῆς αὐτοῦ.

42. Specifically, ℵ*vid, (ar*), and (Cl) (NA[27], 547).

43. Specifically, K, 565, 892, *al*, it, sy[hmg] (NA[27], 24).

44. Among the manuscripts that contain Luke 10:7, NA[27] lists 147 majuscules and miniscules, not counting M. These represent three text-types, and date from the third to the sixteenth centuries (NA[27], 684–713). In spite of the number of manuscripts (more than 1,300), the representation of various text-types, and the wide range of dates from which these manuscripts originate, there is no variant on record for this remark as found in Luke's gospel.

45. NA[27], 150–246. Barton also calls attention to "the striking uniformity among New Testament texts in the early manuscript tradition," writing, "It does not at all suggest a lengthy period of tentative acceptance leading eventually to 'canonization,' but a very rapid attribution of supreme authority. In that sense the Church entered the second century with a core New Testament already enjoying 'scriptural' status, and never found any reason to change it" (Barton, *Holy Writings, Sacred Text*, 26).

In addition to these observations, it will be recalled from chapter 3 that 1 Timothy exhibits at least five features that suggest a possible prior familiarity with a written form of Luke's gospel on the part of both writer and recipient.[46] The first such instance entails the only two occurrences of νομοδιδάσκαλος in the NT outside of 1 Timothy 1:7, one of which may be found in Luke 5:17, while the other appears in Acts 5:34.[47]

Second, it was noted in the analysis of 4:1–5 that Paul's reference to λόγος θεοῦ in connection with his sanctioning of all food suggested a significant correspondence to Jesus' words concerning both matters as found in Luke's gospel.[48] The lesson that addresses the acceptability of foods is found in Luke 11:37–41, in which Jesus is invited to share a meal with a Pharisee. When Jesus does not perform the ceremonial pre-meal washing, the Pharisee registers some astonishment, and Jesus responds by chiding the Pharisee for his obsession with outward and ritual purity considering the Pharisee's neglect of genuine purity of person, character, and conduct. Jesus concludes his response to the Pharisee with an invective against the Pharisees for their habitual hypocrisy in the things over which they obsess as well as those they neglect. In the midst of this censure (11:41), Jesus declares, καὶ ἰδοὺ πάντα καθαρὰ ὑμῖν ἐστιν. For the host in this encounter, the issue chiefly concerns practices that either leave one pure or defiled. Accordingly, in delivering his response, Jesus seeks to redirect his hosts' attention away from washing *per se* and more toward what truly defiles an individual, in the process of which he declares all things "clean."[49] Matthew and Mark also include a version of this encounter.[50]

---

46. Moule also observes these corresponding points of contact, though he finds in them evidence of Lukan composition of the PE. Moule in fact observes three classes of correspondence between Luke-Acts and the PE: "significant word, or uses of words," "significant phrases, or collocations of words," and "significant ideas," instances of each of which are adduced here (Moule, "Problem of the Pastoral Epistles," 441, 443, 445). See also Witherington, *Letters and Homilies*, 57–61; Wolfe, "Sagacious Use of Scripture," 213.

47. Collins, *Timothy and Titus*, 29; Oberlinner, *Erster Timotheusbrief*, 19; Pirot and Clamer, *La Sainte Bible*, 207.

48. Recall from the previous chapter the remarks by Fee, Mounce, and Towner (chapter 3, note 81).

49. Geldenhuys, *Gospel of Luke*, 341–42; Nolland, *Luke*, 2:664–65; Plummer, *Gospel According to Saint Luke*, 310–11.

50. These versions appear in Matt 15:1–20 and Mark 7:1–23, each of which also contains Jesus' explanation to his disciples.

Third, and in a similar manner, the Synoptic Gospels also convey a teaching of Jesus that addresses the sanctity of marriage, which corresponds to Paul's sanction of marriage also argued on the basis of λόγος θεοῦ. Specifically, Luke 16:18, for instance, reads, πᾶς ὁ ἀπολύων τὴν γυναῖκα αὐτοῦ καὶ γαμῶν ἑτέραν μοιχεύει, καὶ ὁ ἀπολελυμένην ἀπὸ ἀνδρὸς γαμῶν μοιχεύει.[51] In all three versions of this teaching, Jesus firmly speaks against divorce and the casual treatment of the marriage contract and relationship.

In view of these instances, it is most probable that Paul's reference to λόγος θεοῦ as the mediator that sanctified or sanctioned marriage and all food serves as an allusion to Jesus' words concerning such matters as they appear in Luke 11 and 16, as well as in similar passages of Matthew and Mark. Such allusions also point to a familiarity with a fixed gospel tradition, whether written or oral, on the part of both author and recipient. Furthermore, Paul's remarks suggest not only that he may have drawn upon the gospel tradition as we find it in the Synoptics, but also that he may have been familiar with what had already become a conventional interpretation of that tradition. At the same time, he does not cite any particular version of either lesson, though his statement, ἁγιάζεται . . . διὰ λόγου θεοῦ, might legitimately be perceived as an allusion either to Luke's ἰδοὺ πάντα καθαρὰ ὑμῖν ἐστιν, or to Mark's explanatory καθαρίζων πάντα τὰ βρώματα.[52] Not only is this so, but the inclusion of material so reflective of Jesus' teachings on food and marriage also suggests that when the gospel message was proclaimed, it was comprised not only of the central teaching regarding what God accomplished through Jesus (like that appearing in 1 Tim 1:15 or 2:5–6), but also of the story about Jesus that

51. Geldenhuys, *Gospel of Luke*, 421; Liefeld, *Luke*, 990; Nolland, *Luke*, 2:821–22; Plummer, *Gospel According to Saint Luke*, 389–90. Again, slightly different versions of this passage appear in Matt 5:31–32, 19:1–12 and Mark 10:11–12.

52. It seems beyond mere coincidence that in Luke, one may find both of these topics addressed in a manner entirely consistent with Paul's remarks in 1 Timothy. Furthermore, as noted in the previous chapter, the informal nature of the allusions to food and marriage in 4:3–4, their explicit association with λόγος θεοῦ and the correlation of its interpretation with the Synoptic tradition, along with the absence of any direct literary dependence, would seem indicative of something more complex than a simple Logion source lying behind Paul's words in this passage. In addition to these details, it is worth noting that many commentators appear drawn to an explanation of λόγος θεοῦ that permits it to refer to Scripture, even though they do not reflect the specific solution offered here. Consequently, one can observe that the broad impulse is to read λόγος θεοῦ as a reference to the written word, even while the prevailing views of Christian writings tend to rule out the consideration of any written gospel.

culminated in his death and resurrection. Such an account would have included events and teachings associated with Jesus' earthly life and ministry.[53] While such a document may not have acquired the technical *genre* designation of "gospel" at the time, it nevertheless stood as a gospel account, complete with facts, historical reference points, and doctrine, and therefore would have served as an appropriate mainstay in the apostolic proclamation and teaching.[54]

Fourth, it was noted with respect to 1 Tim 4:13 that Paul writes of ἡ ἀνάγνωσις ("the reading") that Timothy is to uphold, and it was argued further that this "reading" is linked directly with "the teaching," and thus likely entailed a written form of the apostolic proclamation concerning Jesus. This point has special significance to the primary topic of this study, for a fundamental trait of anything that functions as the referent of ἡ ἀνάγνωσις is that it also must be something recorded in writing.[55] The correspondence between ἡ διδασκαλία and ἡ παράκλησις in this passage has already been established; both serve as signifiers of the apostolic message. However, Paul writes of three elements that form the content of Timothy's instruction to be given to the church, ἡ ἀνάγνωσις being the first of the three. Ἀνάγνωσις formed the initial source from which ἡ διδασκαλία and ἡ παράκλησις derived. Since ἡ ἀνάγνωσις appears in a cluster of three terms in this letter, the remaining two of which appear to denote the gospel message, it would seem to be an arbitrary shift in subject matter if ἡ ἀνάγνωσις were to serve as a designation for the OT alone. On the other hand, as previously discussed, Paul's citations of and allusions to the Torah suggest that ἡ ἀνάγνωσις must include at least the writings of the OT. Consequently, the most likely referent of "the reading" entails some written form of the apostolic gospel message

---

53. Barton, *Holy Writings, Sacred Text*, 67; Stonehouse, *Origins of the Synoptic Gospels*, 117, 132–33; Stonehouse, *Witness of Luke to Christ*, 26. Also, even though he offers no support for a *written* gospel, Helmut Koester nevertheless asserts about the gospel content, "The oldest Gospels are built around the narratives of the passion and death of Jesus" (Koester, "Writings and the Spirit," 368).

54. Barton suggests, "The first Christians had books about Jesus and his first disciples, and they used them as authoritative sources of information about the central events of salvation" (Barton, *Holy Writings, Sacred Text*, 67).

55. Cothenet, "Directives pastorales dan les Épîtres a Timothée," 18–19; BDAG, 206b; Knight, *Pastoral Epistles*, 234; Louw and Nida, *Greek-English Lexicon of the New Testament*, 33.53; Meier, "What Counts as Scripture?" 77; Schrenk, "γράφω, γραφή, γράμμα, κ.τ.λ.," 749–51.

in conjunction with the OT.[56] This gospel, it now is proposed, is the one written by Luke. At the very least, this explanation would certainly account for the exact match between Luke 10:7 and the citation of 1 Tim 5:18, and it does so more compellingly than positing a more vague and varied Logion tradition.

Finally, in 1 Tim 6:13–14, Paul admonishes Timothy, τηρῆσαί σε τὴν ἐντολὴν ἄσπιλον ἀνεπίλημπτον μέχρι τῆς ἐπιφανείας τοῦ κυρίου ἡμῶν Ἰησοῦ Χριστοῦ. The *modus operandi* or vantage point that Timothy must assume so as to "keep the commandment" Paul describes is the same as that of Jesus, ὁ μαρτυρήσας ἐπὶ Ποντίου Πιλάτου τὴν καλὴν ὁμολογίαν.[57] Now, while all four gospel accounts give witness to Jesus' encounter with Pilate, only Luke, apart from a variant reading for Matt 27:2, makes reference to Pilate's family name, "Pontius": once in his gospel (3:1) and once in Acts (4:27). These two occurrences, along with the one here in 1 Tim 6, are the only instances of Pilate's surname in the New Testament. If this point, along with the matched expressions shared by 1 Tim 5:18 and Luke 10:7, is taken into due consideration, the likelihood increases that λόγος θεοῦ and ἡ ἀνάγνωσις may also serve as references to a written gospel. Thus, there are at least five plausible instances of literary correlation between the Gospel of Luke and 1 Timothy.

Considering the points just reviewed, the exact replication of Jesus' words as found in Luke 10:7 provides not one uniquely plausible point of correspondence between 1 Timothy and Luke's gospel, but the fourth of at least five such links. While one could note any one of these points of correlation without drawing weighty conclusions, the presence of five such instances within the same document seems extraordinary. Thus, apart from the widespread presumption of a tight literary dependence linking the Synoptic Gospels and of the relatively late date of their final composition, *prima facie* data would likely carry more weight, and the possibility of a circulating written form of Luke's gospel would not receive such a summary dismissal.[58]

56. Bernard maintains that ἀνάγνωσις, while certainly referring to the OT, could denote the apostolic letters as well (Bernard, *Pastoral Epistles*, 71–72). See also Lock, *Pastoral Epistles*, 53; Spicq, *Les Épîtres Pastorales*, 148.

57. Knight, *Pastoral Epistles*, 265–66; Towner, *Letters to Timothy and Titus*, 413–14; Witherington, *Letters and Homilies*, 289–90, 293–94. Furthermore, as noted above, in the case of the Lukan expressions found in 1 Timothy, while they also appear in some Matt manuscripts as variant readings, the Matthean versions of these same passages do not appear in any Lukan manuscript.

58. As Robinson notes, "Much more than is generally recognized, the chronology

As it is, while Luke clearly drew upon sources for his gospel, a reasonable case may be made that he exercised more literary independence than is typically allowed, and that he composed his work at a relatively early date. To begin with, as John Robinson has pointed out, there exists no truly compelling reason to place the composition of any NT book after A.D. 70, since such a catastrophic and momentous occasion as the fall of Jerusalem and the destruction of the Temple would hardly escape mention in subsequent Jewish and Christian literature.[59] While this provides a helpful criterion, the timeframe for the composition of Luke's gospel may be pressed even further. Again referencing Robinson, one searches in vain for any account in Acts of the persecution of Nero (A.D. 64) or of the death of James, the brother of Jesus (A.D. 62), both of which should appear in Luke's report of critical happenings attending the infancy of the church and the progress of the gospel across the Roman Empire, assuming it were written after these events.[60] In fact, in agreement with Harnack, Robinson maintains that Acts could not have been written later than the latest event recorded, which accounts at least in part for the relatively abrupt ending, with Paul still in prison and with no

---

of the New Testament rests on presuppositions rather than facts . . . What seemed to be firm datings based on scientific evidence are revealed to rest on deductions from deductions. The pattern is self-consistent but circular" (Robinson, *Redating the New Testament*, 2–3, 8–9). See also Hemer, *Hellenistic History*, 311; Kümmel, *Introduction to the New Testament*, 52–80; Wenham, *Redating Matthew, Mark and Luke*, xxii; Zahn, *Introduction to the New Testament*, 2:400–426. In particular, it is interesting to note the language that Kümmel uses as he sets up his presentation as an adherent of the Two-Source Theory. As he writes, "We *cannot be sure* that the Synoptic Gospels have been preserved for us in their original wording . . . *In all probability* the stream of oral tradition, first in Aramaic and then in Greek as well, continued for a long time . . . On the basis of the resulting *presupposition* indicated by this evidence—that Mk could be the common source for Mt and Lk—the omission of small bits of Markan special material by Mt and Lk is thoroughly comprehensible," he telegraphs how slim the actual evidence base may be upon which the entire hypothesis rests (Kümmel, *Introduction to the New Testament*, 52–53, 56–57, emphasis mine).

59. Robinson is most emphatic on this point, and indeed, once it is proposed, it seems so patently obvious that one might wonder why it has received so little consideration in the examination of the NT (Robinson, *Redating the New Testament*, 10–13). Furthermore, as Robinson also observes (citing C. C. Torrey), "It is perhaps conceivable that *one* evangelist writing after the year 70 might fail to allude to the *destruction of the temple* by the Roman armies . . . but that *three* (or four) should thus fail is quite incredible" (ibid., 30). See also Moule, *Birth of the New Testament*, 5, 173–76; Wenham, *Redating Matthew, Mark and Luke*, 224.

60. Robinson, *Redating the New Testament*, 89.

resolution relative to his trial.[61] Accordingly, this places the composition of Acts at no later than A.D. 62.

In view of these considerations, the *terminus ad quem* for the composition of Luke must fall even earlier. As Luke himself informs his reader, Acts is the second of two corresponding works, which necessarily requires that his gospel had been written and released before the subsequent work. Reckoning for the gathering of information, even as Luke remarks in the prologue of his gospel, and for some time to craft his document (which also is implied in the prologue),[62] it still seems reasonable to place the writing of the Gospel of Luke no later than the the 50s.[63] Indeed, while the absence of more certain data forbids pressing this date further, there does not seem to be any compelling reason to deny the plausibility that Luke's gospel could have been written in the early 50s.[64]

In 2 Cor 8:18, Paul also provides a plausible indication that a written gospel lay behind some of his instructions to the Corinthians. John Wenham has argued that Paul's remarks in 2 Cor 8:18, in which he refers to a brother who is "renowned in the gospel," provide additional information that signal the existence of a written version of Luke's gospel.[65] The text

---

61 Ibid., 90–91; Liefeld, *Luke*, 807–8; Schnabel, *Early Christian Mission*, 1:31; Wenham, *Redating Matthew, Mark and Luke*, 223.

62. Stonehouse, *Origins of the Synoptic Gospels*, 116.

63. In fact, Robinson proposes that the "final stages" of all of the Synoptic Gospels should not be placed later than the 50s (Robinson, *Redating the New Testament*, 101–8).

64. Gerhardsson hints at this as he writes, "As early as the oldest preserved documents of the young Church, the epistles of Paul, of which the majority were written in the fifties, we see that early Christianity had a tradition (παράδοσις) which was regarded as authoritative. Further, we can see that at least some collections of gospel material belonged to the material classified in this way" (Gerhardsson, *Memory and Manuscript*, 13). Also, as Robinson once again notes, "The objection will doubtless still be raised that all this allows too little time for the development in the theology and practice of the church presupposed by the gospels and Acts. But this judgment is precariously subjective. It is impossible to say *a priori* how long is required for any development, or for the processes, communal and redactional, to which scholarly study has rightly drawn attention. We have noted how much could happen within three years of the crucifixion—and we are allowing a further thirty for the full flowering of the synoptic tradition. There is nothing, I believe, in the theology of the gospels or Acts or in the organization of the church there depicted that requires a longer span, which was already long enough, if we are right, for the creation of the whole Pauline corpus, including the Pastoral Epistles." (Robinson, *Redating the New Testament*, 116). See also Wenham, *Redating Matthew, Mark and Luke*, 223, 237.

65. Indeed, reflecting upon the implications of what he deems a likely reference

lies in the midst of a statement in which Paul expresses his intent to send Titus to Corinth so as to assist the Corinthians in the task of completing their collection on behalf of the believers in Judea.[66] It reads,

> And we have sent along with him the brother whose fame in the gospel [is] through all the churches; and not only [is this so], but being appointed by the churches, he [is]our fellow traveler with us in this grace, which is being administered by us for the glory of the Lord Himself, and for our readiness.

The first vital element is Paul's reference to τὸν ἀδελφὸν, whom he is sending with Titus to Corinth. In this, he endorses this unnamed colleague as a partner with himself and Titus.[67] He then adds a further description, οὗ ὁ ἔπαινος ἐν τῷ εὐαγγελίῳ, by which he further defines or distinguishes this "brother." Specifically, this individual has attained fame with respect to "the gospel." Taken by itself, this could refer to someone known for his preaching of the gospel message, for his labor on behalf of the gospel, or someone known for his written gospel work.[68]

---

to Luke in 2 Cor 8:18 (τὸν ἀδελφὸν οὗ ὁ ἔπαινος ἐν τῷ εὐαγγελίῳ διὰ πασῶν τῶν ἐκκλησιῶν), he writes, "The Gospel of Luke was written before 56, the approximate date of 2 Corinthians. It is difficult to say how long it would take for the fame of the book to spread through 'all the churches.' The expression suggests more than just the churches of Macedonia and Achaia, so we should probably allow at least a year, and say therefore that its writing had taken place by 55 at the latest" (Wenham, *Redating Matthew, Mark and Luke*, 223, 237).

66. Furnish, *2 Corinthians*, 402, 414–15, 422, 433–34; Harris, *Second Epistle to the Corinthians*, 569–70, 600–602; Martin, *2 Corinthians*, 255, 274; Matera, *2 Corinthians*, 187–96.

67. Furnish, *2 Corinthians*, 434; Harris, *Second Epistle to the Corinthians*, 600; Matera, *2 Corinthians*, 196.

68. Though Martin summarily dismisses the latter possibility, stating, "[Luke] is ruled out by the fact that there is no clear evidence before A.D. 150 of τὸ εὐαγγέλιον ("the Gospel") being used of a written composition" (Martin, *2 Corinthians*, 274; see also Harris, *Second Epistle to the Corinthians*, 602). Two things may be said in response to Martin, however. First, an absence of clear positive evidence is not the same as clear evidence to the contrary; Martin's position essentially reduces to an argument from silence. Second, there is in fact evidence of the term τὸ εὐαγγέλιον being used to designate a literary genre prior to A.D. 150. In the Didache (ca. A.D. 100), one may find four direct references to τὸ εὐαγγέλιον as a collection of teachings that Christians are exhorted to follow. While these instances seem to suggest a written work as a source, the language is admittedly equivocal (Ehrman, *Apostolic Fathers*, 1:411; *Did.*, 8.2, 11.3, 15.3, 15.4). However, David Warren has uncovered an unambiguous reference to "the reading of the holy Scripture, which the Christians call the Gospel," within a Syriac copy of an apology written to the Emperor Hadrian by the Christian apologist Aristides probably sometime before A.D. 125, though Warren estimates before A.D.

However, the possibilities narrow significantly when Paul adds that this brother's recognition extends διὰ πασῶν τῶν ἐκκλησιῶν. In other words, the brother who will accompany Titus is not only a close partner of Paul's, but he also is a coworker who has gained recognition all over the church specifically because of the gospel, or possobly *his* gospel.[69] Finally, in perhaps one of the most telling elements of all, Paul also characterizes this brother as συνέκδημος ἡμῶν σὺν τῇ χάριτι ταύτῃ. While Paul writes in his letters of many different partners and coworkers in the faith, there are relatively few who fit the full profile drawn from these verses.[70] In fact, based upon available data, the only individual who easily fits all the criteria noted is Luke, Paul's faithful companion and the author of a gospel that appears to have been written from the outset as a teaching document for the church.[71] Consequently, this passage supports the suggestion that indeed, Luke had written and published his gospel at least as early as A.D.

---

140 (Warren, "Who Originated the Term 'Gospel' as a Genre?"). While this does not confirm the hypothesis being proposed in this study, it nevertheless does testify to an earlier use of τὸ εὐαγγέλιον as a designation of a literary genre than is commonly attested ("Aristides," 102; Birley, "Hadrian," 662–63; Eusebius, *Ecclesiastical History*, 4.3.3; Ferguson, *Backgrounds of Early Christianity*, 37; Grant, "Aristides," 382).

69. Contra Lenski, *Epistle to the Corinthians*, 1151. Wenham writes, "The 'brother whose fame in the gospel is throughout the churches' is evidently Luke, and his fame derives from his gospel-book . . . If . . . Luke's gospel had been circulating in the churches of Greece for a year or two, he would indeed have been famous for one very special service to the gospel" (Wenham, *Redating Matthew, Mark and Luke*, 223, 236).

70. Wenham lists several possible candidates, maintaining that only Luke and Tychicus could reasonably fit the criteria, but determining in the final analysis that it must refer to Luke, who has "a strong backing of tradition behind him" (ibid., 231–34).

71. Contra Furnish, *2 Corinthians*, 435–36, and Lenski, *Epistle to the Corinthians*, 1151. Similarly to Wenham, Richard Anderson writes, "In Second Corinthians 8:18 we read these words: 'With him we are sending the brother who is famous among all the churches for his preaching of the gospel.' Wenham has argued persuasively that this passage can only refer to Luke and the fame that followed the publication of his gospel. Paul does not describe the life of Jesus because Luke has already done so" (Anderson, "Theophilus: A Proposal," 206). Also, in enumerating the four canonical gospels, Eusebius appears to reference 2 Cor 8:18 as he writes, "And thirdly, that according to Luke, who writes, for those who from the Gentiles [came to believe], the Gospel that was praised by Paul" (Eusebius, *Ecclesiastical History*, 6.2.6). The long recension of the letter of Ignatius to the Ephesians (ca. fourth century) also includes the remark, ὁ κύριος ἡμῶν καὶ θεὸς Ἰησοῦς ὁ Χριστίς, ὁ υἱος τοῦ θεοῦ τοῦ ζῶντος, πρῶτον ἐποίησεν καὶ τότε ἐδίδαξεν, ὡς μαρτυρεῖ Λουκᾶς οὗ ὁ ἔπαινος ἐν τῷ εὐαγγελίῳ διὰ πασῶν ἐκκλησιῶν (Lightfoot, *Apostolic Fathers* 2, 3:262). See also Ehrman, *Apostolic Fathers*, 1:211–12; Chrysostom, *Homilies on the Epistles of Paul*, 363–64; Stonehouse, *Origins of the Synoptic Gospels*, 116–17; Stonehouse, *Witness of Luke to Christ*, 45.

55, and that it had circulated διὰ πασῶν τῶν ἐκκλησιῶν, likely meaning throughout at least Achaia, Macedonia, and Judea, where Luke had traveled with Paul, as well as Asia Minor, the most probable destination of Paul's letters to Timothy.[72]

With respect to the content and historical merits of Luke's gospel itself, Ned Stonehouse points to the prologue,[73] in which Luke declares his intent and something of his method. In 1:1–4, one reads,

> Inasmuch as many have attempted to compile a report of the things fulfilled among us, just as those who were eyewitnesses and servants of the word from the beginning handed down to us, it seemed (right) to me also, having followed all things closely from the beginning, to write accurately an orderly (account) for you, most excellent Theophilus, so that you might know the certainty of the things regarding which you were instructed.

In this opening, Luke makes known his intent to report accurately for the assurance of Theophilus and he acknowledges that, while not an eyewitness himself, he conducted research among those who were. In other words, Luke offers attestation of his qualifications to carry out the particular enterprise he intends. As to the latter point, Luke also presents himself as an associate of, or at least one acquainted with, the eyewitnesses and "servants of the word," who may be supposed to have been some of the original apostles.[74]

At least two conclusions may be drawn from these remarks. First, while acknowledging his familiarity with sources and other attempts to write down a record of the events touching upon "the things that Jesus began to do and teach," Luke also presents himself not as a mere compiler

72. Wenham even points out regarding 1 Tim 5:18, "We should note also the possible quotation of Luke's gospel in 1 Timothy 5:18, which cites verbatim the dominical saying 'The labourer deserves his wages' after the quotation from Deuteronomy 25:4 'You shall not muzzle an ox when it is treading out the grain,' introducing both by the quotation-formula 'the Scripture says.' The saying could of course have been known by oral tradition, but its wording is exactly that of Luke 10:7. Such exactitude of quotation is striking, since . . . apparent allusions to the words of Jesus in the gospels are seldom verbatim even in the apostolic fathers. Such precision of wording with reference to a saying from 'Scripture' certainly suggests quotation of a writing" (Wenham, *Redating Matthew, Mark and Luke*, 237).

73. Stonehouse, *Witness of Luke to Christ*, 24–31.

74. Bauckham, *Jesus and the Eyewitnesses*, 119; Wenham, *Redating Matthew, Mark and Luke*, 209. Liefeld also notes, "The honesty of the writer in distinguishing himself from the eyewitnesses and the care he took to provide an orderly, accurate account cannot be overlooked" (Liefeld, *Luke*, 807).

and editor of other reports, but as a researcher and an original writer in his own right.[75] Thus, while it cannot be said that he was operating in complete independence, neither would it be accurate to paint his work as entirely literarily dependent upon previous accounts. Second, by mentioning his affiliation with the apostles, Luke gives the impression that he sees himself also as guardian of the apostolic tradition.[76] Therefore, unless one finds clear reason to dismiss Luke's self-attestation, his self-effacing candor at the beginning of his gospel and his forthright declaration of his agenda both commend his credibility as a witness. The significance of the far-reaching implications of this adjusted perspective of the composition and dating of Luke's gospel may be elevated even further when one considers two additional pieces of data relative to the Lukan writings.

The first comes from a succession of several remarks proffered by Tertullian in his treatise against Marcion. Tertullian writes,

> If that is evidently more true which is earlier, if that is earlier which is from the very beginning, if that is from the beginning which has the apostles for its authors, then it will certainly be quite as evident that that comes down from the apostles, which has been kept as a sacred deposit in the churches of the apostles . . . I say, therefore, that in them (and not simply such of them as were founded by apostles, but in all those which are united with them in the fellowship of the mystery *of the gospel of Christ*) that Gospel of Luke which we are defending with all our might has stood its ground from its very first publication . . . The same authority of the apostolic churches will afford evidence to the other Gospels also, which we possess equally through their means, and according to their usage—I mean the Gospels of John and Matthew—whilst that which Mark published may be affirmed to be Peter's, whose interpreter Mark was. For even

75. Bauckham also observes, "Luke means that he has thoroughly understood everything that the eyewitnesses have passed on to him. His 'informed familiarity' (Moessner's phrase) is his qualification for writing a history based on these eyewitness accounts and, probably, for doing so more satisfactorily than his predecessors who have already done so" (Bauckham, *Jesus and the Eyewitnesses*, 123). However, on the last point, it is only fair to point out that Stonehouse sees Luke's comments as reflecting no criticism of his predecessors (Stonehouse, *Witness of Luke to Christ*, 31–32). See also Stonehouse, *Witness of Luke to Christ*, 34; Wenham, *Redating Matthew, Mark and Luke*, xxiii, 56, 209.

76. Barton goes even further, maintaining, "It is hard to resist the conclusion that the Gospels were intended from the first as the supreme religious writings of the Christians" (Barton, *Holy Writings, Sacred Text*, 25). See also Stonehouse, *Origins of the Synoptic Gospels*, 116–17; Stonehouse, *Witness of Luke to Christ*, 45.

> Luke's form of the Gospel men usually ascribe to Paul. And it
> may well seem that the works which disciples publish belong
> to their masters . . . If the (Gospels) of the apostles have come
> down to us in their integrity, whilst Luke's which is received
> amongst us, so far accords with their rule as to be on a par with
> them in permanency of reception in the churches, it clearly fol-
> lows that Luke's gospel also has come down to us in like integrity
> until the sacrilegious treatment of Marcion.[77]

While Tertullian does not place the composition of Luke's gospel at
a specific point in time, he makes it patently clear not only that this work
was viewed as one of great eminence among the writings of the church,
but also that it derived its authority from Paul, whose disciple Luke was.
At the very least, readers must acknowledge Tertullian's thesis that the
Gospel of Luke wields an authority comparable with that ascribed to the
Pauline writings, and it would appear from his writing that this was an
authority understood from the origin of the document, not something
formulated and ascribed only in Tertullian's own age. Furthermore, and
as suggested elsewhere, the reputedly close association between Luke and
Paul may account for the frequently similar lexis that one may observe in
the PE, as well as Paul's decision to present a citation in 1 Tim 5:18 that
so exactly reflects Luke's gospel.[78]

Second, according to Eldon Epp, it may be inferred from the evidence gathered from among the Oxyrhynchus papyri that the circulation of documents was quite efficient in the Greco-Roman world of the
first century. In his survey of the papyrus manuscripts of New Testament
documents, he observes,

> In Egypt, during the first centuries of the Christian era, there
> was a lively and vigorous movement of people back and forth
> between Alexandria and the Greco-Roman world to the east
> and west and north, as well as between Alexandria and the
> upper regions of Egypt, especially the Fayum and centers like
> Oxyrhynchus.[79]

---

77. *Marc.* 4.5, 349–50, emphasis in original. See also Clarke, "Problem of Pseudonymity," 455. Irenaeus likewise writes, "Luke also, the companion of Paul, recorded
in a book the Gospel preached by him" (*Haer.* III 1:1, 414).

78. Knight, *Pastoral Epistles*, 50–51; Moule, "Problem of the Pastoral Epistles,"
430–52.

79. Epp, "Papyrus Manuscripts," 8.

Offering several examples of the "movement" noted in the non-Christian papyri themselves, he writes further,

> Letters traveled 800 miles from Asia Minor to Alexandria in two months; from Transjordan to Alexandria, about 350 miles, in thirty-six days; from Philadelphia to Syria, some 400 miles, in fourteen days; 150 miles from Alexandria to Philadelphia, one in four days and another in seven days; from Alexandria to another Delta city in nineteen days; and from Memphis to Alexandria, about 125 miles, in three weeks. Thus this prompt transfer of letters by casual means—finding, for example, someone sailing up the river to the destination of the letter—operated not only within Egypt (i.e., between the Delta, the Fayum, and Upper Egypt), but also between Egypt and places far removed, such as Ostia in Italy, Cilicia in Asia Minor, Sidon in Syria, and Arabia (to use some actual examples in addition to those cited earlier), and it functioned both in the Hellenistic and Roman periods.[80]

Finally, he concludes the discussion, remarking,

> NT writings, wherever they might have originated in the vast Mediterranean region, could rapidly have made their way to any other part of that Roman world—in a matter of days or weeks. No longer, therefore, do we have to assume a long interval of years between the time a NT letter or Gospel was written and its appearance in another place—even a far-off place.[81]

Thus, on the basis of the research of Robinson, Stonehouse, and Wenham (among others), one learns that the dates and composition theories commonly attached to the Synoptic Gospels (and especially to Luke) do not do the greatest justice to actual data, and that in fact it is not unreasonable to place the date of the composition of Luke's gospel in the early- to mid-50s. This would render plausible the existence and availability of a written and circulating form of the Gospel of Luke at least by the time of Paul's missionary journey to Ephesus, Macedonia, and Greece (Acts 18:23—21:15), sometime in A.D. 52 to 57.[82] From Tertullian's tes-

80. Ibid., 9.

81. Ibid.

82. This range is suggested by a composite survey of Pauline chronologies as proposed by Alexander, Schnabel, and Witherington (Alexander, "Chronology of Paul," 115–23; Schnabel, *Early Christian Mission*, 1:41–52; Witherington, *Paul Quest*, 307–28).

timony, a close correspondence between the apostolic commission and preaching of Paul emerges on the one hand, and the Gospel writing of Luke, on the other. This effectively tightens the nature of their association and increases the likelihood that Paul would have had an intimate acquaintance with Luke's writings and that he would have readily recognized them as an authoritative composite witness to God's gospel message. The work of Epp shows that documents could circulate all over the empire with relative ease and regularity, which at least makes it plausible that a gospel written sometime in the 50s, in a relatively short time—perhaps no more than three months—could have reached the Galatian cities where Timothy grew up and no doubt received his first instruction in the apostolic message. This fact not only testifies to the wide exposure that such a document would have received, but it would also account for Paul's implicit expectation that Timothy would have known the gospel and recognized the force of any citation taken from it.

Therefore, based upon a survey of the literary context and reflection upon the evidence pointing to the possible existence and plausibly early circulation of Luke's gospel, a reasonable case does in fact exist for the argument that Paul intends to cite a written version of the Gospel of Luke alongside Deuteronomy and that he refers to both of these sources as ἡ γραφή.

1 Timothy and ἡ γραφή

While other aspects of the hypothesis proposed in this study remain to be considered, a provisional conclusion is offered at this point, based chiefly upon the evidence found in the fabric of the text and discourse of 1 Timothy. First, it has been noted that the *prima facie* testimony indicates that Paul likely used ἡ γραφή in 1 Timothy to refer to texts found in both the OT and the NT: specifically, Deut 25:4 and Luke 10:7.

Second, by tracing the multitude of terms and expressions by which Paul refers to the apostolic gospel message entrusted to him, as well as the syntax within which these terms and expressions lie, one observes that ἡ γραφή, which is a clear reference to God's word, at the very least stands on equal footing with Paul's apostolic proclamation—also God's word entrusted to his apostle.[83] Consequently, it is maintained here that ἡ γραφή

83. Knight states plainly, "Paul regards ἡ γραφή as holy Scripture, i.e., as God directly speaking" (Knight, *Pastoral Epistles*, 233). Witherington suggests as well, "What

also serves as a reference to that same apostolic proclamation, which also stands in parity with the Law, Prophets, and Writings. Much of this parity rests upon the authority that Paul attributes to his own teaching and instruction with respect to the gospel, for he attaches a great deal of significance to his appointment as a κῆρυξ καὶ ἀπόστολος . . . διδάσκαλος, and this by the command of God.[84] At the same time, the lack of explanation and apparent expectation that Timothy will recognize the authority both of Paul's instruction and of the citations offered as evidentiary support of that instruction also argues for such parity. Consequently, for Paul, ἡ γραφή denotes those writings that convey the authority of God's own word and instruction, which are comprised of the Law, Prophets, and Writings, along with his own teachings and those of other members of the apostolic company.

Together, the points discussed in this chapter lead to the provisional conclusion that Paul actually cites Luke's gospel as ἡ γραφή. This conclusion is further reinforced by the additional data adduced pertaining to the circulation of documents in the first-century Greco-Roman world, the plausibility of an early composition of the Gospel of Luke, along with Tertullian's testimony concerning the close association between Luke and Paul and the comparable authority ascribed to their writings. Therefore, over the course of the analysis of 1 Timothy,

---

I would stress is the rhetorical effect of the quotations. They provide a strong warrant for remunerating the elders as well as respecting them, a warrant that in rhetorical terms is the strongest one possible: an inartificial proof—that is, *evidence cited from a previous recognized authority*, not an argument made up by the speaker" (Witherington, *Letters and Homilies*, 275, emphasis mine). Schnabel sees added significance in the assertion here, writing, "The expression 'the Scripture says' (*legei he graphe*, Rom 9:17; 4:3; 10:11; 1 Tim 5:18; John 7:42; 19:37; Jas 2:23; also Gal 3:8: Scripture 'declares') implies a personification of Scripture . . . What Scripture says is identical with what God says. Scripture has immediate divine authority. The speech of Scripture is interchangeable with the speech of God" (Schnabel, *Inspiration und Offenbarung*, 125–26). Spicq likewise affirms, "The Scripture that speaks is synonymous with God" (Spicq, *Les Épîtres Pastorales*, 176).

84. Blum makes this precise point, observing, "The New Testament writers viewed their authority as coming from God. Paul, in particular calls himself an apostle, a herald, a witness and an ambassador (Rom 1:1, 5; Gal 1:8, 9; 1 Thess 2:13; 1 Tim 2:7) . . . First Corinthians 2:13 reads, 'This is what we speak, not in words taught us by human wisdom but in words taught by the Spirit, expressing spiritual truths in spirituals words.' The sentence probably does not refer directly to Paul's writing ministry but rather to his preaching and teaching. His primary point is that the Spirit teaches him, so that what he teaches is not his own human wisdom but divine" (Blum, "Apostles' View of Scripture," 51).

coupled with a careful consideration of the dating and composition of Luke's gospel, it has been established as plausible that when Paul uses ἡ γραφή, he intends it as a reference to both the OT writings and at least some of the writings produced by the apostolic company. In the next two chapters, this same question shall be examined relative to the one occurrence of ἡ γραφή in 2 Timothy.

CHAPTER 5

2 Timothy: Tracing Discourse
and Semantics Relative to γραφη

SIMILARLY TO THE INVESTIGATION of 1 Timothy in chapter 3, the primary objective of this chapter lies in tracing and evaluating the discourse and prevailing semantic streams running through 2 Timothy. It will be argued that γραφή, while occurring only at 3:16, lies embedded within the primary semantic thread of this letter, once again one that is associated with securing the apostolic gospel message. Furthermore, to a greater extent than with 1 Timothy, the importance of this assessment lies in the influence that the discourse flow of 2 Timothy exerts over the construal of γραφή.

Second Timothy does not exhibit conspicuously neat structural elements such as the *inclusio* that frames 1 Timothy. Nevertheless, it does feature some of its own discrete markers that telegraph the prevailing tone and intent of the letter as a whole, as Paul employs sufficient repetition at key junctures that permit him to forge semantic or conceptual links between units, while he also assembles more extended semantic streams.[1] As with 1 Timothy, the most important such set of associated terms is comprised of expressions that trace Paul's preoccupation with the apostolic gospel proclamation. This chapter will be concerned chiefly with tracing and highlighting features of this particular stream through 2 Timothy, along with the material that supports and propels it through the letter, while also observing the authority that Paul attaches to his own ap-

---

1. As with reference to 1 Timothy (chapter 3), see Van Neste, *Cohesion and Structure*, 11–12; Reed, "Cohesive Ties in 1 Timothy," 131–47; Reed, "Discourse Features," 228–52.

ostolic teaching. Prominent among several sets of parallel expressions in 2 Timothy are two occurrences each of forms of συγκακοπαθέω (1:8; 2:3) and κακοπαθέω (2:9; 4:5), in addition to one instance of πάσχω (1:12).[2] Complementing these expressions, three instances of ἐπαισχύνομαι (1:8, 12, 16) and one occurrence of ἀνεπαίσχυντος (2:15) also are dispersed over the first half of the letter.[3] Together, these elements strike a palpable tone of urgency and struggle—established early in the letter—as Paul beckons Timothy to courage and faithfulness in the face of opposition.[4] Furthermore, while working through the document, one may discern a developing sense of resolution coupled with resignation, as if this letter shall serve as a final piece of correspondence from Paul, in which he passes responsibility for the apostolic gospel message to Timothy, which message is variously designated τὸ εὐαγγέλιον, ὁ λόγος, ἡ διδασκαλία, ἡ ἀλήθεια, ἡ πίστις, and παραθήκη.[5] This gospel message Timothy also must

2. These terms are discussed in BDAG, 500b, 785–86a, 951a; Louw and Nida, *Greek-English Lexicon of the New Testament*, 24.78, 24.84, 24.89. Towner identifies Paul's legacy of suffering passed on to Timothy as one of the vital thematic motifs, also writing, "Paul's calling and willing suffering for Christ mirror Christ's own experience of death (1:8–10; 2:8–10) . . . These vignettes . . . mark the path that Timothy is to follow, in full awareness of the suffering ahead and the promises of relief and vindication, as he takes up (or resumes) his ministry with renewed heart in the knowledge that Paul's course is finished" (Towner, *Letters to Timothy and Titus*, 80). See also Aageson, "Pastoral Epistles, Apostolic Authority," 10.

3. Van Neste observes, "The two key verbs in v. 8 and v. 12 are related (lexically and semantically) and occur in chiastic order. Timothy is urged not to be ashamed (ἐπαισχύνομαι) but to 'suffer with' Paul (συγκακοπαθέω) for the gospel, and Paul suffers (πάσχω) in his role of proclaiming the gospel and is not ashamed (ἐπαισχύνομαι)" (Van Neste, *Cohesion and Structure*, 154). See also Mounce, *Pastoral Epistles*, 479.

4. Johnson writes, "The letter clearly communicates a sense of urgency about his close associate Timothy's commitment to the cause . . . He suggests that Timothy may be fearful out of shame at Paul and the message he proclaims (1:8). He begs Timothy to 'take a share of the suffering' for the good news (1:8) . . . Paul writes to Timothy, then, in order to encourage his delegate in his struggles and persuade him to stay the course . . . At the heart of Paul's conception of Timothy's ministry is a call to endurance and suffering . . . So Paul calls on Timothy repeatedly to *endure* (2:13; 3:14; 4:15), convinced that suffering is a consequence of witnessing to the good news" (Johnson, *Letters to Timothy*, 320, 327). Marshall also proposes, "The letter . . . becomes an appeal for readiness to suffer in the course of Christian witness" (Marshall, *Pastoral Epistles*, 700).

5. Guthrie observes, "Much stress is laid, for instance, on the occurrence of such expressions as the faith, the truth, the teaching, the commandment, the charge, the deposit, all of which appear to refer to the whole body of doctrine" (Guthrie, *Mind of Paul*, 17). Regarding the prevailing tone, Johnson writes, "In 2 Timothy, the mood is much grimmer. Paul does not express any hope of this-life deliverance, but sees his death as imminent (4:6) . . . The image of an aging—indeed, dying—religious leader

entrust to a subsequent generation of ministers and leaders (2:2). Over
the course of surveying the virtually interchangeable terms noted above,
a good deal of data emerges that contributes significantly to the construal
of γραφή that concerns this study.

1:1–2—The Prooemium

As with his first letter, and per his conventional salutations, Paul opens this
correspondence to Timothy with a declaration of his apostleship, standing in the service of Χριστὸς Ἰησοῦς, and brought about διὰ θελήματος
θεοῦ κατ᾽ ἐπαγγελίαν ζωῆς τῆς ἐν Χριστῷ Ἰησοῦ. The phrase διὰ θελήματος
θεοῦ reflects a typical Pauline qualifier, while κατ᾽ ἐπαγγελίαν ζωῆς τῆς ἐν
Χριστῷ Ἰησοῦ likely represents an effort to define the primary purpose of
Paul's apostolic commission: namely, to advance the "promise of life that
is in Christ Jesus."[6] Thus, Paul's position and calling entails serving as the
designated representative of Christ Jesus and a primary bearer of the message that testifies of him. At the same time, Paul's apostolic commission is
in keeping with and due to the authority of God himself.[7] Consequently,
the material that follows under this aegis will likewise carry the weight

---

who before his death instructs his follower on the struggles that lie ahead and warns
of the necessity for perseverance in the face of opposition reminds many scholars of
the literary genre known as the testament or farewell discourse" (Johnson, *Letters to
Timothy*, 319, 320–21). See Weiser, *Der zweite Brief an Timotheus*, 38–39.

6. Regarding Paul's language here, as opposed to 1 Tim, Fee notes, "It is not at
all surprising, given the nature of this letter, with its more intensified eschatological
outlook, that Paul should reflect on his apostleship in such eschatological terms at the
outset" (Fee, *Timothy and Titus*, 219). Marshall also writes, "1 Tim further traces [the]
command back to 'Christ Jesus our *hope*' alongside God, but 2 Tim states that it is in
accordance with the *promise of life* which is in Christ Jesus. There is thus an allusion
to salvation as a gift of God in both salutations" (Marshall, *Pastoral Epistles*, 683).
Towner's assessment goes beyond all of these, and locates the head of the semantic
stream pertaining to the apostolic gospel in the expression ἐπαγγελίαν ζωῆς τῆς ἐν
Χριστῷ Ἰησοῦ. Towner writes, "In this passage, 'the promise of life that is in Christ
Jesus' is an abbreviation for Paul's gospel (1:9–11) . . . Paul's self-description breathes
an air of authority—originating in the will of God—and redemptive purpose, in that
Paul's gospel is the linchpin in God's plan of salvation" (Towner, *Letters to Timothy
and Titus*, 439). See also Agnew, "Origin of the Term *Apostolos*," 53; Spicq, *Les Épîtres
Pastorales*, 305.

7. Barrett asserts, "*By the will of God* corresponds to 'by command of God' in 1 Tim
1:1, and is another way of expressing the divine origin of Paul's apostleship" (Barrett,
Pastoral Epistles, 91, emphasis Barrett's). See also Oberlinner, *Zweiter Timotheusbrief*,
6; Weiser, *Der zweite Brief an Timotheus*, 78.

of God's authority. Also, and as noted with respect to 1 Timothy, Paul's assertion in this letter is not given as an introduction to Timothy, who is already quite familiar with Paul and his calling. Rather, the expression of this claim likely establishes a tone of solemnity and gravity that befits the letter as a whole and prepares the reader for the weighty instructions to come.[8]

1:3–7 — Remembering and Reminding

Paul opens the main body of his correspondence by calling Timothy's attention to several matters for remembrance. Paul himself ἀδιάλειπτον ἔχει τὴν [Τιμοθεοῦ] μνείαν in his daily and nightly prayers, while μεμνημένος Timothy's tears (presumably at their last parting) and the affection to which these bore witness, and while ὑπόμνησιν λαβὼν of Timothy's sincere faith: the legacy handed down from his mother and grandmother.[9] All of this prepares the ground and establishes a basis (δι᾽ ἣν αἰτίαν) from which Paul then ἀναμιμνῄσκει Timothy, ἀναζωπυρεῖν τὸ χάρισμα τοῦ θεοῦ, ὅ ἐστιν ἐν σοὶ διὰ τῆς ἐπιθέσεως τῶν χειρῶν μου.[10] In the process of deliver-

8. Marshall hints at this when he proposes, "[Paul] is giving instructions that are authoritative both for his junior colleague and for the congregations under his care. Even a communication to a colleague is more than a personal letter, since the gospel is at stake" (Marshall, *Pastoral Epistles*, 684–85).

9. Though he terminates this literary unit at the end of 1:5, Van Neste writes, "In vv. 3–5, the topic and genre center on thanks and remembrance" (Van Neste, *Cohesion and Structure*, 147). Later, in discussing 1:6–14, he adds, "[The] shift to Timothy as subject is also seen in the use of 'remembrance' language (ἀναμιμνῄσκω), but, whereas in 1.3–5 it was Paul who was doing the remembering, now it is Timothy who is called to remember" (ibid., 149). Relative to Timothy's legacy of faith, Kelly writes, "Paul's point is that, just as his own religious life had powerful family roots, so Timothy's was grounded in that of his mother and grandmother . . . The context makes it clear that faith means faith in Christ" (Kelly, *Pastoral Epistles*, 157).

10. Fee observes, "Paul is about to urge Timothy to loyalty (to himself) and perseverance (in the gospel), especially in the face of hardship. In so doing he will appeal to his (Paul's) own example (e.g., 1:11–12; 2:9–10; 3:10–11), to their long association (e.g., 3:10–11), and to Timothy's own spiritual history (e.g., 1:6–7, 13–14; 3:10–15)" (Fee, *Timothy and Titus*, 221). Marshall likewise suggests, "The purpose of a thanksgiving in the Pauline correspondence is not to offer an actual prayer to God but rather to *report* what Paul says in his prayers as a means of encouragement and exhortation to the readers. Here the intent of the 'prayer-report' is not simply to give news of Paul's concern for him to Timothy but rather to give him strong encouragement through the knowledge of the fact that Paul remembers him ceaselessly in prayer and that Paul is convinced of the reality of his faith. This will then form the basis for the appeal to him

ing this initial summons, he calls Timothy to fresh courage and resolve, arguing, οὐ γὰρ ἔδωκεν ἡμῖν ὁ θεὸς πνεῦμα δειλίας ἀλλὰ δυνάμεως καὶ ἀγάπης καὶ σωφρονισμοῦ.[11] In these clauses occur forms of ἀναμιμνήσκω, μιμνήσκω, μνείαν, and ὑπομιμνήσκω, all of which function as references to remembrance and recollection, and together form a cluster of semantically related terms. Therefore, one might say that the governing motif of these first few verses consists in the importance of remembering and reminding, probably employed so as to provide a foundation or inspiration for perseverance.[12] These details prepare the epistolary ground for the more pointed material to come: material acutely concerned with the gospel message, which will also provide a basis for assessing Paul's use of γραφή in 2 Timothy.

1:8–18—Suffering with and Being Unashamed

Framing this literary unit while also bracing its center, three negated instances of ἐπαισχύνομαι sound the dominant note of 1:8–18. Paul, in his first direct admonition to Timothy, urges him, μὴ οὖν ἐπαισχυνθῇς τὸ μαρτύριον τοῦ κυρίου ἡμῶν μηδὲ ἐμὲ τὸν δέσμιον αὐτοῦ. Paul then balances this prohibition with the positive exhortation, συγκακοπάθησον τῷ εὐαγγελίῳ κατὰ δύναμιν θεοῦ.[13] Here, ἐπαισχύνομαι is construed as a reference to Timothy's probable impulse to conceal an association or affinity with Paul and his gospel, as much to avoid or diminish his own suffering by virtue of persecution or opposition, as to avoid internal dis-

that will follow" (Marshall, *Pastoral Epistles*, 689).

11. Barrett, *Pastoral Epistles*, 93–94; Collins, *Timothy and Titus*, 197–98; Fee, *Timothy and Titus*, 226–27; Guthrie, *Pastoral Epistles*, 139–40; Johnson, *Letters to Timothy*, 352; Marshall, *Pastoral Epistles*, 695–96; Witherington, *Letters and Homilies*, 313.

12. Collins, *Timothy and Titus*, 194; Lenski, *St. Paul's Epistles*, 752–53; Marshall, *Pastoral Epistles*, 699–700; Scott, *Pastoral Epistles*, 90; Van Neste, *Cohesion and Structure*, 147–48; Witherington, *Letters and Homilies*, 312.

13. Johnson writes, "Paul weaves together three things: the good news that both Paul and Timothy were called to proclaim, Paul's willingness to bear the suffering ingredient to his role as a teacher, and his exhortation to Timothy to claim his own 'special gift for service' with its attendant suffering. The extended kerygmatic statement in 1:9–10 is bracketed on one side by the commands 'do not be ashamed' and 'take your share of suffering' for the good news (1:8) and on the other side by the declaration that although Paul 'suffers even these things' for the good news, he is 'not ashamed' (1:12)" (Johnson, *Letters to Timothy*, 353). See also Aageson, "Pastoral Epistles, Apostolic Authority," 18.

tress or embarrassment.[14] In the absence of an explicit explanation from Paul, this understanding is inferred, based upon the coordinate alternative relationship (signaled by ἀλλά) that lies between οὐκ ἐπαισχύνομαι and συγκακοπαθέω (1:8), and between οὐκ ἐπαισχύνομαι and πάσχω (1:12). In each case, the response or antithesis to "being ashamed" consists in embracing the suffering—or the "suffering with" Paul—that comes with an unambiguous association with τὸ εὐαγγέλιον. That "the gospel" serves as the effective cause of the affliction mentioned is clear on the basis of three factors.

First, forging the most explicit connection that links the gospel and its proclamation directly to the suffering that Timothy is to embrace, Paul exhorts Timothy, συγκακοπάθησον τῷ εὐαγγελίῳ.[15] In this instance, Timothy is to suffer κατὰ δύναμιν θεοῦ, likely meaning that he must rest upon God's power for him as he bears up under suffering.[16] Extending this train of thought a little further, in 1:9–10, Paul describes God as,

> ... τοῦ σώσαντος ἡμᾶς καὶ καλέσαντος κλήσει ἁγίᾳ, οὐ κατὰ τὰ ἔργα ἡμῶν ἀλλὰ κατὰ ἰδίαν πρόθεσιν καὶ χάριν, τὴν δοθεῖσαν ἡμῖν ἐν Χριστῷ Ἰησοῦ πρὸ χρόνων αἰωνίων, φανερωθεῖσαν δὲ νῦν διὰ τῆς ἐπιφανείας τοῦ σωτῆρος ἡμῶν Χριστοῦ Ἰησοῦ, καταργήσαντος μὲν τὸν θάνατον φωτίσαντος δὲ ζωὴν καὶ ἀφθαρσίαν διὰ τοῦ εὐαγγελίου.

In the process of attaching these points to his admonition, Paul here rehearses core elements of the gospel message for which he has already suffered, and on account of which Timothy also must fortify himself to bear suffering. These include God's acts of saving and calling his people to holiness, the denial that this salvation and calling derives from one's own works, and the corresponding affirmation that such salvation and calling stem from God's own unmerited favor and purpose. Following these points, Paul offers the reminder that God confers his grace, by which he saves and calls, upon the objects of his favor "in Christ Jesus," and that this this grace has been active for eternity. In the next three relative clauses of these verses, Paul brings the whole report full circle, affirming that

14. Johnson, *Letters to Timothy*, 357–59; Spicq, *Les Épîtres Pastorales*, 313; Towner, *Letters to Timothy and Titus*, 463.

15. Kelly, *Pastoral Epistles*, 161; Lenski, *St. Paul's Epistles*, 758–59; Lock, *Pastoral Epistles*, 86; Marcheselli-Casale, *Le Lettere Pastorali*, 655; Mounce, Pastoral Epistles, 480–81; Witherington, *Letters and Homilies*, 316.

16. Collins, *Timothy and Titus*, 199; Fairbairn, *1 and 2 Timothy and Titus*, 318; Marshall, *Pastoral Epistles*, 704; Scott, *Pastoral Epistles*, 92.

the saving and calling grace of God just described now stands revealed by means of the appearance of Christ Jesus himself, the "Savior" in whom this work is embodied, who, in the process of making his appearance, also abolished death and brought life and immortality to light by means of "the gospel."[17] The entirety of the complex thought contained in these verses opens and closes with a form of τὸ εὐαγγέλιον. Between these two occurrences in 1:8 and 1:10, Paul has crafted a lengthy and complex series of relative clauses that convey the content of τὸ εὐαγγέλιον.[18] Rhetorically, this has the effect of raising the prominence of τὸ εὐαγγέλιον in the letter. Also, as Paul already suffers for this gospel, Timothy is to do likewise. The all-important matter of the gospel proclamation must govern Timothy's assessment of his situation.[19]

Second, as Paul continues his instruction through the remaining relative clauses of his admonition, found in 1:11–12, he explicitly describes the gospel, on the one hand, as that εἰς ὃ ἐτέθην ἐγὼ κῆρυξ καὶ ἀπόστολος καὶ διδάσκαλος, while on the other hand, declaring with equal clarity, δι' ἣν αἰτίαν καὶ ταῦτα πάσχω.[20] In response to these two realities—Paul's appointment unto the gospel and his suffering on its account—Paul then asserts on his own behalf, ἀλλ' οὐκ ἐπαισχύνομαι.[21]

17. Barrett, *Pastoral Epistles*, 95; Bernard, *Pastoral Epistles*, 110–11; Brox, *Die Pastoralbriefe*, 231–32; Knight, *Pastoral Epistles*, 375–76; Lock, *Pastoral Epistles*, 87; Weiser, *Der zweite Brief an Timotheus*, 121.

18. Collins also notes this as significant (Collins, *Timothy and Titus*, 201). Towner infers from the final reference to διὰ τὸ εὐαγγέλιου, "This activity is clearly perceived as the normative way of mediating salvation" (Towner, *Goal of Our Instruction*, 95).

19. Fee states, "Aware of Timothy's character and of the difficulties ahead, Paul adds the dimension of divine help: by the power of God (the same word as in v. 7). This mention of God launches Paul into a creedlike expression of the gospel itself (vv. 9–10; the first loyalty), which is followed in turn by Paul's own examples (vv. 11–12; the second loyalty), and a final exhortation to 'guard the deposit' (vv. 13–14; cf. 1 Tim 6:20; the third loyalty)" (Fee, *Timothy and Titus*, 229).

20. Knight maintains, "εἰς ὃ refers to that 'for which' Paul was appointed, with the antecedent of ὃ being εὐαγγέλιου" (Knight, *Pastoral Epistles*, 377). Later, Knight adds, "δι'ἣν αἰτίαν functions as a causal conjunction with the meaning 'for which reason,' 'therefore,' 'because of' Paul's service in the gospel ministry he suffers these things, because suffering is tied up with the gospel in this evil world (cf. v. 8; 3:12)" (ibid., 378). Van Neste likewise states, "The relative pronoun, ὃ, clearly refers back to εὐαγγέλιου, in v. 10. The mention of the gospel prompts a statement connecting it with the work of Paul as is common in the Pastorals (e.g., 1 Tim 1.11; 2.7; Titus 1.3) . . . 1.11 does not function to present new, previously unknown information but fits a larger pattern in the larger passage of connecting the proper message with Paul" (Van Neste, *Cohesion and Structure*, 153).

21. Barrett, *Pastoral Epistles*, 96; Guthrie, *Pastoral Epistles*, 144; Kelly, *Pastoral*

While both of the arguments surveyed above are fairly explicit, the third link between τὸ εὐαγγέλιον and the suffering that visits those associated with it also begins to build the first direct point of contact between 2 Timothy and the analysis of γραφή that impels this study. Immediately following his assertion, οὐκ ἐπαισχύνομαι, Paul then justifies his lack of shame, arguing, οἶδα γὰρ ᾧ πεπίστευκα καὶ πέπεισμαι ὅτι δυνατός ἐστιν τὴν παραθήκην μου φυλάξαι εἰς ἐκείνην τὴν ἡμέραν.[22] Along with the causal function of γάρ, the most critical interpretive element in this statement depends on the construal of ἡ παραθήκη μου. According to Paul's words as recorded in 1:12, his confidence in God's capacity to guard his "trust" or "deposit" provides the grounding reason that he may declare his disposition toward the gospel in the statement, οὐκ ἐπαισχύνομαι, even though that gospel serves as the effective cause of his sufferings.[23] Many presume that, with ἡ παραθήκη μου, Paul here refers to his own future hope, kept secure by God εἰς ἐκείνην ἡμέραν.[24] However, while the conventional construal of ἡ παραθήκη μου has some merit within the scope of this one verse alone, the wider literary context suggests a more likely intent.

Immediately following 1:12, Paul then exhorts Timothy, ὑποτύπωσιν ἔχε ὑγιαινόντων λόγων ὧν παρ' ἐμοῦ ἤκουσας ἐν πίστει καὶ ἀγάπῃ τῇ ἐν Χριστῷ Ἰησοῦ· τὴν καλὴν παραθήκην φύλαξον διὰ πνεύματος ἁγίου τοῦ ἐνοικοῦντος ἐν ἡμῖν. The two admonitions contained here in 1:13–14 cast παραθήκη in a very different light from the conventional treatment of 1:12. In the first admonition, Paul refers to a ὑποτύπωσις ὑγιαινόντων λόγων, suggesting that he has in mind a very specific and apparently

---

Epistles, 165; Marshall, *Pastoral Epistles*, 709; Towner, *Letters to Timothy and Titus*, 475; Van Neste, *Cohesion and Structure*, 154.

22. Barrett, *Pastoral Epistles*, 96; Collins, *Timothy and Titus*, 211; Fee, *Timothy and Titus*, 231; Kelly, *Pastoral Epistles*, 165; Knight, *Pastoral Epistles*, 378–79; Marshall, *Pastoral Epistles*, 710.

23. Regarding this, Collins asserts, "Paul is convinced that the one in whom he trusted will be able to maintain the treasure that has been entrusted to him. With this conviction Paul can offer himself as an example for Timothy to follow" (Collins, *Timothy and Titus*, 211). Marshall also writes, "Here the thought must be of a knowledge which conveys the fact that God is trustworthy, and a line between personal experience of God and knowledge about him would be hard to draw. Either way, the knowledge leads to a conviction about what God will do in the future for Paul" (Marshall, *Pastoral Epistles*, 710).

24. See, for instance, Conybeare and Howson, *Life and Epistles of Saint Paul*, 837–38; Fee, *Timothy and Titus*, 231–32; Knight, *Pastoral Epistles*, 380; Lock, *Pastoral Epistles*, 88.

exclusive report or message.[25] He further qualifies this message with the relative clause, ὧν παρ' ἐμοῦ ἤκουσας, indicating that Timothy already has acquired a familiarity with these "sound words," because he learned them from Paul himself.[26] Timothy is now advised to "hold" or "keep" this "pattern" (or "standard") of "sound words" that he has learned from Paul.[27] In the second admonition, Paul next urges Timothy, τὴν καλὴν παραθήκην φύλαξον. In the absence of an explicit conjunction, it is understood here that the relationship between 1:13 and 1:14 is paratactic, virtually presuming an elliptical καί. This would make ὑποτύπωσιν ἔχε ὑγιαινόντων λόγων and τὴν καλὴν παραθήκην φύλαξον parallel expressions, indicating two ideas occurring in progression or sequence.[28] In this case, the most apparent sense of these two admonitions would be on the one hand, "hold" or "maintain the pattern of sound words," and on the other hand, "guard the good trust," which consists of the very pattern of sound words Timothy learned and to which he himself must adhere.[29]

25. Collins, *Timothy and Titus*, 212–13; Guthrie, *Pastoral Epistles*, 145; Hanson, *Pastoral Letters*, 80; Knight, *Pastoral Epistles*, 381; Marshall, *Pastoral Epistles*, 712; Spicq, *Les Épîtres Pastorales*, 318–19.

26. Marshall describes this message as "the Christian teaching of Paul which Timothy has frequently heard directly from him" (Marshall, *Pastoral Epistles*, 712–13). See also Weiser, *Der zweite Brief an Timotheus*, 129.

27. As Spicq writes, "This is an exhortation to maintain a correct form of the Christian doctrine" (Spicq, *Les Épîtres Pastorales*, 319). See also Marcheselli-Casale, *Le Lettere Pastorali*, 673.

28. Fee writes, "Since what was entrusted is described as good, it almost certainly refers to the 'sound teaching' of the gospel" (Fee, *Timothy and Titus*, 233). Knight concurs, stating, "That which Timothy is to 'keep' or 'preserve' (v. 13) he is now urged to 'guard (φυλάσσω,** also in v. 12 and 1 Tim 6:20), i.e., guard against it being lost or damaged, (BDAG s.v. 1c), especially against false teachers and false teaching" (Knight, *Pastoral Epistles*, 381).

29. Marcheselli-Casale writes, "The term 'deposit-*paratheke*' was used by Paul so as to indicate the gospel that must be kept without alterations until the return of Christ" (Marcheselli-Casale, *Le Lettere Pastorali*, 679). Likewise, Mounce states, "The παραθήκην, 'deposit,' is the gospel . . . Its emphatic position before the verb φύλαξον, 'guard' (on which, see v. 12) and its description as καλήν, 'good' (see 1 Tim 1:8), roughly paralleling ὑγιαινόντων λόγων, 'healthy words,' firmly separate it from the opponents' teachings" (Mounce, *Pastoral Epistles*, 494). Similarly, Towner maintains, "*Paratheke* is closely associated with *euangelion* in 2 Tim 1.6–14. The emphasis in this term is more on the preservation and accurate transmission to succeeding generations of 'the gospel' that was entrusted to Paul. In terms of content, *paratheke* may be generally described as *euangelion*, but greater precision is probably implied" (Towner, *Goal of Our Instruction*, 123).

In addition to these points, within the clause containing the imperative, ὑποτύπωσιν ἔχε ὑγιαινόντων λόγων, one finds the first occurrence of λόγος in 2 Timothy. The logical connection between this idea and the preceding one may be found in 1:11. In the prepositional phrase, εἰς ὃ ἐτέθην ἐγὼ κῆρυξ καὶ ἀπόστολος καὶ διδάσκαλος, the relative pronoun, ὅ, corresponds to τὸ εὐαγγέλιον in 1:10. Here, Paul indicates his own apostolic appointment in the ministry of, and responsibility for, the proclamation of the gospel.[30] Thus, in the process, he also anticipates his reference in 1:13 to ὑποτύπωσις . . . ὑγιαινόντων λόγων ὧν παρ᾽ ἐμοῦ ἤκουσας, for he states plainly that his apostolic task lay in preaching and teaching "the gospel." Consequently, with respect to the material of 1:13, it is the position of this study that ὑποτύπωσις . . . ὑγιαινόντων λόγων ὧν παρ᾽ ἐμοῦ ἤκουσας corresponds to the teachings associated with τὸ εὐαγγέλιον.[31] Because of the prepositional phrase εἰς ὃ ἐτέθην ἐγὼ κῆρυξ καὶ ἀπόστολος καὶ διδάσκαλος, which indicates a trust conferred personally upon Paul, it is inferred here that τὸ εὐαγγέλιον represents a particular set of ideas or teachings that Timothy received and learned from Paul directly, and which are authorized or authenticated by him.[32] So far then, Paul has issued two affirmative commands to Timothy: "Suffer with [me] for the gospel . . . for which I was appointed a preacher and an apostle and a teacher," and "hold the pattern of sound words which you have heard from me." In view of the two occurrences of τὸ εὐαγγέλιον, along with the subsequent reference to ὑποτύπωσις . . . ὑγιαινόντων λόγων ὧν παρ᾽ ἐμοῦ ἤκουσας, that precede the second imperative, παραθήκη in 1:14 surely corresponds to

30. Barrett, *Pastoral Epistles*, 96; Bernard, *Pastoral Epistles*, 111; Collins, *Timothy and Titus*, 209–10; Marshall, *Pastoral Epistles*, 708–9; Spicq, *Les Épîtres Pastorales*, 317; Towner, *Goal of Our Instruction*, 50; Weiser, *Der zweite Brief an Timotheus*, 121.

31. Collins writes, "The 'model of sound words' is the precious treasure that had been entrusted to Timothy. That treasure, whose import is emphasized by the adjective 'precious' appropriate to the metaphor 'treasure,' is the treasure that had been entrusted to Paul (v. 12). Acting to ensure the proper transmission of the treasure for safekeeping from one generation to the next is the Holy Spirit" (Collins, *Timothy and Titus*, 213). Johnson also points out "This phrase echoes 1:13, where Paul speaks of the healthy words 'which you heard from me' . . . The real key to the passage is 2:1–2. Indeed, it is the key to the function of the Pastorals as a whole: Timothy is instructed to 'entrust' the things he heard from Paul to other faithful men, who, in turn, can teach them to others" (Johnson, *Letters to Timothy*, 364, 369).

32. Fairbairn, *1 and 2 Timothy and Titus*, 326; Knight, *Pastoral Epistles*, 377, 381; Marshall, *Pastoral Epistles*, 708, 712–13; Oberlinner, *Zweiter Timotheusbrief*, 51; Van Neste, *Cohesion and Structure*, 153; Weiser, *Der zweite Brief an Timotheus*, 129.

τὸ εὐαγγέλιον, εἰς ὃ ἐτέθην ἐγὼ κῆρυξ καὶ ἀπόστολος καὶ διδάσκαλος, which also may be designated, ὑποτύπωσις ὑγιαινόντων λόγων.[33] Thus, the two instances of ἡ παραθήκη in 1:12 and 1:14 fall in close literary proximity to one another, both lie in the midst of a semantic sequence corresponding to the apostolic gospel proclamation, and the one instance (τὴν καλὴν παραθήκην φύλαξον) in 1:14 is construed widely as a reference to the gospel message. Furthermore, Paul's most apparent pressing interest through these verses concerns the perpetuation and bold advancement of the gospel message (even to the point of suffering himself while also calling on Timothy to suffer). It is most probable that this same meaning also lies in ἡ παραθήκη μου in 1:12.[34] In other words, it is understood in this analysis that in both cases παραθήκη serves as a reference to the gospel message and proclamation entrusted to Paul, on account of which he remains unashamed (or unafraid of the persecution it incites), precisely because God is capable of preserving and sustaining that message until it is no longer necessary: namely, until the end of all things.[35]

As in 1 Timothy, in this letter Paul employs several different expressions as references to the one gospel message that has been entrusted to him and for which he stands appointed as an apostle. Thus far in 2 Timothy, these expressions include τὸ εὐαγγέλλιον, ὑποτύπωσις ὑγιαινόντων λόγων ὧν παρ' ἐμοῦ ἤκουσας, and ἡ καλὴ παραθήκη.[36] Paul closes this segment with reflections upon the faithfulness of Onesiphorus, who remained "unashamed" in his service of the apostle and his gospel.[37]

33. Accordingly, Hanson proposes, "It seems better to understand it of 'the deposit of faith,' the substance of the gospel message. God will keep Paul faithful to that message" (Hanson, *Pastoral Letters*, 80). Knight also writes, "Since Timothy is the one commanded to guard the παραθήκην, 'the deposit,' it is something entrusted to his care (cf. the parallel in 1 Tim 6:20), i.e., 'the standard of sound words that he heard' from Paul" (Knight, *Pastoral Epistles*, 381).

34. Spicq maintains, "Given this consistent parallelism, it seems necessary that 'the deposit' in vv. 12 and 14 be understood in same sense as the object of the Christian proclamation" (Spicq, *Les Épîtres Pastorales*, 318).

35. Bernard, *Pastoral Epistles*, 111; Collins, *Timothy and Titus*, 211–13; Guthrie, *Pastoral Epistles*, 144; Kelly, *Pastoral Epistles*, 165–66.

36. As Van Neste proposes, "In 1.13 what is to be kept is the 'standard of sound words,' and in 1.14 what is to be guarded is the 'deposit' which most likely refers to the gospel. Thus these exhortations are united as appeals to Timothy to be faithful regarding the gospel" (Van Neste, *Cohesion and Structure*, 156).

37. Bassler, *1 Timothy, 2 Timothy, Titus*, 136–37; Johnson, *Letters to Timothy*, 363; Marshall, *Pastoral Epistles*, 719; Scott, *Pastoral Epistles*, 98–99; Witherington, *Letters and Homilies*, 323–25.

2:1–7—Suffering with and Entrusting

In 2:1, Paul resumes his direct instructions to Timothy, building upon the preceding remembrance of Onesiphorus,[38] and writing, Σὺ οὖν, τέκνον μου, ἐνδυναμοῦ ἐν τῇ χάριτι τῇ ἐν Χριστῷ Ἰησοῦ, which he then follows with, καὶ ἃ ἤκουσας παρ’ ἐμοῦ διὰ πολλῶν μαρτύρων, ταῦτα παράθου πιστοῖς ἀνθρωποις, οἵτινες ἱκανοὶ ἔσονται καὶ ἑτέρους διδάξαι. In the first imperative, Paul exhorts Timothy to "be strong in the grace that is in Christ Jesus." However, relative to the predominant line of discourse in the letter, it is the second imperative of 2:1–2 that provides the more critical details.

The first of these details appears in the relative clause, ἃ ἤκουσας παρ’ ἐμοῦ, also the first of two semantic elements linking this literary unit with the preceding one.[39] This expression, which funtions as the direct object of παράθου, readily recalls ὑποτύπωσις . . . ὑγιαινόντων λόγων ὧν παρ’ ἐμοῦ ἤκουσας as it appears in 1:14, and doubtless refers to the very same body of teaching, or "pattern of sound words, mentioned there."[40] Thus, it is understood that the "sound words" of the gospel proclamation that comprise a body of teaching to be embraced and protected are now to be passed on and entrusted to others.[41] The second detail, which also provides the second semantic link with the preceding passage, lies in the imperative, ταῦτα παράθου πιστοῖς ἀνθρωποις. The imperatival form of παρατίθημι found here, the verbal cognate of παραθήκη, recalls the two instances of παραθήκη occurring in 1:12 and 1:14.[42] Consequently,

38. Guthrie, *Pastoral Epistles*, 149; Johnson, *Letters to Timothy*, 364, 367; Lock, *Pastoral Epistles*, 92–93; Witherington, *Letters and Homilies*, 328.

39. Marshall, *Pastoral Epistles*, 724–25; Spicq, *Les Épîtres Pastorales*, 341.

40. Knight's opening statement on this unit reflects the position here regarding the cumulative effect of Paul's prevailing concern and multiple interchangeable expressions by which he designates his gospel. He writes, "This section begins with 'therefore' (οὖν), gathers up the preceding concerns, commands, and examples, and turns to a renewed direct address to Timothy (v. 1) . . . God's power (and one's need to appropriate it) and God's gospel (and the need to faithfully pass it on) are the objective realities on which Paul bases his continual appeal to Timothy to suffer for the gospel . . . Paul uses ἀκούω to refer to his apostolic message because that message was so often given in oral preaching and teaching" (Knight, *Pastoral Epistles*, 388–89).

41. Collins, *Timothy and Titus*, 213; Johnson, *Letters to Timothy*, 364, 369; Towner, *Goal of Our Instruction*, 118, 124–26.

42. Towner observes this as well, noting, "The command itself, 'entrust [*parathou*] [these things] to reliable people,' which comes in the next phrase, picks up and echoes the language of 'deposit' and 'guarantor' (*parathēkē*) introduced in 1:12–14 and earlier

Paul has been appointed as a herald, apostle, and teacher, making him a steward of the gospel that constitutes his apostolic trust (παραθήκη), which God is capable of sustaining. This same (παραθήκη) also functions as something that Timothy must first guard, and then must entrust (παρατίθημι) to other faithful men.[43] Ταῦτα in this passage stands in apposition with ἃ ἤκουσας παρ᾽ ἐμοῦ, further indicating that the things that Timothy is to "entrust" to faithful men consists of those very teachings or words that he learned from Paul.[44] The third detail concerns Paul's obvious aim that Timothy entrust what he has heard and learned from Paul to other faithful men, so that they in turn ἱκανοὶ ἔσονται καὶ ἑτέρους διδάξαι.[45] Here one finds testimony that implies Paul's sense that the church likely must continue for some time beyond his own lifetime and thus will need the apostolic gospel by which it may be sustained and instructed.[46] Paul's remarks here also indicate that he views his own teaching—the "pattern of sound words," or "the gospel" entrusted to him—as an authoritative teaching destined for the church into the future.[47]

Finally, binding this unit even more tightly to the previous one in terms of content and lexis, Paul then urges Timothy once again, Συγκακοπάθησον ὡς καλὸς στρατιώτης Χριστοῦ Ἰησοῦ.[48] Similarly to the previous occurrence in 1:8, which appeared in close proximity with τὸ εὐαγγέλιον (which also consists of the ὑποτύπωσις . . . ὑγιαινόντων λόγων ὧν παρ᾽ ἐμοῦ ἤκουσας that Timothy is to maintain and guard), συγκακοπαθέω this time falls shortly after ἃ ἤκουσας παρ᾽ ἐμοῦ, suggesting that Paul here reiterates the idea of suffering that comes on account

---

in 1 Tim 1:18; 6:20 to describe the succession of Paul's ministry to his follower" (Towner, *Letters to Timothy and Titus*, 490).

43. Belleville, "Canon of the New Testament," 378; Fiore, *Pastoral Epistles*, 147; Spicq, *Les Épîtres Pastorales*, 342; Towner, *Goal of Our Instruction*, 123–25.

44. See Marcheselli-Casale, *Le Lettere Pastorali*, 687; Van Neste, *Cohesion and Structure*, 165–66.

45. Johnson, *Letters to Timothy*, 365, 369; Marshall, *Pastoral Epistles*, 726; Spicq, *Les Épîtres Pastorales*, 342.

46. Guthrie states, "The apostle is depicted as solicitous for the preservation of Christian teaching, and it cannot be imagined that he would ever have overlooked this necessity. He must at the end of his life have conceived of the teaching being in a form sufficiently fixed to be transmitted" (Guthrie, *Pastoral Epistles*, 151).

47. Guthrie, *Pastoral Epistles*, 151; Knight, *Pastoral Epistles*, 392; Marshall, *Pastoral Epistles*, 726–27.

48. Fee, *Timothy and Titus*, 241; Guthrie, *Pastoral Epistles*, 152; Johnson, *Letters to Timothy*, 365; Marshall, *Pastoral Epistles*, 727.

of association with the gospel and its proclamation.[49] Paul makes it clear that Timothy shall consider his summons, like a military commission, as a matter of single-minded commitment, while he forsakes all other interests or ambitions that might distract him from gospel service.[50]

So far in the survey of 2 Timothy, while no direct information explicitly connected with γραφή has arisen, a complex and concentrated semantic network is already taking shape, formed by multiple instances of τὸ εὐαγγέλιον, ἡ παραθήκη, and ἃ ἤκουσας παρ᾽ ἐμοῦ (or ὑποτύπωσις . . . ὑγιαινόντων λόγων ὧν παρ᾽ ἐμοῦ ἤκουσας), and this network lays an essential foundation for the evaluation of γραφή. In addition to this, Paul's use of λόγος also begins to exhibit a correspondence with the other terms previously listed: a correspondence that will persist as the letter progresses.

2:8–14—The Word of God and the Faithful Word

The main ideas of 2 Tim 2:8–15, the next literary unit containing some form of λόγος, once again are carried by two imperatives directed to Timothy: μνημόνευε Ἰησοῦν Χριστὸν . . . , and ταῦτα ὑπομίμνῃσκε . . . This section also features two instances of λόγος, one of which forms a part of the single occurrence of πιστὸς ὁ λόγος in 2 Timothy. The imperative that opens this unit admonishes Timothy, μνημόνευε Ἰησοῦν Χριστὸν ἐγηγερμένον ἐκ νεκρῶν, ἐκ σπέρματος Δαυίδ, κατὰ τὸ εὐαγγέλιόν μου. While Paul has previously referred to the apostolic message entrusted to him as "the sound words, which you heard from me," and as "the good trust," he now writes of it as, "my gospel."[51] By employing this expression, Paul conveys some sense of the personal nature of his apostolic investment in the message of χάριν, τὴν δοθεῖσαν ἡμῖν ἐν Χριστῷ Ἰησους, as he writes in 1:9. In the process, however, he also discloses additional details regarding the material that forms the content of "his gospel," or the "sound words," namely, Ἰησοῦν Χριστὸν ἐγηγερμένον ἐκ

49. Barrett, *Pastoral Epistles*, 101; Collins, *Timothy and Titus*, 220; Kelly, *Pastoral Epistles*, 174–75; Lenski, *St. Paul's Epistles*, 779–80; Marshall, *Pastoral Epistles*, 727.

50. Fairbairn, *1 and 2 Timothy and Titus*, 334; Scott, *Pastoral Epistles*, 101–2.

51. Collins affirms, "The words 'in accordance with my proclamation (*kata to euangelion mou*)' have a formulaic ring. They indicate that Timothy is to recall the traditional Christian creed such as it had been proclaimed by Paul. For the Pastor, who would have Timothy know this, Paul's preaching is the norm of the believer's faith" (Collins, *Timothy and Titus*, 224).

νεκρῶν, ἐκ σπέρματος Δαυίδ.[52] Here one finds a direct link not only with the work that Jesus performed by means of the cross and resurrection, but also with the hopes of Israel rooted in God's promise to the house of David, and with the resurrection of Christ, which also may serve to buttress Paul's summons to Timothy to embrace suffering even as Jesus suffered.[53] Consequently, Paul's gospel would seem to include details concerning who Jesus was, and even some of πάντων . . . ὧν ἤρξατο ὁ Ἰησοῦς ποιεῖν τε καὶ διδάσκειν, as Luke writes (Acts 1:1).

Paul has indicated in earlier remarks, such as ἐμὲ τὸν δέσμιον αὐτοῦ (1:8) and δι'ἣν αἰτίαν καὶ ταῦτα πάσχω (1:12), that he suffers on account of the gospel. Also, he has twice urged Timothy to suffer for the sake of this same gospel, writing, συγκακοπάθησον τῷ εὐαγγελίῳ (1:8), and συγκακοπάθησον ὡς καλὸς στρατιώτης Χριστοῦ Ἰησοῦ (2:3). He explicitly states again in 2:9 that he suffers for that gospel, writing of τὸ εὐαγγέλιόν μου, εν ᾧ κακοπαθῶ μέχρι δεσμῶν ὡς κακοῦργος.[54] However, at this point (2:9), he also takes the unprecedented step in 2 Timothy of referring to the gospel entrusted to him as God's word, writing, ἀλλὰ ὁ λόγος τοῦ θεοῦ οὐ δέδεται. In other words, Paul points out that while he suffers imprisonment for the gospel, "the word of God," unlike Paul, is not imprisoned, bound, nor constrained in any way.[55] Far more significantly,

52. Fee writes, "Together these two realities, Jesus Christ risen from the dead and Jesus Christ of the seed of David form a brief epitome of 'my gospel'" (Fee, *Timothy and Titus*, 246). Johnson likewise views these as elements of Paul's gospel, even while remarking, "When Paul summarizes his gospel as 'raised from the dead . . . from the seed of David,' his point is not immediately clear" (Johnson, *Letters to Timothy*, 380).

53. Johnson proposes this latter intent with greater confidence than is exhibited here, writing, "Paul begins his gospel summary with the resurrection of Jesus, for that is the source of the power of life that he and Timothy share (1:10). The rapid turn to Jesus' human origins, and the immediate connection to Paul's imprisonment, in contrast, point Timothy to the reality that the delegate's present call—as Paul's own—is to share the human suffering of Jesus that preceded his resurrection." (Johnson, *Letters to Timothy*, 380).

54. Bernard, *Pastoral Epistles*, 119; Collins, *Timothy and Titus*, 224; Johnson, *Letters to Timothy*, 374, 381; Knight, *Pastoral Epistles*, 398; Quinn and Wacker, *Letters to Timothy*, 645–46.

55. Indeed, Barrett affirms, "Whatever be the fate of the missionaries, *the word of God* (the Gospel message preached by the apostles and their helpers) *is not shut up. The word is what matters*" (Barrett, *Pastoral Epistles*, 103, emphasis Barrett's). Fiore writes, "The inability to chain God's word (v. 9) coordinates with Paul's assurance of God's guardianship over the Gospel words entrusted to Paul (1:12) and serves as a comment on Timothy's task to entrust the Gospel to other teachers (2:2)" (Fiore, *Pastoral Epistles*, 154). Similarly, Holtz maintains, "It would be intended for the progress

however, Paul plainly equates "my gospel," "the things you have heard from me," and "the pattern of sound words that you heard from me" with God's own revelatory word or teaching, explicitly declaring what, up to this point, has been only implied by his apostolic claim: Paul's teaching is God's teaching.[56] After declaring that he stands ready to endure any difficulty for the sake of God's elect and their attainment of salvation, Paul delivers the affirmation, πιστὸς ὁ λόγος. Based upon the literary and semantic stream of the letter thus far, there can be little doubt that this λόγος is precisely ὁ λόγος τοῦ θεοῦ of which Paul has just written, which in turn represents τὸ εὐαγγέλιον that comprises his apostolic trust.[57] This affirmation of the faithfulness or trustworthiness of the apostolic word of God is then justified by a series of conditional expressions that serve as truths deriving from the implications of that "faithful word," for indeed, "if . . . we die with him, we also shall live with him; if we endure,

───────────

of the mission in spite of the imprisonment of Paul" (Holtz, *Die Pastoralbriefe*, 166). In addition, Oberlinner is unequivocal in equating τὸ εὐαγγέλλιον with ὁ λόγος τοῦ θεοῦ (Oberlinner, *Zweiter Timotheusbrief*, 80).

56. As Schlatter writes, "'His message' is 'the word of God'" (Schlatter, *Die Kirche der Griechen*, 236). Spicq also states plainly, "The word of God, it (ἀλλά)—which here is personified (cf. 1 Thess 2:13; 2 Thess. 3:1) and identical to the 'gospel'—is not bound, nor can it be bound" (Spicq, *Les Épîtres Pastorales*, 347). Wolfe also remarks, "(ὁ λόγος τοῦ θεοῦ) is God's word, not man's. He is responsible for its existence and its ongoing effectiveness. This is clearly an affirmation that for the author there is an authority at work, greater than that even of the apostles, in the revelation and proclamation of the gospel" (Wolfe, *Place and Use of Scripture*, 144).

57. In this instance, Johnson shows agreement with the argument presented here, noting, "The phrase *pistos ho logos* (2:11) does not appear to be simply a formal introduction to a traditional fragment, for the immediate antecedent to *logos* is the *logos tou theou* (word of God) in 2:9! Paul is saying that the word of God is faithful! Paul and his delegate can trust the pattern of suffering now, glory later, because it is confirmed in the story of Jesus. Jesus was born of the seed of David, a human among others: he endured; he suffered; he died. But he was raised from the dead. And his gift, the Holy Spirit, now indwells and strengthens his followers (1:14; 2:1) as they undergo experiences of shame and suffering for the sake of that same good news" (Johnson, *Letters to Timothy*, 381). Rendall, following his summation of the three occurrences of this clause in 1 Timothy, comments regarding 2 Timothy, "The second epistle dwells with equal earnestness on the value of the Gospel whereunto he had been appointed a preacher and an apostle, on the sound words which Timothy had heard of him, and the good thing committed to Timothy, which he charges him to commit in his turn to faithful men who should be able to teach others also. For its sake he gladly suffers as an evildoer, even unto bonds: He exults in the contrast between his own bonds and the freedom of the Word of God, which is not bound, but has power to save; and breaks out once more into the ejaculation, 'Faithful is the Word' (ii.11)" (Rendall, "Faithful is the Word," 319). See also Van Bruggen, "Vaste grond onder de voeten," 44.

we also shall reign with him; if we deny him, he shall deny us; if we prove faithless, he will remain faithful, for he cannot deny himself."[58] As will be shown, the apostolic gospel message begins to gain greater prominence among the motifs running through 2 Timothy.

2:15–26—The Word of Truth

In 2:15, Paul urges Timothy, σπούδασον σεαυτὸν δόκιμον παραστῆσαι τῷ θεῷ, ἐργάτην ἀνεπαίσχυντον, ὀρθοτομοῦντα τὸν λόγον τῆς ἀληθείας. In this exhortation, the "word of God" and "faithful word" is now designated, "the word of truth"; it testifies to the activity of "God who saves us," and it is comprised of "the pattern of sound words."[59] Naturally then, it would be a matter of great importance that one who would show himself a "worker unashamed" would also prove anxious to handle correctly this precious ὁ λόγος τῆς ἀληθείας. At the same time, while the phrase, ὁ λόγος τῆς ἀληθείας (2:15) preserves a semantic link to the preceding literary unit with the use of λόγος, the chief apparent concern occupying these verses consists in "the truth," further marked by two additional instances of ἡ ἀλήθεια (2:18, 25).[60] Furthermore, while Timothy must exert great effort to present himself as approved to God, a key element of which entails his appropriate handling of "the word of truth," his conduct and handling of that word stands in direct contrast to those who are characterized by αἱ βέβηλοι κενοφωνίαι,[61] who also περὶ τὴν ἀλήθειαν ἠστόχησαν. Thus, while

58. Consistent with his previous analysis of 2:8, Johnson also sees these lines as additional reinforcement for Paul's call for Timothy to suffer (Johnson, *Letters to Timothy*, 381).

59. Fee states, "Paul is not urging that he correctly interpret Scripture, but that he truly preach and teach the gospel, the word of truth, in contrast to the 'word battles' (v. 14) and 'godless chatter' (v. 16) of the others" (Fee, *Timothy and Titus*, 255). Knight reflects this assessment as well, observing, "In Col 1:5 and Eph 1:13 εὐαγγέλιον is used to identify 'the word of truth' as 'the gospel.' This fits the context here, where Paul has used 'gospel' (τὸ εὐαγγέλλιον) as the central concept (1:8, 10; 2:8). He has used the phrase 'the word of God' (v. 9) and now refers to God's word as 'the word of truth.' 'Truth' he uses in an absolute sense to contrast it with the error of the false teachers, the false teaching that contradicts and stand over against the word of God, the gospel" (Knight, *Pastoral Epistles*, 412).

60. Johnson, *Letters to Timothy*, 385; Knight, *Pastoral Epistles*, 412; Towner, *Goal of Our Instruction*, 122; Van Neste, *Cohesion and Structure*, 168–69.

61. Collins, *Timothy and Titus*, 231–32; Fee, *Timothy and Titus*, 255; Johnson, *Letters to Timothy*, 385–86; Kelly, *Pastoral Epistles*, 183–84.

the opposition is characterized by abandoning "truth," Timothy's good standing rests upon representing it faithfully.[62]

Later (2:22), after urging Timothy, Τὰς δὲ νεωτερικὰς ἐπιθυμίας φεῦγε, δίωκε δὲ δικαιοσύνην πίστιν ἀγάπην εἰρήνην μετὰ τῶν ἐπικαλουμένων τὸν κύριον ἐκ καθαρᾶς καρδίας τὰς δὲ μωρὰς καὶ ἀπαιδεύτους ζητήσεις παραιτοῦ, Paul then reminds him to adopt an unassuming and gentle posture before those whom he encounters, writing, δοῦλον δὲ κυρίου οὐ δεῖ μάχεσθαι ἀλλὰ ἤπιον εἶναι πρὸς πάντας, διδακτικόν, ἀνεχίκακον ἐν πραΰτητι παιδεύοντα τοὺς ἀντιδιατιθεμένους.[63] As the rationale behind this counsel, Paul explicitly suggests that, with respect to the very people who have rejected the truth, δώῃ αὐτοῖς ὁ θεὸς μετάνοιαν εἰς ἐπίγνωσιν ἀληθείας.[64] The possible, even hoped-for result of this gracious work of God is that these people ἀνανήψωσιν ἐκ τῆς τοῦ διαβόλου παγίδος, ἐζωγρημένοι ὑπ' αὐτοῦ εἰς τὸ ἐκείνου θέλημα. In other words, Paul's expression, "repentance unto the knowledge of the truth," serves as a designation for salvation.[65]

While the recurring refrain of ἡ ἀλήθεια sounds the dominant semantic and thematic note of these verses, Paul also uses ἡ ἀλήθεια as yet another reference to the "faithful" word of the gospel proclamation entrusted to him, which he also entrusts to Timothy.[66] The critical link that merges ἡ ἀλήθεια, a stand-alone reference to the gospel, with ὁ [πιστὸς] λόγος occurs in 2:15, when Paul draws upon the previous usage of ὁ λόγος and modifies it with ἡ ἀλήθεια. This link is then strengthened by his subsequent and consistent use of ἀλήθεια as the remedy for those who oppose the gospel.[67]

---

62. Towner notes regarding the nature of the opposition, "It is clear from the verbal assault that the false teachers rejected, undermined, diluted, or otherwise perverted the apostolic gospel" (Towner, *Goal of Our Instruction*, 25). See also Van Neste, *Cohesion and Structure*, 200.

63. Barrett, *Pastoral Epistles*, 108–9; Collins, *Timothy and Titus*, 238, 241–42; Marshall, *Pastoral Epistles*, 765–66; Witherington, *Letters and Homilies*, 340.

64. Fairbairn, *1 and 2 Timothy and Titus*, 358–59; Guthrie, *Pastoral Epistles*, 166; Kelly, *Pastoral Epistles*, 190; Witherington, *Letters and Homilies*, 340–41.

65. Barrett, *Pastoral Epistles*, 109 (implicit); Collins, *Timothy and Titus*, 243 (though Collins seems to avoid the term, "salvation," preferring to refer to "a kind of redemption"); Fairbairn, *1 and 2 Timothy and Titus*, 359; Kelly, *Pastoral Epistles*, 190–91; Knight, *Pastoral Epistles*, 425; Marshall, *Pastoral Epistles*, 766–67; Weiser, *Der zweite Brief an Timotheus*, 235.

66. Knight, *Pastoral Epistles*, 412, 425; Van Neste, *Cohesion and Structure*, 168.

67. Towner, *Goal of Our Instruction*, 122; Van Neste, *Cohesion and Structure*,

3:1–9—Men of Corrupt Mind

In the material that occupies 3:1–9, Paul resumes his criticism of the men who set themselves against "the truth." In their depravity, they serve as emblems of καιροὶ χαλεποί. They are ἄνθρωποι κατεφθαρμένοι τὸν νοῦν, who also are characterized as ἔχοντες μόρφωσιν εὐσεβείας τὴν δὲ δύναμιν αὐτῆς ἠρνημένοι.[68] However, these men also masquerade as ministers or legitimate authorities, preying upon γυναικάρια σεσωρευμένα ἁμαρτίαις, ἀγόμενα ἐπιθυμίαις ποικίλαις, πάντοτε μανθάνοντα καὶ μηδέποτε εἰς ἐπίγνωσιν ἀληθείας ἐλθεῖν δυνάμενα.[69] While the precise dynamic that Paul presents in this description is difficult to determine, the situation at least would appear to concern women who take dubious refuge from sin in empty "learning" that ultimately leads to no true knowledge at all, and that certainly fails to attain salvation.[70] This in turn would indicate that Paul uses ἀλήθεια here, as in 2:15–26, as much more than a designation for accurate doctrine or information. It entails, in fact, a knowledge that also results in wisdom and salvation: a knowledge that transforms character and the soul.[71] In addition, while the women these false teachers mislead render themselves "unable to come to a knowledge of the truth," the men themselves also ἀνθίστανται τῇ ἀληθείᾳ, for which reason Paul declares them ἀδόκιμοι περὶ τὴν πίστιν.[72] Thus, they set themselves against "the truth," in which they might find salvation, even while they also mislead others into failing to attain salvation. In every respect then, these men are precisely as Paul describes them: "worthless as regards the faith." They have no genuine faith of their own, and Paul's prior remarks indicate that they leave in their wake others who are held captive by their own

---

168–69, 200.

68. Bernard, *Pastoral Epistles*, 131; Collins, *Timothy and Titus*, 244–45; Fee, *Timothy and Titus*, 268; Marshall, *Pastoral Epistles*, 769, 775; Scott, *Pastoral Epistles*, 118–19.

69. Barrett, *Pastoral Epistles*, 110; Fee, *Timothy and Titus*, 268, 270–71; Johnson, *Letters to Timothy*, 406–7; Kelly, *Pastoral Epistles*, 195–96.

70. Bernard, *Pastoral Epistles*, 131–32; Fee, *Timothy and Titus*, 272; Johnson, *Letters to Timothy*, 411–14; Kelly, *Pastoral Epistles*, 195–96; Marshall, *Pastoral Epistles*, 777–78; Scott, *Pastoral Epistles*, 121.

71. Kelly writes, "With the mention of the truth, which in his usage stands for the authentic gospel, Paul reverts to the false teachers, claiming that they in fact withstand the truth" (Kelly, *Pastoral Epistles*, 196).

72. Fee, *Timothy and Titus*, 272–73; Marshall, *Pastoral Epistles*, 779–80; Mounce, *Pastoral Epistles*, 550; Towner, *Goal of Our Instruction*, 25.

hardness.[73] Here, it is important to note as well that Paul adds yet another term that might well stand as synonymous with the other references to the apostolic gospel proclamation: namely, ἡ πίστις. This expression very likely performs double duty, designating as well the whole of the tradition and ethos that derives from the apostolic proclamation. Thus, to "come to a knowledge of the truth," also implies that one has attained "the faith."[74]

3:10–17—Persecution, [τὰ] ἱερὰ γράμματα, and ἡ γραφή

In contrast with the men he has just described (3:1–9) in a commentary that constitutes the primary motif of the preceding unit, Paul now reflects for Timothy upon his own life and conduct, reminding him,

> Σὺ δὲ παρηκολούθησάς μου τῇ διδασκαλίᾳ, τῇ ἀγωγῇ, τῇ προθέσει, τῇ πίστει, τῇ μακροθυμίᾳ, τῇ ἀγάγῃ, τῇ ὑπομονῇ, τοῖς διωγμοῖς, τοῖς παθήμασιν, οἷά μοι ἐγένετο ἐν Ἀντιοχείᾳ, ἐν Ἰκονίῳ, ἐν Λύστροις, οἵους διωγμοὺς ὑπήνεγκα καὶ ἐκ πάντων με ἐρρύσατο ὁ κύριος.

Two relatively small but significant details arise here. First, while Paul draws attention to various aspects of what Timothy already has seen in him, he places particular emphasis on the sufferings he sustained while proclaiming the gospel among the cities of South Galatia.[75] As a citizen of Lystra, Timothy likely heard Paul's preaching and teaching even as he witnessed firsthand the persecutions he endured.[76] Among other things, this reminder no doubt serves to reinforce for Timothy once again the principle that association with the gospel and its proclamation brings with it persecution. Indeed, as if to make the point perfectly clear, Paul declares, οἱ θέλοντες εὐσεβῶς ζῆν ἐν Χριστῷ Ἰησοῦ διωχθήσονται.[77]

---

73. Fairbairn, *1 and 2 Timothy and Titus*, 369–71; Mounce, *Pastoral Epistles*, 549–50; Scott, *Pastoral Epistles*, 122.

74. Fairbairn, *1 and 2 Timothy and Titus*, 371; Knight, *Pastoral Epistles*, 434–36; Mounce, *Pastoral Epistles*, 549–50.

75. Blevins, "Acts 13–19: The Tale of Three Cities," 442; Collins, *Timothy and Titus*, 257–58; Fee, *Timothy and Titus*, 276–77; Johnson, *Letters to Timothy*, 417; Witherington, *Letters and Homilies*, 356–57.

76. Collins, *Timothy and Titus*, 258 (though Collins suggests that "the Pastor" was familiar with Luke's account of these events); Marshall, *Pastoral Epistles*, 785; Quinn and Wacker, *Letters to Timothy*, 741–44; Spicq, *Les Épîtres Pastorales*, 373; Witherington, *Letters and Homilies*, 357.

77. Collins, *Timothy and Titus*, 259; Fee, *Timothy and Titus*, 277; Guthrie, *Pastoral*

Second, it is in keeping with both the previously noted semantic configuration and the predominant interest driving the letter that Paul specifically and prominently mentions his διδασκαλία, and that he reminds Timothy of his own history, as he παρακολούθησεν Paul's ministry and teaching. This remark not only recalls two previous and similar references to ὑποτύπωσις . . . ὑγιαινόντων λόγων ὧν παρ' ἐμοῦ ἤκουσας (1:13) and ἃ ἤκουσας παρ' ἐμοῦ (2:2), but it also implies Timothy's existing investment in the gospel message that comprised Paul's teaching and that was validated by his life.[78]

The most vital section of 2 Timothy relative to the research question of this study is found in 3:14–17. It is anticipated by one more instance in which Paul mentions the false teachers, of whom he writes, πονηροὶ δὲ ἄνθρωποι καὶ γόητες προκόψουσιν ἐπὶ τὸ χεῖρον πλανῶντες καὶ πλανώμενοι. These men continue to provide a foil for Paul's sustained admonitions to Timothy as he exhorts him, Σὺ δὲ μένε ἐν οἷς ἔμαθες καὶ ἐπιστώθης.[79] In this charge, the relative clauses, οἷς ἔμαθες καὶ ἐπιστώθης (in which οἷς serves as the object of both ἔμαθες and ἐπιστώθης and carries forward the notion of the διδασκαλία that Timothy παρακολούθησεν from 3:10) together form yet another reference to the apostolic gospel message, otherwise designated ὑποτύπωσις . . . ὑγιαινόντων λόγων ὧν παρ' ἐμοῦ ἤκουσας, ἃ ἤκουσας παρ'ἐμοῦ, ὁ λόγος τῆς ἀληθείας, ἡ ἀλήθεια, ἡ παραθήκη, ὁ [πιστὸς] λόγος, ὁ λόγος τοῦ θεοῦ, and τὸ εὐαγγέλιον.[80]

In 3:14–15, Paul justifies the admonition, "remain in the things that you have learned and [in the things that] you have come to believe," with two causal expressions. In the first, occurring in the latter part of 3:14, he argues for Timothy's perseverance on the merits of the sources

Epistles, 173; Mounce, _Pastoral Epistles_, 559–60.

78. Kelly, _Pastoral Epistles_, 198; Knight, _Pastoral Epistles_, 438–39; Marshall, _Pastoral Epistles_, 783; Towner, _Letters to Timothy and Titus_, 570.

79. Bernard, _Pastoral Epistles_, 135; Collins, _Timothy and Titus_, 260–61; Guthrie, _Pastoral Epistles_, 174; Witherington, _Letters and Homilies_, 358.

80. Fee remarks, "By way of contrast (but as for you), Timothy is urged to remain faithful to the apostolic gospel (continue in what you have learned; both referring back to vv. 10–11 and anticipating what is about to be said). What you have learned, Paul hopefully affirms, is also that which you have become convinced of" (Fee, _Timothy and Titus_, 278). Marshall also asserts, "Here the locus is expressed by ἐν οἷς, referring to the items of teaching which constitute the Scripture. This doubtless includes baptismal teaching (Holtz, 186) but goes beyond it to include the teaching given by one Christian leader to another. It has not only been taught to Timothy. It has also been committed to him as a sacred trust, so that he can then pass it on unchanged to others" (Marshall, _Pastoral Epistles_, 787).

of Timothy's instruction, writing, εἰδὼς παρὰ τίνων ἔμαθες. In view of Paul's use of plural τίς, one question that arises here concerns exactly who these people are from whom Timothy has received the "things [he has] learned and has come to believe."[81] With respect to the immediate literary context, it has already been noted that Timothy attended closely to Paul's teaching and life. Furthermore, Paul has referred to Timothy's acquaintance with his teaching in at least two other locations in the letter (1:13; 2:2). However, in 1:5, Paul also credited Timothy's mother and grandmother with rearing him in his ἀνυπόκριτος πίστις. Consequently, it may be said with some confidence that Timothy gained his "knowledge of the truth" at least from his mother, his grandmother, and his mentor: the Apostle Paul.[82]

The second causal expression, occupying 3:15, consists of [εἰδὼς] ὅτι ἀπὸ βρέφους τὰ ἱερὰ γράμματα οἶδας, τὰ δυνάμενά σε σοφίσαι εἰς σωτηρίαν διὰ πίστεως τῆς ἐν Χριστῷ Ἰησοῦ, and is connected to the one preceding it by καί. In this case, εἰδὼς is understood, largely because this permits the καί to retain its typical coordinate function while at the same time avoiding treating ὅτι (construed here as an indicator of indirect discourse) as superfluous.[83] This is the second time in 2 Timothy that Paul either makes use of or refers explicitly to an authoritative written source of teaching or instruction, the previous incident having occurred in 2:19, when Paul drew upon Numbers and Joel.[84] Τὰ ἱερὰ γράμματα, as a definite noun, designates a specific collection of writings.[85] In addition, because of Paul's

81. Indeed, Collins observes, "The plural 'from whom' (*para tinon*) suggests that in addition to Paul, Timothy had other teachers" (Collins, *Timothy and Titus*, 261).

82. Cook suggests that the plural could indicate "those teachers in the church, the chief of whom was Paul, who taught right doctrine" (Cook, "Scripture and Inspiration," 57). Johnson however remarks succinctly, "The plural points back to Timothy's maternal forebears (1:5), as well as Paul" (Johnson, *Letters to Timothy*, 419).

83. Bernard is explicit in this, asserting, "*And that*, not 'because'; ὅτι depends upon εἰδὼς" (Bernard, *Pastoral Epistles*, 135, emphasis Bernard's). Similarly, Knight observes, "This verse adds another object of the participle εἰδὼς (v. 14), as the conjunctions καί and ὅτι indicate (cf. Ellicott). Timothy also knows that (καί ὅτι) he has known (οἶδας) from childhood not only his teachers but also the source of the teaching itself, the 'holy Scriptures'" (Knight, *Pastoral Epistles*, 443). Also, while Marshall does not specify this syntactical configuration, he does refer to this clause as an additional source of "motivation," implying a causal function (Marshall, *Pastoral Epistles*, 788).

84. Johnson, *Letters to Timothy*, 387.

85. Even if the article was not part of the original text, the adjective ἱερός, along with the affirmation of Timothy's familiarity with this body of literature, almost certainly renders the noun definite (Fee, *Timothy and Titus*, 278; Wolfe, *Place and Use of*

earlier references to Numbers and Joel, there is an explicit indication that
he viewed the OT as authoritative and that he expects Timothy to recognize both the material and its authority. Consequently, τὰ ἱερὰ γράμματα
almost certainly refers broadly to the Law, Prophets, and Writings, in
which Timothy would have received instruction throughout his childhood.[86] Furthermore, it seems clear that these writings integrate well
with—or perhaps even form part of—the gospel proclamation, in that
they have the capacity to σοφίσαι εἰς σωτηρίαν, which comes διὰ πίστεως
τῆς ἐν Χριστῷ Ἰησοῦ.[87]

So far then in 3:14–15, Paul has written of two important bodies
of teaching and revelation: the apostolic gospel message, indicated by
οἷς ἔμαθες καὶ ἐπιστώθη (which he designates throughout the letter by
means of various expressions, and for which he has suffered and continues to do so), and the Law, Prophets, and Writings with which Paul and
Timothy have both been familiar since childhood.[88] The last three ideas
of the unit, occupying 3:16–17, contain the one occurrence of γραφή in 2
Timothy, the chief topic of interest in this study alongside the previously
examined occurrence in 1 Tim 5:18. After commending οἷς ἔμαθες καὶ
ἐπιστώθη (3:14) and τὰ ἱερὰ γράμματα (3:15), Paul now affirms, πᾶσα
γραφὴ θεόπνευστος καὶ ὠφέλιμος πρὸς διδασκαλίαν, πρὸς ἐλεγμόν, πρὸς
ἐπανόρθωσιν, πρὸς παιδείαν τὴν ἐν δικαιοσύνῃ, ἵνα ἄρτιος ᾖ ὁ τοῦ θεοῦ
ἄνθρωπος, πρὸς πᾶν ἔργον ἀγαθὸν ἐξηρτισμένος.

In evaluating the meaning and significance of πᾶσα γραφή relative
to τὰ ἱερὰ γράμματα, it must be acknowledged that the vastly prevailing

Scripture, 120).

86. Though Marcheselli-Casale suggests that ἱερὰ γράμματα may in fact include
the early writings of the NT as well as the Hebrew Canon, (Marcheselli-Casale, *Le
Lettere Pastorali*, 766). Marshall affirms, "[τὰ] ἱερὰ γράμματα is found as a set phrase
for the Scriptures. There is, therefore, nothing unusual about the phrase, although in
the present context it may perhaps stress that the OT is a textbook to be read by a
child spelling out the letters. The reference is purely to the OT Scriptures, although
later this and similar phrases were used for the Bible as a whole" (Marshall, *Pastoral
Epistles*, 789).

87. Johnson, *Letters to Timothy*, 419–20 (though Johnson prefers to read this as a
reference to Jesus' OT faith as he demonstrated it toward God, rather than as a statement regarding the OT witness to the Messiah, fulfilled in the Christ event). See also
Fee, *Timothy and Titus*, 278–79; Guthrie, *Pastoral Epistles*, 174–75; Wolfe, *Place and
Use of Scripture*, 123–24.

88. This is implicit in most sources, even when it is not explicitly stated (see, for instance, Fee, *Timothy and Titus*, 278–79; Johnson, *Letters to Timothy*, 419; Kelly, *Pastoral
Epistles*, 200–201; Marshall, *Pastoral Epistles*, 790; Spicq, *Les Épîtres Pastorales*, 375).

treatment of πᾶσα γραφή construes it as a synonym of τὰ ἱερὰ γράμματα, with the result that πᾶσα γραφή is taken as another reference to the OT Scriptures that permits Paul to offer additional descriptive commentary upon those Scriptures.[89] Certainly, Paul frequently draws upon various expressions to designate the same substantive at other points in the letter, a point that has been argued throughout this survey with regard to the apostolic gospel message. Consequently, it would not be out of character for him to continue this practice here. However, several subtle details may tell against the prevailing interpretation and suggest that πᾶσα γραφή signals the integration of οἷς ἔμαθες καὶ ἐπιστώθη with τὰ ἱερὰ γράμματα without blurring the distinction between the two bodies of instruction—a point that will be examined more closely in the next chapter. It is certainly clear at least that Paul deems both πᾶσα γραφή and τὰ ἱερὰ γράμματα as compatible with the apostolic gospel tradition with which he stands entrusted. Furthermore, while the elevation of Timothy's own summons probably functions as the central idea of the unit, cued by two emphatic occurrences of Σὺ δέ (3:10, 14), the abrupt double reference to vital written and authoritative material also registers powerfully.

4:1–8—Final Charges

Paul's last chapter opens with the solemn declaration, Διαμαρτύρομαι ἐνώπιον τοῦ θεοῦ καὶ Χριστοῦ Ἰησοῦ τοῦ μέλλοντος κρίνειν ζῶντας καὶ νεκρούς, καὶ τὴν ἐπιφάνειαν αὐτοῦ καὶ τὴν βασιλείαν αὐτοῦ. Even before an actual charge issues forth, the tone and urgency signaled from the early moments in the letter find confirmation in what feels like a final weighty word.[90] In 4:2, Paul commands Timothy, κήρυξον τὸν λόγον.

---

89. While he rightly observes that Paul's point in this passage lies in affirming the *worth* of Scripture, as opposed to formulating ontological affirmations about it, Johnson is most emphatic on this point, dismissing any possibility that γραφή could have any NT writing as its referent (Johnson, *Letters to Timothy*, 421–25). Marshall also apparently assumes this position without argument, as he provides an extensive discussion on whether the expression should be construed as a reference to every single passage of OT Scripture, to OT Scripture as a whole, or to specific passages (Marshall, *Pastoral Epistles*, 790–92). Witherington simply declares, "This is of course a reference to the Old Testament, for there was no New Testament as of yet" (Witherington, *Letters and Homilies*, 359). However, see also Cothenet, "Directives pastorales dan les Épîtres a Timothée," 19.

90. Johnson comments, "The beginning of Paul's final summons to his delegate is very solemn . . . The expression serves to call God and Christ as witnesses in order to

Against the observations of semantic links noted throughout the analysis of the entire letter up to this point, it is inconceivable that ὁ λόγος that Timothy must proclaim could represent anything except "the word of truth" he learned from Paul, "the good trust," "the word of God," and indeed, the "faithful" word.[91] The semantic thread detected earlier has gained prominence through the document, and a careful tracing of the ideas as Paul has strung them together leads naturally to the conclusion that "the word" that so captivates him and that Timothy must preach consists precisely in the apostolic trust given to him: the essential apostolic gospel message. As he proceeds with his instructions, Paul specifies some of the more critical tasks that κήρυξον must entail.

In the remainder of 4:2, he writes, ἐπίστηθι εὐκαίρως ἀκαίρως, ἔλεγξον, ἐπιτίμησον, παρακάλεσον, ἐν πάσῃ μακροθυμίᾳ καὶ διδαχῇ. As Paul presents his list of duties, he writes of objectives reminiscent of διδασκαλία, ἐλεγμός, ἐπανόρθωσις, παιδεία ἡ ἐν δικαιοσύνῃ, which appear in 3:16.[92] In other words, ὁ λόγος that Timothy is to κηρύξαι becomes the means to accomplish all that πᾶσα γραφή is profitable to perform. Furthermore, it seems the reason for the importance of such functions as ἔλεγξις, ἐπιτιμία, and παράκλησις lies in the fact that ἔσται . . . καιρὸς ὅτε

---

enhance the gravity of Paul's exhortation" (Johnson, *Letters to Timothy*, 427). Marshall also states, "A further, final exhortation forms the climax of the instructions and tends to recapitulate them. It imparts a sense of urgency to all that has been said already" (Marshall, *Pastoral Epistles*, 797).

91. Barrett writes, "The message (λόγος) which Timothy must proclaim is found, for example, in the 'faithful saying (λόγος)' of 1 Tim 1:15, 'Christ Jesus came into the world to save sinners.' This is the Gospel (v. 5)" (Barrett, *Pastoral Epistles*, 116). Collins likewise writes, "In the Pastor's circles, 'the word' (*ho logos*) was used as a cipher for the Christian message. 'The word' is the word of God (2:9; 1 Tim 4:5; Titus 1:3; 2:5), the message of truth (2:15), the words of faith (1 Tim 4:6). This word is summarized in trustworthy sayings (*pistos ho logos*). Charged with preaching the word, Timothy is to proclaim Paul's gospel message. The ministry of the word of God is the one ministry without which a Christian community cannot exist" (Collins, *Timothy and Titus*, 269).

92. Fiore comments, "Further admonition directed toward Timothy solemnly instructs him to persist in all facets of moral exhortation (4:1–2 and 4, which repeat 3:14–17)" (Fiore, *Pastoral Epistles*, 180). Johnson also writes, "In a manner similar to the earlier presentation of Paul's example in 3:10–11, the charge spells out three (or four) modes of discourse involved in the 'preaching of the word,' as well as an attitude" (Johnson, *Letters to Timothy*, 428). See also Marshall, *Pastoral Epistles*, 800–801. Bernard, however, insists, "The apparent parallelism between the clauses of this verse and those of iii. 16 is not to be pressed" (Bernard, *Pastoral Epistles*, 140). Nevertheless, it may be significant that Bernard determined it necessary to offer such a corrective remark, as he also observes the "apparent parallelism" (ibid.).

τῆς ὑγιαινούσης διδασκαλίας οὐκ ἀνέξονται.[93] While this is just the second time in 2 Timothy that ὑγιαίνω has appeared, and it is the only time that it directly modifies διδασκαλία, it seems most probable that ὑγιαίνουσα διδασκαλία in 4:3 extends the previously observed semantic thread and that it corresponds to ὑποτύπωσις . . . ὑγιαινόντων λόγων ὧν παρ' ἐμοῦ ἤκουσας (1:13).[94]

Just as he used ἡ ἀλήθεια in construct with ὁ λόγος in 2:15–26, Paul reprises it here in 4:4. This time however, even though it occurs in close proximity with ὁ λόγος and ἡ διδασκαλία, ἡ ἀλήθεια yet stands alone, as in 2:18, 25, and 3:7, a sufficient signifier of all that is expressed by ὑποτύπωσις . . . ὑγιαινόντων λόγων ὧν παρ' ἐμοῦ ἤκουσας, ἃ ἤκουσας παρ'ἐμοῦ, ὁ λόγος τῆς ἀληθείας, ἡ ἀλήθεια, ἡ παραθήκη, ὁ [πιστὸς] λόγος, ὁ λόγος τοῦ θεοῦ, τὸ εὐαγγέλιον, and ὑγιαίνουσα διδασκαλία.[95] Shortly afterward in 4:5, Paul offers a last summary of Timothy's calling, writing, Σὺ δὲ νῆφε ἐν πᾶσιν, κακοπάθησον, ἔργον ποίησον εὐαγγελιστοῦ, τὴν διακονίαν σου πληροφόρησον. While it is noteworthy that even here at the end of the main body of his correspondence Paul continues to call Timothy to endure suffering, more significant for this study is the first occurrence of εὐαγγελιστής, a personal cognate of τὸ εὐαγγέλιον. As a characterization of Timothy's commission from Paul, it confirms what has been proposed from the beginning of the chapter: Timothy is to suffer in the process of proclaiming the apostolic gospel message. However, while suffering seems to comprise the attendant circumstance, the focal point remains the gospel itself.[96]

<hr/>

93. Fee, *Timothy and Titus*, 285–86; Kelly, *Pastoral Epistles*, 206; Marshall, *Pastoral Epistles*, 801.

94. Johnson remarks, "Since healthy teaching is precisely what Paul and Timothy have to offer (1:13), they face continuing rejection, and will require all the patience and long-suffering they can muster" (Johnson, *Letters to Timothy*, 429). As Marshall also maintains, "The phrase ὑγιαίνουσα διδασκαλία is repeated from 1 Tim 1.10; Titus 1.9; 2.1; cf. 2 Tim 1.13" (Marshall, *Pastoral Epistles*, 802).

95. Johnson writes, "Paul makes a very strong claim. Truth (*aletheia*) is the defining characteristic of the message of Paul and Timothy, which implies that resistance to their message is opposing the truth (compare 2:15, 18, 25; 3:7, 8)" (Johnson, *Letters to Timothy*, 430).

96. Bernard, *Pastoral Epistles*, 141–42; Fairbairn, *1 and 2 Timothy and Titus*, 388; Fee, *Timothy and Titus*, 286–87; Marshall, *Pastoral Epistles*, 803–4.

4:9–22—Closing Admonitions

This literary unit is marked clearly by the two framing occurrences of Σπούδασον ἐλθεῖν in 4:9 and 4:21. It contians a significant number of personal recollections and references, including a request that Timothy bring with him a cloak and some of Paul's parchments, and an expressed concern that Timothy arrive before winter. Paul has already begun to review his own ministry as one taking final stock as he prepares to die.[97] However, Paul refers once more to the cause that has consumed his apostolic career, writing, ὁ δὲ κύριός μοι παρέστη καὶ ἐνεδυνάμωσέν με, ἵνα δι' ἐμοῦ τὸ κήρυγμα πληροφορηθῇ καὶ ἀκούσωσιν πάντα τὰ ἔθνη.[98] Even now, his chief concern is that "the proclamation (τὸ κήρυγμα)" be fulfilled.

2 Timothy Discourse and Semantic Overview—Concluding Remarks

At the beginning of this chapter, it was suggested that on the one hand, 2 Timothy exhibits a conspicuous and fairly persistent concern for suffering hardship and persecution for the sake of faithfully proclaiming the apostolic gospel message. It was also proposed that distinct semantic streams would reveal themselves over the course of the letter, particularly the thread that traces Paul's overwhelming preoccupation with his apostolic teaching and gospel proclamation.[99] While both of these hypotheses have been corroborated in the process of conducting the discourse and semantic analysis of this chapter, it is the second hypothesis that provides the most significant contribution to this study.

In addition, it has been noted that, as with 1 Timothy, Paul has used a wide range of expressions in 2 Timothy by which to designate the proclamation that forms the heart of his apostolic mission. In 2 Timothy, Paul has referred to this message as ὑποτύπωσις . . . ὑγιαινόντων λόγων ὧν

---

97. Bernard, *Pastoral Epistles*, 142–43; Fee, *Timothy and Titus*, 288; Johnson, *Letters to Timothy*, 450–51; Spicq, *Les Épîtres Pastorales*, 388.

98. Collins, *Timothy and Titus*, 286; Johnson, *Letters to Timothy*, 442; Marshall, *Pastoral Epistles*, 824–25; Towner, *Goal of Our Instruction*, 123.

99. With respect to this concern relative to 3:16, Cook shows no hesitation to affirm, "The teaching on the inspiration of Scripture in our passage is a part of the larger Pastoral concern for orthodoxy noted above. This concern is manifested in Paul's repeated urging of Timothy to guard the tradition entrusted to him and to teach it to those in his charge (1 Tim 4:6; 6:20; 2 Tim 1:14; 2:2)" (Cook, "Scripture and Inspiration," 56).

παρ᾽ ἐμοῦ ἤκουσας, ἃ ἤκουσας παρ᾽ἐμοῦ, ὁ λόγος τῆς ἀληθείας, ἡ ἀλήθεια, ἡ παραθήκη, ὁ [πιστὸς] λόγος, ὁ λόγος τοῦ θεοῦ, τὸ εὐαγγέλιον, ὑγιαίνουσα διδασκαλία, ἡ πίστις, and finally, τὸ κήρυγμα.[100] However, even more noticeably, Paul has utilized more personal expressions to speak of this message than were seen in 1 Timothy: expressions drawing upon first-person personal pronouns (ὑποτύπωσις . . . ὑγιαινόντων λόγων ὧν παρ᾽ ἐμοῦ ἤκουσας, ἃ ἤκουσας παρ᾽ἐμοῦ, τὸ εὐαγγέλλιόν μου). In addition, this highly personal association is matched by Paul's elevated determination (in comparison with that exhibited in 1 Timothy) to equate this message—his gospel, his teaching, the pattern of sound words that Timothy learned from him—with God's own utterances, conveyed most clearly by the designation, ὁ λόγος τοῦ θεοῦ.

With respect to the variety of expressions used to denote the one apostolic gospel message with which Paul is preoccupied, and with respect to that preoccupation itself, general agreement is apparent among the multitude of sources cited here, even as was noted relative to 1 Timothy. Furthermore, it is significant that such broad agreement may be found among representatives of a wide range of assumptions regarding the authorship and dating of these letters and differing treatments of γραφή.

The next chapter will offer a close examination of γραφή in 2 Tim 3:16 against the literary survey of the whole of 2 Timothy just presented, especially as it relates to τὰ ἱερὰ γράμματα. Over the course of the close analysis of 3:14–17, this study's divergence from the majority view of γραφή in 2 Timothy will assume sharper contours than it has in this chapter. At the same time, it is clear that the distinct position of this work rests largely upon a foundation of widely shared premises. At this point, it remains the position of this study that, as with 1 Tim 5:18, Paul uses γραφή in 2 Tim 3:16 to denote the Law, Prophets, and Writings, as well as written apostolic material by which the gospel message is conveyed, explained, taught, or defended. The discourse and semantic thread just traced will be crucial to the following analysis.

---

100. Towner summarizes the prevailing concern of these letters as expressed in various traditional formulae thusly, "From the standpoint of the letters as a corpus the tradition exemplifies the 'sound teaching', that is, the apostolic gospel which the author seeks to safeguard from the onslaught of the false teachers" (Towner, *Goal of Our Instruction*, 118). See also ibid., 121–26; Van Neste, *Cohesion and Structure*, 216–17.

CHAPTER 6

Γραφη with Reference
to the Immediate Literary Context of 2 Timothy

IT WAS OBSERVED IN the previous chapter that 2 Timothy, much like 1 Timothy, exhibits a prominent and widely recognized concern for the preservation and advancement of the apostolic gospel proclamation. This preoccupation manifests itself primarily by means of a readily discernible semantic thread that carries the gospel motif through the entire letter. Over the course of 2 Timothy, Paul refers to that gospel message and its contents as ἡ ἀλήθεια, τὸ εὐαγγέλιον, τὸ κήρυγμα, ὁ λόγος τῆς ἀληθείας, ὁ λόγος τοῦ θεοῦ, ὁ [πιστὸς] λόγος, ἡ παραθήκη, ἡ πίστις, and ὑγιαίνουσα διδασκαλία. In addition, and uniquely in 2 Timothy, Paul makes it clear that the gospel advances at the expense of perseverance under hardship, a motif that provides an additional subtext that contributes to the construal of γραφή in 3:15-16. It also has been noted that Paul draws upon more personal expressions to speak of this message than were observed in 1 Timothy. For instance, he refers to the gospel message now entrusted to Timothy as ὑποτύπωσις . . . ὑγιαινόντων λόγων ὧν παρ᾽ ἐμοῦ ἤκουσας (1:13), ἃ ἤκουσας παρ᾽ἐμοῦ (2:2), τὸ εὐαγγέλλιόν μου (2:8). In the latter example, Paul also implicitly equates this message with God's own utterances or revelatory word (ὁ λόγος τοῦ θεοῦ).[1]

While most of these observations find ample corroboration among the various sources consulted, this study departs from the mainstream chiefly in the implications it extracts from the grammatical and syntactical

1. Collins, *Timothy and Titus*, 224; Guthrie, *Pastoral Epistles*, 156; Knight, *Pastoral Epistles*, 398; Schlatter, *Die Kirche der Griechen*, 236; Spicq, *Les Épîtres Pastorales*, 347; Towner, *Goal of Our Instruction*, 123-24; Wolfe, *Place and Use of Scripture*, 144.

structure of 3:14–17. It also differs from most other studies in its assessment of the relationship between τὰ ἱερὰ γράμματα and πᾶσα γραφή in 3:15–16, both of which are construed by most scholars as synonymous references to the Law, Prophets, and Writings with which Timothy was familiar and had studied from childhood.[2] In all fairness, it must be acknowledged that on the strict basis of lexis and common suppositions regarding what materials would have been written, published, and distributed during or shortly after Paul's lifetime, the majority opinion is certainly plausible. However, several other factors—both textual and historical—suggest that the construal represented by the prevailing view relative to both τὰ ἱερὰ γράμματα and πᾶσα γραφή may be precipitous.

First, the conspicuous and widely acknowledged preoccupation with the gospel message conveyed in this letter, coupled with almost no direct comment relative to the writings of the OT, would seem to signal at the outset that the gospel enjoys a more elevated level of importance in this piece of correspondence than do the Law, Prophets, and Writings.[3] By itself, this fact makes it rather unlikely that Paul would depart significantly from his established epistolary course so as to commend the merits of the OT writings uniquely, as several sources seem to allege.

Second, while the widely supposed improbability of the existence in Paul's lifetime of writings that now form part of the NT plays a very considerable role in common assessments of γραφή, it rests largely upon assumptions rather than upon hard facts.[4] Indeed, as demonstrated in

2. Aageson, "Pastoral Epistles, Apostolic Authority," 25; Belleville, "Canon of the New Testament," 377; Collins, *Timothy and Titus*, 262–63; Cook, "Scripture and Inspiration," 58; Guthrie, *Pastoral Epistles*, 175; Lock, *Pastoral Epistles*, 110; Weiser, *Der zweite Brief an Timotheus*, 281.

3. See, for example, Belleville, "Canon of the New Testament," 377; Collins, *Timothy and Titus*, 262–63; Fiore, *Pastoral Epistles*, 171; Johnson, *Letters to Timothy*, 423–24; Towner, *Letters to Timothy and Titus*, 586–87.

4. For instance, Johnson seems to fall victim to his own critique concerning "construal," as he dismisses the possibility that γραφή can refer to anything but the OT, writing, "It should be obvious that Paul cannot be making a statement about the Christian Bible, for the New Testament collection was not yet in existence" (Johnson, *Letters to Timothy*, 419). At the same time, Johnson neglects to address the possible existence of some Christian writings at the time of this letter's composition. In a more moderated assertion, Towner writes, "The only question would be whether the contents go beyond the OT to include writings of the early church already in circulation, but this does not seem very likely" (Towner, *Letters to Timothy and Titus*, 587). On the other hand, Witherington remarks even more tersely than Johnson regarding γραφή, "This is of course a reference to the Old Testament, for there was no New Testament as of yet" (Witherington, *Letters and Homilies*, 359). This study takes exception to the positivism of these comments, especially since no source consulted has troubled to

chapter 4, this position does not fit all of the available data. For instance, Spicq provides an argument against the prevailing assumption, writing,

> All of the books of the New Testament, if one excepts the two of St. John (Rev., John), and perhaps a few others, already were known when St. Paul wrote these words. Doubtless, he understood and embraced them as "Scripture," when it says that "all Scripture is divinely inspired," since he could in no way ignore, and did not ignore, in effect, that they were part of this divine Scripture, which he celebrates here, along with its authority and excellent usefulness.[5]

Representing a more moderate position, Ferguson, referencing Barton, offers,

> It may claim too much "to say that the canon was fixed" already at the end of the first century, "since its edges were still quite fuzzy; yet it would be equally mistaken to say that 'there was no Christian Scripture other than the Old Testament'" at this time, "for much of the core [of the New Testament] already had as high a status as it would ever have." In terms of the significance of scriptural status, there is no time when Christians did not treat the writings that would become the New Testament as Scripture.[6]

Consequently, whereas assuming the absence of apostolic writings from the early church's authoritative collection of teaching once may have

---

present evidence or argument for the premise indicated. This is the case particularly with Johnson and Witherington. Indeed, it is precisely the question of the possibility of extant Christian writings and their recognition as Scripture that is at stake here. Wolfe offers an assessment of the prevailing position and its assumptions, writing, "Denials are usually on the basis of the interpreters' *a priori* judgement [*sic*] as to whether or not NT documents or sayings sources could have been considered as Scripture during the NT period. The burden of proof, however, is certainly on those who would deny an extension of *graphe* to include some NT writings, or sayings sources, especially in light of some grammarians' understanding of the construction in 2 Timothy 3:16" (Wolfe, "Scripture in the Pastoral Epistles," 14).

5. Spicq, *Les Épîtres Pastorales*, 377.

6. Ferguson, "Factors Leading to the Selection," 298. Similarly, Schnabel writes, "If Christ and the apostles lived and worshipped with a normative list of authoritative books which they regarded as 'holy' (Rom 1:2; 2 Tim 3:15; cf. Rom 7:12), we may further conclude that it is by no means impossible that the notion of a new and additional set of normative Scripture for the 'new covenant' on a par with the Scriptures of the 'old covenant' was born already in early apostolic times" (Schnabel, "History, Theology," 18a).

ruled out the consideration of such documents as "Scripture," the amendment of that assumption as argued in this study reinstates some of these very writings (such as the letters of Paul and Luke's gospel), setting them firmly within the domain of possible referents for γραφή.

Third, Paul employs two lexically similar expressions in 3:15–16— τὰ ἱερὰ γράμματα and πᾶσα γραφή,[7] which occur without preface or explanation—to achieve his primary objective of commending the gospel teaching that Timothy is charged to uphold with renewed vigor, and for which he is called to suffer.[8] The abrupt appearance of these terms suggests that Paul understands them to fit coherently within the existing rhetorical scheme of the letter. However, this chapter will argue that the construal of γραφή as a reference to the OT alone may in fact disrupt Paul's rhetorical scheme.

Fourth, as mentioned in the previous chapter, Paul actually refers to two distinct bodies of authoritative instruction in 3:14–15: namely, οἷς ἔμαθες καὶ ἐπιστώθης and τὰ ἱερὰ γράμματα. Thus, it will be argued here that, their virtual lexical equivalence notwithstanding, Paul does not use τὰ ἱερὰ γράμματα and πᾶσα γραφή as synonyms referring to one body of revelation (as is commonly held). Rather, they serve as two of *three* expressions that on the one hand, help to differentiate between two bodies of authoritative teaching (οἷς ἔμαθες καὶ ἐπιστώθης and τὰ ἱερὰ γράμματα), and that on the other hand, signal the integration of both authorities into one body of Scripture (πᾶσα γραφή).

---

7. For instance, BDAG lists for γράμμα, "*A document, piece of writing*; a relatively long written publication, *writing, book*," while noting, "A brief piece of writing, writing; sacred Scripture; Scripture in its entirety" for γραφή (BDAG, 205b, 206b, emphasis mine). Schrenk includes among his comments regarding γράμμα, "The use of γράμμα is parallel to that of γραφή. Γράμμα is properly what is 'inscribed' or 'engraven' and then what is 'written' in the widest sense" (Schrenk, "γράφω, γραφή, γράμμα, κ.τ.λ.," 742–73). With respect to γραφή, Schrenk's remarks include, "'writing,' 'what is written'" (ibid., 753–54). Furthermore, with respect to various occurrences in John's Gospel, Schrenk writes, "There can hardly be any doubt whatever that . . . we are to think of the unified totality of Scripture. Similarly, it is impossible to take 1 Pet 2:6 . . . or 2 Pet 1:20 in any other way" (ibid., 754–55). Louw and Nida record "any kind of written document, whether in book or manuscript form, with focus upon the content—'writings, what has been written'" for γράμμα, and "a particular passage of the OT—'Scripture, Scripture passage'" for γραφή (Louw and Nida, *Greek-English Lexicon of the New Testament*, 33.50, 33.53).

8. Regarding this, Mounce writes, "Verses 14–17 are yet another appeal that Timothy remain loyal to what he has learned, and earlier in this letter this means the gospel message" (Mounce, *Pastoral Epistles*, 564).

In view of these several considerations, this chapter isolates 2 Tim 3:14–17 and offers a close analysis of it within its immediate literary context. It shall build largely upon the semantic overview provided by the preceding chapter and will be conducted as follows.

First, a detailed grammatical analysis of 3:14–17 shall be presented, comprised of an appraisal of the main and dependent clauses found in these verses. In the process, it will be argued that within the scope of 3:14–17, γραφή is most coherently understood as a reference to the combined bodies of the OT and apostolic gospel message based upon the grammar and syntax of this literary unit. Second, the assessment of 3:14–17 as a whole literary unit shall be considered relative to the literary units on either side of these verses: namely, 3:10–13 and 4:1–4. This review will demonstrate that the construal of γραφή proposed here integrates this literary unit with the units that precede and follow it in a smoother and more coherent fashion than the conventional treatment is able to achieve.

Thus, on the basis of the evaluation of 3:14–17 in isolation and then in light of the two literary units on either side of these verses, it will be proposed that, on a tight exegetical basis, the most defensible reading lies in construing γραφή as a composite reference to the Law, Prophets, and Writings together with the gospel message proclaimed by Paul and the rest of the apostles—a message that apparently was attaining written form and scriptural status by the time Paul composed his letters to Timothy.

Grammatical Analysis of 3:14–17

While some of the interpretive details that follow may seem self-evident, it is worth noting them explicitly to establish firmly the basis for this chapter's distinct arguments.[9] In 3:14–17, Σὺ δὲ μένε ἐν οἷς ἔμαθες καὶ

9. At times, it is difficult to weigh precisely the exegetical merits of a commentator's interpretive solution. For instance, while Johnson does not comment at all upon the grammatical structure, his paraphrase seems to treat 3:15a as a main clause, along with 3:14a and 3:16 (Johnson, *Letters to Timothy*, 416). Lock also offers little commentary upon the grammar, though his paraphrase treats 3:14a and 3:16 as main clauses, each modified as proposed here (Lock, *Pastoral Epistles*, 104). On the other hand, while Towner does propose a syntactical arrangement, he does not explicitly justify his position grammatically, writing, "The instructions, which carry through to v. 17, are carefully constructed: (1) the basic instruction (v. 14a); (2) two causes, motives, or reasons for obeying the instructions, followed by a statement of the Scriptures' salvific power that validates the motives (vv. 14b–15ab); (3) a supporting argument for the

ἐπιστώθης serves as the first of two main clauses. In addition to the subject and main verb (Σὺ . . . μένε), it contains two relative clauses, οἷς ἔμαθες καὶ ἐπιστώθης , with οἷς serving as the object of both ἔμαθες and ἐπιστώθης. The main clause is modified by two subordinate clauses found in 3:15, εἰδὼς παρὰ τίνων ἔμαθες, and [εἰδὼς] ὅτι ἀπὸ βρέφους τὰ ἱερὰ γράμμα οἶδας, τὰ δυνάμενά σε σοφίσαι εἰς σωτηρίαν διὰ πίστεως τῆς ἐν Χριστῷ Ἰησοῦ. In the second subordinate clause, εἰδώς is understood elliptically so as to preserve coherency, while ὅτι introduces indirect discourse, signaling the content of what Timothy knows. These two relative clauses are linked by καί, indicating a paratactic or series relationship between them, and both are construed as causal.[10]

The second main clause, which appears in 3:16, is πᾶσα γραφὴ θεόπνευστος καὶ ὠφέλιμος πρὸς διδασκαλίαν, πρὸς ἐλεγμόν, πρὸς ἐπανόρθωσιν, πρὸς παιδείαν τὴν ἐν δικαιοσύνῃ. Two grammatical details lead to the designation of 3:16 as a main clause, rather than an additional dependent clause that either explains or justifies the preceding material. First, in the absence of an explicit conjunction between 3:15 and 3:16, it seems most sensitive to authorial intent to infer a syntactical relationship that follows the text rather than directing it.[11] In this case, the sense of καί would impose least upon the text. Furthermore, because 3:15 functions as part of the indirect discourse introduced in 3:14b, and there are no indications that 3:16 does likewise, 3:16 must stand in series with 3:14a. The second detail lies in the use of ἡ γραφή in 3:16, instead of τὸ γράμμα. When combined with the lack of a conjunction that explicitly links the

power of the Scriptures, based on their nature and function (v. 16) . . . The statement that follows (v. 16) clearly adheres logically to the argument that has been developing, supporting the assertion of the Scriptures' power (v. 15b) by emphasizing their divine source and usefulness" (Towner, *Letters to Timothy and Titus*, 580, 585). The claim that 3:16 "supports" the preceding clauses is an especially important interpretive decision, for if Towner is correct, then he has proposed an assessment that directly opposes that offered in this study, which in turn could affect the resulting construal of γραφή. However, while Towner's proposal seems to be a plausible interpretive option on the surface, Paul has not drawn upon any of the critical conjunctions or participles in 3:16 that would be necessary to justify Towner's syntactical assessment. Thus, while his rendering of 3:15–16 seems a reasonable option with respect to content, Towner assumes a syntactical intent not explicitly signaled by Paul.

10. Bernard offers the most explicit reflection of the construal proposed here, saying, "καὶ ὅτι *and that*, not 'because'; ὅτι depends upon εἰδώς" (Bernard, *Pastoral Epistles*, 135). See also Marshall, *Pastoral Epistles*, 788; Quinn and Wacker, *Letters to Timothy*, 756; Spicq, *Les Épîtres Pastorales*, 374; Towner, *Letters to Timothy and Titus*, 581.

11. As Towner does by inferring a causal link between 3:15 and 3:16 (See note 9 above).

ideas contained in these verses, an alteration in the subject would seem
to signal a new set of ideas. Additional arguments for this interpretive
decision will emerge as the exegesis develops.

Tracing out the remainder of the clause, the adjectives θεόπνευστος
and ὠφέλιμος are construed here as predicate nominatives, incorporating
an elliptical ἐστίν. The main idea is modified by the dependent clause
ἵνα ἄρτιος ᾖ ὁ τοῦ θεοῦ ἄνθρωπος, πρὸς πᾶν ἔργον ἀγαθὸν ἐξηρτισμένος,
in which ἵνα most likely indicates that the following material expresses
contingent result.[12] Furthermore, it is the position here that, while the
main clause features the commentary upon "all Scripture," the point Paul
argues in 3:16–17 concerns the completeness or fully-equipped status
enjoyed by the man of God who adheres to "all Scripture." Thus, the affirmation of the sufficiency of πᾶσα γραφή to equip the man of God is a
parallel idea to the admonition, "continue in what you have learned and
have come to believe," so that the two main clauses of 3:14–17, in company with their discrete dependent ideas, form the bases of two large and
complex ideas (3:14–15 and 3:16–17) that together are intended to fortify
Timothy in both his conviction and confidence as he works to preserve
and advance the true apostolic gospel message.[13] With the participles
rendered in italics so as to reflect their syntactical function, a working
English translation for these verses is,

> [3:14]But you, continue in the things you have learned and have
> come to believe,
>> knowing (*because you know*) [those] from whom you have
>> learned [them],
>> [15]and [knowing (*because you know*)]
>> that, from infancy, you have known the holy writings ([τὰ]
>> ἱερὰ γράμματα) that are able to make you wise unto salva-
>> tion [that is] through faith that [is] in Christ Jesus.
> [16][And] All Scripture (πᾶσα γραφή) [is] God-breathed and prof-
> itable for teaching, for reproof, for restoration, for training in
> righteousness;
>> [17]so that the man of God may be qualified,
>> standing equipped (*in that he stands equipped*) for every
>> good work.[14]

12. Guthrie, *Pastoral Epistles*, 176–77; Johnson, *Letters to Timothy*, 425; Spicq, *Les
Épîtres Pastorales*, 378; Witherington, *Letters and Homilies*, 361.

13. While Knight does not explicitly concur with this analysis, his treatment of
the material of 3:14–17 does reflect a similar appraisal (Knight, *Pastoral Epistles*, 398).
Again, see note 9 above.

14. Indentation to the right (inside) indicates a supporting or subordinate function,

Several details relative to this translation help establish the arguments and implications that follow from this point. First, there is broad agreement that οἷς ἔμαθες καὶ ἐπιστώθης refers to the gospel proclaimed by the apostles and that τὰ ἱερὰ γράμματα refers to the Law, Prophets, and Writings, and the present study stands in agreement with the prevailing opinion on both points.[15] This means that in 3:14–15, Paul explicitly mentions two distinct (though apparently compatible) bodies of instruction, a detail that frequently goes unmentioned in interpretive discussions concerning 3:14–17.

Second, because of the literary structure detailed in the above analysis, in which the two main clauses are Σὺ δὲ μένε ἐν οἷς ἔμαθες καὶ ἐπιστώθης and πᾶσα γραφὴ θεόπνευστος . . . τὴν ἐν δικαιοσύνῃ, it is clear that τὰ ἱερὰ γράμματα and πᾶσα γραφή do not stand in *syntactically* equivalent positions, whatever may be said of their semantic similarity. Taking this point even further, it is equally clear that Paul's remarks concerning "the holy writings" are offered in the first place as partial justification for his admonition to Timothy to "continue in the things you have learned and have come to believe." Thus, the authority and God-given nature of τὰ ἱερὰ γράμματα are qualities that Timothy already takes as a matter of fact, for his confidence in these writings provides part of the basis for his continued allegiance to the apostolic gospel (alongside his confidence in those from whom he received that message), even while he labors in the midst of difficulties. Indeed, it is precisely these qualities already presumed to adhere to τὰ ἱερὰ γράμματα that also provide a warrant for Timothy's confidence in οἷς ἔμαθες καὶ ἐπιστώθης. This means that it would hardly be necessary for Paul to utilize the time or space to state that these writings are "God-breathed and profitable for teaching, for reproof, for restoration, for training in righteousness."[16] On the

---

while supported or main ideas lie to the left (outside).

15. Quinn and Wacker, *Letters to Timothy*, 755–56; Schlatter, *Die Kirche der Griechen*, 257–58; Spicq, *Les Épîtres Pastorales*, 375; Towner, *Letters to Timothy and Titus*, 580–81; Weiser, *Der zweite Brief an Timotheus*, 277; Witherington, *Letters and Homilies*, 358–59.

16. Guthrie seems to experience some reservation over this question as well, as he reflects, "It is difficult to see why the apostle should need to assure Timothy that inspired Scriptures are profitable. On the other hand, it is not easy to see why Timothy should need to be assured, at this point, of the inspiration of the Scriptures. One explanation is that it is the profitableness not the inspiration which Paul is pressing on Timothy (cf. Bernard). After all he must have been assured of the inspiration of Scripture since his youth" (Guthrie, *Pastoral Epistles*, 175–76). However, to follow up

other hand, if πᾶσα γραφή were to refer to the OT writings *in conjunction with* the apostolic gospel, then Paul's remarks concerning "all Scripture" provide an additional affirmation that may stand alongside the admonition to Timothy and that would be based in part upon the acknowledged worth and authority of τὰ ἱερὰ γράμματα.

Third, the interpretation of 3:16 depends to some extent upon accounting for Paul's use of πᾶς to modify γραφή. To this end, when evaluating the construal of τὰ ἱερὰ γράμματα against that of πᾶσα γραφή, it seems important to note at the outset that τὰ ἱερὰ γράμματα is already a collective term, apparently referring to the whole of "the holy writings."[17] In other words, Paul does not write that Timothy was reared and instructed from infancy in *some* of the holy writings, so that now he must affirm the worth of the collection as a whole. Rather, he indicates that Timothy grew up under the instruction found in "the holy writings," to

---

on Guthrie's own observation, one also must wonder why, if Timothy were trained in the Scriptures from his childhood, he would need to be reassured of their profitability any more than their inspiration. Note also Lock's attempts to account for Paul's use of γράμματα in 3:15, as he writes, "Possibly also he wishes to hint at an antithesis both to the unwritten myths and genealogies of the false teachers and to the Ἐφεσία γράμματα, the sacred books and charms of the magicians at Ephesus, Acts 1919 (*Encycl. B.* ii. col. 1304). 'Your text-books were Scriptures, *not* tradition'; 'they were ἱερά, not βέβηλα'" (Lock, *Pastoral Epistles*, 109). In other words, while Lock does not reflect the analysis proposed here, he nevertheless sees Paul differentiating between the Law, Prophets, and Writings, and some additional tradition, even as proposed in this study. Mounce likewise observes, "In some places it appears that he is referring to the OT; in other places it appears that he is referring to the gospel message. Because of the flow of the discussion, it appears that Paul does not talk about the OT in distinction from the gospel message, or the gospel message apart from its heritage in the OT" (Mounce, *Pastoral Epistles*, 561). Mounce concludes his discussion on this point by suggesting, "Paul could be saying that of all the world's writings, those coming from God are uniquely profitable for Timothy's ministry. But the consistent use of γραφή in the NT to refer to the OT argues against this possibility" (ibid.,565). However, against Mounce, it is maintained in this study that it is precisely in the recognition of the typical usage of γραφή that Paul's use of it in 2 Timothy has such power to convey forcefully that scriptural standing also applies to his own apostolic teaching.

17. Mounce, arguing for a construal of πᾶς as "all," or referring to the whole, nevertheless writes, "It should also be noted that the singular πᾶσα γραφή, 'all Scripture,' is parallel to the plural ἱερὰ γράμματα, 'sacred writings,' *which refers to the entire OT*" (Mounce, *Pastoral Epistles*, 567, emphasis mine). While he also offers his argument in defense of his construal of πᾶς as "every," Towner states regarding [τὰ] ἱερὰ γράμματα, "Paul has echoed specific OT texts and stories in the near context (2:19; 3:8–9, 11; cf. 2:7; 4:14, 17–18) for the purpose of correction and instruction (see 16b), and has referred to *the entirety of the Scriptures* (albeit uniquely as instructional materials) in the plural in v. 15" (Towner, *Letters to Timothy and Titus*, 587, emphasis mine).

all appearances referring to them as a complete collection. Consequently, reading πᾶσα γραφή as simply a more inclusive or more expansive reference to τὰ ἱερὰ γράμματα, as several commentators suggest, would seem to result in a redundancy between 3:15 and 3:16. Put another way, if τὰ ἱερὰ γράμματα and πᾶσα γραφή denote the same body of teaching, the collective (and already all-inclusive) sense of τὰ ἱερὰ γράμματα would seem to render πᾶς superfluous as a modifier of γραφή.[18]

In view of the preceding arguments, it is proposed here that πᾶσα γραφή signals the gathering together and classification of οἷς ἔμαθες καὶ ἐπιστώθης with τὰ ἱερὰ γράμματα into a single, more expansive, and integrated category that Paul now designates γραφή ("Scripture"). Indeed, the very reason behind using γραφή lies in Paul's desire to differentiate from τὰ ἱερὰ γράμματα so that he may remind Timothy that the gospel message that he learned and received, and which he is to guard and entrust to another generation of faithful men, holds the very same standing in the apostle's estimation as τὰ ἱερὰ γράμματα, or the OT Scriptures.[19]

This point may also provide some insight into one of the more commonly recurring interpretive discussions associated with the adjective πᾶς. Most discussions begin with the assumption that the referent of γραφή is the OT, and that the real question concerns whether πᾶς should be translated as "every" or "all."[20]

---

18. This is all the more the case if one were to take the presence of the definite article as more strongly attested than its absence.

19. Spicq writes, "πᾶσα γραφή, according to the context, evidently designates all of the holy books of the Old Testament that Timothy had learned and known from his infancy . . . Consequently, one cannot exclude the writings produced by the Apostles or approved by them . . . If the Old Testament is useful, how much more will be the word coming from the mouth of Christ himself, and contained in the New Testament" (Spicq, *Les Épîtres Pastorales*, 377, 379). House ventures a bit further, suggesting, "It may be that γραφή in 2 Timothy 3:16 extends beyond the γράμμα under which Timothy was reared . . . γραφή may refer to the Word of God accepted by the Apostle Paul, and probably by the church, at the time of the writing of 2 Timothy *and also that which was expected to come later under the inspiration of God*" (House, "Biblical Inspiration," 56–57, emphasis mine). Cook, on the other hand, while maintaining that γράμμα and γραφή share the same referent, nevertheless explicitly discloses the correspondence he observes between οἷς ἔμαθες καὶ ἐπιστώθης and γραφή, as he writes, "The teaching on the inspiration of Scripture in our passage is a part of the larger Pastoral concern for orthodoxy noted above. This concern is manifested in Paul's repeated urging of Timothy to guard the tradition entrusted to him and to teach it to those in his charge" (Cook, "Scripture and Inspiration," 56).

20. See, for instance, Bover, "Uso de Adjetivo Singular πᾶς en San Pablo," 411–34; Collins, *Timothy and Titus*, 263; Fee, *Timothy and Titus*, 279; Johnston, *Use of Πᾶς in*

However, it is proposed that this question may not be the most important inquiry pertaining to πᾶς after all; the more critical issue concerns the effect of the singular πᾶσα γραφή when considered against two previously mentioned sources of revelation (both expressed in plural terms) that appear over the preceding four clauses.[21] Thus, on the one hand, Paul does employ πᾶς so as to clarify the scope of the church's authoritative writings, as most scholars maintain. On the other hand, and more precisely, since Paul has already referred to the "holy writings" collectively, affirming their worth as a whole, he now uses γραφή modified by πᾶς so as to convey that this referent is broader and even more inclusive than all of τὰ ἱερὰ γράμματα; it includes as well the οἷς ἔμαθες καὶ ἐπιστώθης that so occupy his attention through the letter. Accordingly, Paul signals that his apostolic gospel teaching—the "pattern of sound words" which Timothy learned from him, the "word of God," and the "word of truth," the "faithful" word, the "good trust," and "the things that you heard from me"—shares the same standing accorded to "the holy writings," for it is Scripture.[22]

---

the New Testament; Towner, *Letters to Timothy and Titus*, 585–86; Weiser, *Der zweite Brief an Timotheus*, 279–81.

21. Knight argues, "In this letter Paul has praised Timothy for following his teaching (v. 10), has urged Timothy to continue in what he has learned form Paul (v. 14), has commanded Timothy to retain 'the standard of sound words' that he has heard from Paul (1:13), has commanded him to entrust what he has heard from Paul to faithful men so that they could teach others (2:2), and has insisted that Timothy handle accurately 'the word of truth' (2:15) . . . It seems possible, therefore, that Paul by his use of πᾶσα γραφή is expanding the earlier reference to the OT . . . This understanding also fits well in this context. It provides a reason for Paul's use of πᾶσα and for his change from ἱερὰ γράμματα an OT designation, to πᾶσα γραφή, a possibly more inclusive term" (Knight, *Pastoral Epistles*, 448).

22. Thus, Cothenet asserts, "It is clear, however, that the Jewish reading cannot be the same as the Christian reading according to which Scripture 'leads to salvation through faith in Christ Jesus' (2 Tim 3:15). The reference to the Scripture is part of the oldest preaching (1 Cor 15:3 s.) and it will expand in numerous spoken expressions of fulfillment, as witnessed extensively in the gospels of Matthew and John" (Cothenet, "Directives pastorales dan les Épîtres a Timothée," 19). In spite of his differing position concerning γραφή, Towner also affirms, "The Pauline gospel may be seen as continuous with the power and intention of the ancient Scriptures, and it is possible that the usefulness of the OT needed to be reaffirmed in the wake of heretical misuse of it" (Towner, *Letters to Timothy and Titus*, 584). Similarly, Witherington, in spite of his prior dismissal of NT writings, offers, "Notice also that Paul couples his own teachings with those of the Scripture assuming that both conveyed and convey to Timothy the truth. In short, both Pauline teaching and the Scriptures provide the warrant for the exhortations here" (Witherington, *Letters and Homilies*, 355). With respect to each of

When πᾶσα γραφή appears with the rest of the clause, two other considerations ensue. First, Paul characterizes πᾶσα γραφή as θεόπνευστος. While this association has received a good deal of attention as various scholars have sought to pin down the exact semantic value of θεόπνευστος, one thing seems clear. Πᾶσα γραφή comes from God; it is God's γραφή, and it carries his message and speaks with his authority.[23] Not only does this fit the conventional view of τὰ ἱερὰ γράμματα, it also is consistent with the designation of the apostolic gospel proclamation as οἷς ἔμαθες καὶ ἐπιστώθης and as ὁ λόγος τοῦ θεοῦ.[24]

Second, Paul also declares that this γραφή is ὠφέλιμος πρὸς διδασκαλίαν, πρὸς ἐλεγμόν, πρὸς ἐπανόρθωσιν, πρὸς παιδείαν τὴν ἐν δικαιοσύνῃ. While few would deny that this sweeping benefit must pertain to τὰ ἱερὰ γράμματα, it has already been argued here that Timothy would hardly require any reminder of this fact. Consequently, the point behind this assertion more likely lies in the desire to stiffen Timothy's confidence in the worth of the gospel message entrusted to him and for

---

these sources, it is striking that, while all maintain that Paul affirms the authority and God-given quality of the OT alone as γραφή, they all also inject the notion of a Pauline gospel that is essential to the complex witness and efficacy of γραφή, or as Towner states, "continuous with the power and intention of the ancient Scriptures" (Towner, *Letters to Timothy and Titus*, 584). Wolfe provides a somewhat different reflection, maintaining, "The PE uphold the words, or teaching of Jesus as possessing an inherent authority and representing a standard, that is a canon, akin to that of γραφή ... When these epistles are examined in detail, it becomes evident that within them there is a common thread of understanding and description surrounding the relationships of Scripture, Jesus and his teachings, and the apostolic ministry ... This terminology indicates a Christian παράδοσις (tradition) which has come to be recognized as having inherent authority equal to that of Scripture itself. In fact, Scripture could only be properly understood in light of and in accordance with the apostolic tradition" (Wolfe, "Scripture in the Pastoral Epistles," 14–15).

23. Scott writes, "The crucial word means literally 'breathed into by God'—i.e., a divine quality is present in Scripture, distinguishing it from all human utterance. Ordinary language as used in the Bible becomes the vehicle of a message from God" (Scott, *Pastoral Epistles*, 127). See also Artola, "El Momento de la Inspiración," 61–82.

24. As Kelly writes, "All the more exultantly, therefore, sounds his triumphant interjection, 'not that God's word is chained!' As in 1 Thess 2:13; 2 Thess 3:1, 'God's word,' here equivalent to 'my gospel' above, is almost personified" (Kelly, *Pastoral Epistles*, 177). Also, as previously noted, Piñero acknowledges, "In theory, the syntactical scope of πᾶσα γραφή cannot be reduced to the OT ... Πᾶς without the article means 'any' ... Consequently π. γ. could refer to any writing that Christians considered inspired, not only to the OT." (Piñero, "Sobre el Sentido de θεόπνευστος: 2 Tim 3:16," 146, n. 13).

which he shall likely continue to experience trial and difficulty.[25] Furthermore, as he presses on with his lesson concerning πᾶσα γραφή, Paul asserts that the purpose served by γραφή relative to "teaching," "reproof," "restoration," and "training in righteousness" is ἵνα ἄρτιος ᾖ ὁ τοῦ θεοῦ ἄνθρωπος, πρὸς πᾶν ἔργον ἀγαθὸν ἐξηρτισμένος. The apparent implication is two-fold. On the one hand, the text shows that, apart from γραφή, the "man of God" does not stand "prepared" or "equipped for every good work," which makes πᾶσα γραφή essential to godliness. On the other hand, since a knowledge of πᾶσα γραφή makes the "man of God" ἄρτιος and πρὸς πᾶν ἔργον ἀγαθὸν ἐξηρτισμένος, this γραφή is therefore not only *necessary* for godliness; it also is *sufficient* to that end.[26] Thus, taking into consideration both the fervor with which Paul seeks to uphold the gospel message entrusted to him and the urgency with which he calls Timothy to fresh resolve as a determined guardian and trustee of that message, he cannot possibly view τὸ εὐαγγέλιον as merely ancillary or supplemental to the OT writings.[27] Rather, τὸ εὐαγγέλιον, expressed in 3:14 as οἷς ἔμαθες καὶ ἐπιστώθης, must serve as at least one vital part of the referent for πᾶσα γραφή that is so ὠφέλιμος that with it, ὁ τοῦ θεοῦ ἄνθρωπος is in fact ἄρτιος and πρὸς πᾶν ἔργον ἀγαθὸν ἐξηρτισμένος.

25. Lock reflects this position, stating, "Here stress is only laid on such as affect the teacher's task in face of misleading teaching" (Lock, *Pastoral Epistles*, 110). See also Marshall, *Pastoral Epistles*, 795–96; Spicq, *Les Épîtres Pastorales*, 379; Towner, *Letters to Timothy and Titus*, 593–94.

26. Consequently, even as Cothenet, Towner, and Witherington, among others (see note 22 above), maintain that both [τὰ] ἱερὰ γράμματα and πᾶσα γραφή refer only to the OT, they also must presume the presence of the apostolic gospel proclamation in some form alongside the OT as an essential element for leaving the "man of God" ἄρτιος and πρὸς πᾶν ἔργον ἀγαθὸν ἐξηρτισμένος. However, none of these offers a detailed accounting for that gospel message and its role relative to the "man of God."

27. At this point, some sources that equate πᾶσα γραφή with [τὰ] ἱερὰ γράμματα nevertheless exhibit an inconsistency in their analyses, as they also affirm the necessity of the gospel teaching as part of the Christian's instruction. For example, Witherington asserts, "This wisdom, however, comes only through faith in Christ, not just from knowledge of the Hebrew Scriptures" (Witherington, *Letters and Homilies*, 359). The problem with this position lies in the perception, on the one hand, of the need to interpret OT Scripture so as to make it consistent with the gospel, while, on the other hand, acknowledging the existence of only one body of authoritative γραφή: namely, the OT. See also Hasler, *Die Briefe an Timotheus und Titus*, 75.

Reflection upon 3:14–17 Relative to 3:10–13 and 4:1–4

Σὺ δέ, with which Paul opens 3:10–13 (as he also does 3:14–17), emphatically signals a pointed distinction between Timothy and οἱ ἄνθρωποι, whom Paul describes as φίλαυτοι φιλάργυροι ἀλαζόνες ὑπερήφανοι βλάσφημοι, γονεῦσιν ἀπειθεῖς, ἀχάριστοι ἀνόσιοι ἄστοργοι ἄσπονδοι διάβολοι ἀκρατεῖς ἀνήμεροι ἀφιλάγαθοι προδόται προπετεῖς τετυφωμένοι, φιλήδονι μᾶλλον ἢ φιλόθεοι (3:2–4).[28] However, while the godless men are described in terms of unholy behaviors and impulses, Timothy παρηκολούθησεν . . . τῇ διδασκαλίᾳ, τῇ ἀγωγῇ, τῇ προθέσει, τῇ πίστει, τῇ μακροθυμίᾳ, τῇ ἀγάπῃ, τῇ ὑπομονῇ, τοῖς διωγμοῖς, τοῖς παθήμασιν of Paul. In other words, the variable that seems to have anchored Timothy in right conduct was precisely the teaching and example of Paul. Against Timothy's example, the lives and conduct of the godless men stand in sharp relief. When Paul returns from his brief discussion of the godless men and resumes his instructions to Timothy (3:14), he reiterates the Σὺ δέ of 3:10, this time urging him, "Continue in the things you have learned and have come to believe." Considering the two apparently parallel occurrences of Σὺ δέ that initiate two sets of comments directed to Timothy, the first of which reminds Timothy of what he had followed, and the second of which admonishes him to continue in what he has believed, it is most reasonable to equate the "teaching" that Timothy had followed so closely with the "things [Timothy] learned and [had] come to believe."[29] Indeed, one could say that ἡ διδασκαλία—or οἷς ἔμαθες καὶ ἐπιστώθης— has in fact already served to set Timothy apart from the profane men so thoroughly indicted by Paul. Attending to these points of contact between 3:10–13 and 3:14–17—specifically, the twin occurrences of Σὺ δέ and the parallelism between what Timothy followed and that in which he was to remain—permits the coherent integration of the two segments and supports the notion that οἷς ἔμαθες καὶ ἐπιστώθης almost

---

28. Marshall likewise observes, "The instruction proceeds with the familiar reversion to exhortation to the reader with σὺ δέ (3.10) which contrasts him with the ungodly" (Marshall, *Pastoral Epistles*, 787). See also Bassler, *1 Timothy, 2 Timothy, Titus*, 162–63; Bernard, *Pastoral Epistles*, 133; Collins, *Timothy and Titus*, 260–61; Guthrie, *Pastoral Epistles*, 172; Johnson, *Letters to Timothy*, 416–17; Knight, *Pastoral Epistles*, 438; Quinn and Wacker, *Letters to Timothy*, 738–39; Spicq, *Les Épîtres Pastorales*, 372, 375; Towner, *Letters to Timothy and Titus*, 570; Van Neste, *Cohesion and Structure*, 203.

29. Van Neste notes, "Timothy has both a model of 'teaching' (διδασκαλία) in Paul (v. 10), and source of teaching (διδασκαλία) in the Scriptures (v. 16)" (Van Neste, *Cohesion and Structure*, 182).

certainly refers to the apostolic teaching that has held such a prominent position throughout the letter.[30] Not only is this the case, but this stream of ideas bridging 3:10–13 to 3:14–17 also indicates that the topic most on Paul's mind remains this same apostolic gospel message. In other words, there is a kind of rhetorical momentum passing from 3:10–13 to 3:14–17 that is carried by the notion and importance of the gospel message.

Looking to the other side of 3:14–17, 4:1–2 reads, Διαμαρτύρομαι ἐνώπιον τοῦ θεοῦ καὶ Χριστοῦ Ἰησοῦ . . . κήρυξον τὸν λόγον. This solemn charge follows hard upon the affirmation that πᾶσα γραφή leads to a situation in which ἄρτιος ᾖ ὁ τοῦ θεοῦ ἄνθρωπος, πρὸς πᾶν ἔργον ἀγαθὸν ἐξηρτισμένος. In the process, it also features the final occurrence of λόγος in 2 Timothy pertaining to the apostolic proclamation (and which essentially complements the οἷς ἔμαθες καὶ ἐπιστώθης of 3:14),[31] even as Paul initiates his closing exhortations in terms of the principal command, κήρυξον τὸν λόγον. Paul gives this general command additional contouring when he writes, ἐπίστηθι εὐκαίρως ἀκαίρως, ἔλεγξον, ἐπιτίμησον, παρακάλεσον, ἐν πάσῃ μακροθυμίᾳ καὶ διδαχῇ, here construed as specific elements that comprise the preaching of "the word." Three details emerge as especially significant relative to the construal of 3:14–17 proposed above.

First, in spite of all of the critical mass standing behind the prevailing interpretation of πᾶσα γραφή as a reference to the OT only, Paul in fact presses ahead in 4:1–4 undeterred and undistracted in his sustained concentration upon the gospel message entrusted to Timothy. In other

---

30. Johnson, *Letters to Timothy*, 419; Marshall, *Pastoral Epistles*, 787; Spicq, *Les Épîtres Pastorales*, 375.

31. As Collins declares, "In the Pastor's circles, 'the word' (*ho logos*) was used as a cipher for the Christian message. 'The word' is the word of God (2:9; 1 Tim 4:5; Titus 1:3; 2:5), the message of truth (2:15), the words of faith (1 Tim 4:6). This word is summarized in trustworthy sayings (*pistos ho logos*). Charged with preaching the word, Timothy is to proclaim Paul's gospel message. The ministry of the word of God is the one ministry without which a Christian community cannot exist" (Collins, *Timothy and Titus*, 269). Fee writes, "Above all else, Timothy must proclaim the message of the gospel, which here has the same effect as the charge to 'guard the deposit' in 1 Timothy 6:20 and 2 Timothy 1:14. *This is what the whole appeal from 1:6 to 3:17 is all about*" (Fee, *Timothy and Titus*, 284, emphasis mine). Similarly, Marshall also states, "ὁ λόγος (1 Tim 1.15 note) by itself is 'the Christian message'; it is usually qualified in some way as 'the word of God', 'the word of truth', etc. (2.9, 15; 1 Thess 1.6; Gal 6.6; Acts 8.4; 10.36–44; 14.25; 16.6, et al.), but by this point in the letter no fuller description is needed" (Marshall, *Pastoral Epistles*, 800). Also, of the seven instances of λόγος in 2 Tim, two of these refer to speech: Either that of the godless men (2:17), or that of Paul and his ministry partners (4:15).

words, Paul's attention, on the one hand, remains fixed upon the chief topic of his letter, the apostolic proclamation that suffers no rival and for which Timothy stands prepared to suffer. On the other hand, the force and scope of his assertion that πᾶσα γραφή is of such an origin and quality that leaves the "man of God" fully equipped for executing the duties appointed to him would seem out of scale if it were to be viewed only with reference to the OT writings.

Second, if, as so many assert, Paul actually lauds the qualities of the OT writings alone in 3:16–17, one might not only ask why any other proclamation is necessary or desirable, but also why, at this strategic and climactic point in his letter, Paul would suspend his rhetorical movement by briefly digressing upon an excursus concerning the God-given and eminently profitable OT Scripture. In this case, 3:16–17 would tend to divert attention away from the main point of the letter, however briefly, just as Paul was swinging into his closing and climactic admonitions in 4:1–2 and beyond.[32] This would have the added effect of having to restart the prior rhetorical scheme at 4:1 without the benefit of a clear textual warrant.

Third, and as noted in the previous chapter, while πᾶσα γραφή is profitable for διδασκαλία, ἐλεγμός, ἐπανόρθωσις, παιδεία ἡ ἐν δικαιοσύνῃ ("teaching," "reproof," "restoration," "training in righteousness"), the outworking of the principal admonition κήρυξον τὸν λόγον also involves the specific charges ἐπίστηθι εὐκαίρως ἀκαίρως, ἔλεγξον, ἐπιτίμησον, παρακάλεσον, ἐν πάσῃ μακροθυμίᾳ καὶ διδαχῇ ("stand ready in season, out of season," "reprove," "rebuke," "exhort, with all patience and instruction").[33] Accordingly, it must be noted that two of these expressions, ἐλέγχω and διδαχή in 4:2, explicitly recall ἐλέγμος and διδασκαλία of 3:16. More importantly, however, when looking at more than individual terms, the rhetorical products of the two sets of ideas, while not mirror images, must certainly be acknowledged as similar. In other words, it is a simple observation that while "all Scripture" is effective "for teaching, for reproof, for restoration, for training in righteousness," the preaching

32. Fee also sees 4:1–2 as the pinnacle of Paul's argument, writing, "Above all else, Timothy must proclaim the message of the gospel, which here has the same effect as the charge to 'guard the deposit' in 1 Timothy 6:20 and 2 Timothy 1:14. This is what the whole appeal from 1:6 to 3:17 is all about" (Fee, *Timothy and Titus*, 284). At the same time, exactly how a discussion of the merits of the OT in 3:14–17 serves this "appeal" he does not make clear.

33. Guthrie, *Pastoral Epistles*, 178; Johnson, *Letters to Timothy*, 428; Marshall, *Pastoral Epistles*, 801; Spicq, *Les Épîtres Pastorales*, 385.

of ὁ λόγος includes among its elements the responsibilities to "reprove, rebuke, exhort, with all patience and instruction."[34] This strongly suggests that the kinds of duties for which πᾶσα γραφή equips the man of God are in fact executed as part of the process of preaching "the word," or the apostolic gospel proclamation. Further securing the correspondence between λόγος here and the apostolic message, Paul justifies his exhortation in the subsequent clause by tying it to previous references to that same proclamation (this time designated ὑγιαίνουσα διδασκαλία) as he writes ἔσται . . . καιρὸς ὅτε τῆς ὑγιαινούσης διδασκαλίας οὐκ ἀνέξονται (4:3).[35] This would therefore indicate that the proclamation of the word (ὑγιαίνουσα διδασκαλία, ὁ λόγος, and οἷς ἔμαθες καὶ ἐπιστώθης) is in fact equivalent to the proclamation of πᾶσα γραφή that Paul deems so well suited to the tasks appointed to the man of God. Thus, contrary to the prevailing position on the matter, Paul does not distinguish between πᾶσα γραφή and ὁ λόγος.[36]

2 Timothy and γραφή

Over the course of three consecutive literary units (3:10–13, 3:14–17, and 4:1–4), as with the rest of the letter leading into these units, the main topic of Paul's reflection and instruction is the apostolic gospel proclamation that Timothy has been commanded to guard, proclaim, and hand down to other trustworthy men, and for which he is to suffer persecution. Even with Paul's brief reference to τὰ ἱερὰ γράμματα, he remains undeterred in his promotion of the primary subject of concern. Indeed, his remark concerning τὰ ἱερὰ γράμματα itself serves as one of the bases supporting the excellence of οἷς ἔμαθες καὶ ἐπιστώθης (3:14), or the apostolic gospel message. In view of the various criteria examined here, it seems highly

---

34. Van Neste observes, "The four nouns in 3.16 anticipate the imperatives of 4.2. Specifically, διδαχή (4.2) connects with διδασκαλία (3.16) and ἐλέγχω (4.2) picks up on ἐλεγμός (3.16). Both lists seem to alternate: positive, negative, positive, negative. The combination of teaching and rebuking is clear in both verses" (Van Neste, *Cohesion and Structure*, 207).

35. Bernard, *Pastoral Epistles*, 141; Fee, *Timothy and Titus*, 285–86; Johnson, *Letters to Timothy*, 429; Kelly, *Pastoral Epistles*, 206; Marshall, *Pastoral Epistles*, 801–2; Towner, *Goal of Our Instruction*, 122–23.

36. Along with ὁ λόγος τῆς ἀληθείας, ἡ ἀλήθεια, ἡ παραθήκη, ὁ [πιστὸς] λόγος, ὁ λόγος τοῦ θεοῦ, τὸ εὐαγγέλιον, ὑγιαίνουσα ὑγιαίνουσα, ἡ πίστις, τὸ κήρυγμα, ὑποτύπωσις . . . ὑγιαινόντων λόγων ὧν παρ᾽ ἐμοῦ ἤκουσας, ἃ ἤκουσας παρ᾽ ἐμοῦ, τὸ εὐαγγέλιόν μου, and οἷς ἔμαθες καὶ ἐπιστώθης.

unlikely that Paul would privilege τὰ ἱερὰ γράμματα alone as adequate to prepare Timothy for the duties that fall to him as the pastor in Ephesus and as worthy of his confidence. Therefore, on the basis of the close exegetical analysis of 3:14–17 in isolation, and as it fits within the more extended discourse of 3:10—14:4, πᾶσα γραφή in its immediate literary context should be construed as a reference to the combined witness of the apostolic gospel message alongside all of the recognized OT writings.[37]

One final point must be acknowledged here. While the case has been made that πᾶσα γραφή serves as a reference to the integration of the apostolic gospel teaching with the OT writings, unlike ἡ γραφή in 1 Tim 5:18, it has not yet been shown that πᾶσα γραφή in 2 Tim 3:16 must refer to a *written* form of that apostolic message. Certainly, a written form of the gospel message would suit the thesis of this study, as well as the exegetical criteria adduced in 2 Timothy. Indeed, the currently prevailing position concerning πᾶσα γραφή inherently presumes a written referent. However, based strictly upon the literary context of 2 Timothy alone, one need not conclude that γραφή or any of the other terms Paul uses to refer to his apostolic teaching refers to a written gospel. This point shall be addressed further in the final two chapters.

37. In truth, while the argument presented here is distinct, the *position* of the present study concerning this particular point does not differ markedly from that of Knight, who writes, "In this letter Paul has praised Timothy for following his teaching (v. 10), has urged Timothy to continue in what he has learned from Paul (v. 14) has commanded Timothy to retain 'the standard of sound words' that he has heard from Paul (1:13), has commanded him to entrust what he has heard from Paul to faithful men so that they could teach others (2:2), and has insisted that Timothy handle accurately 'the word of truth' (2:15). After his remarks on πᾶσα γραφή he will urge Timothy to 'preach the word' (4:2), i.e., proclaim the apostolic message, about which Paul has said so much in this letter. It seems possible therefore, that Paul by his use of πᾶσα γραφή is expanding the earlier reference to the OT to include those accounts of the gospel that may have been extant and perhaps also his own and other apostolic writings that have been 'taught by the Spirit' (1 Cor 2:13; cf. for this view, e.g., Stott). This understanding also fits well in this context. It provides a reason for Paul's use of πᾶσα and for his change from ἱερὰ γράμματα, an OT designation, to πᾶσα γραφή, a possibly more inclusive term. It would gather together Paul's concern for the preservation and communication of the gospel and the apostolic understanding and application of that gospel and place it on a par with the OT, as 2 Pet 3:16–17 clearly does. And it would provide a clearer background for and transition to his demand that Timothy 'preach the word' (4:2)" (Knight, *Pastoral Epistles*, 448).

CHAPTER 7

Γραφη in Philo, Josephus, the LXX, the New Testament, and the Apostolic Fathers

THUS FAR, IN A comprehensive endeavor to assess γραφή and its intended meaning as it appears in 1 and 2 Timothy, this study has presented a thorough evaluation of the prevailing discourse and semantic streams running through both letters (see chapters 3 and 5), and a synchronic analysis of γραφή in its immediate literary context as it occurs in each letter (see chapters 4 and 6). Now offering an examination of γραφή along a third (and diachronic) axis, this chapter offers an assessment of the wider use of γραφή to provide a stronger sense of both the possibilities and the limits of the semantic domain within which any interpretation must work. Such a perspective is sought by sifting through literature from approximately the same frame of reference as that reflected in the PE: namely, those writings that come from or acknowledge the authoritative materials of the Jewish and early Christian traditions. Accordingly, the following data comprise a survey of γραφή as it is used in Philo, Josephus, the LXX, the whole of the New Testament, and the Apostolic Fathers.[1] In addition, an evaluation of כתב in the Hebrew Masoretic Text will accompany the survey of the LXX.[2] Whereas several sources have put forward partial appraisals similar to that which is presented here, in most cases, the parameters of these works have permitted little more than summaries

1. Sources and scholarly literature for the survey of Philo, Josephus, the New Testament, and the Apostolic Fathers include *Josephus*; NA[27]; *Philo*; Schrenk, "γράφω, γραφή, γράμμα, κ.τ.λ.," 749–73; Ehrman, *Apostolic Fathers*.

2. The HMT, found in the BHS, is based chiefly upon L, the Leningrad Codex B 19A (BHS, xii, xiv; Soulen and Soulen, *Handbook of Biblical Criticism*, 110).

and generalized commentary.[3] By contrast, this study will provide a list of the various ways in which γραφή may most plausibly be translated for each set of writings, with a sample text representing each classification.[4] Among the additional details provided, the examination of כתב shall include an evaluation of the *Kethib-Qere* principle[5] and its effect upon the continuity between כתב and γραφή. In the meantime, analysis of γραφή in the NT will be attended by a brief examination of two texts (1 Cor 15:3–5 and 2 Pet 3:15–16) that may suggest the existence and circulation of a written gospel during the life and ministry of Paul.[6] At the end of this discussion, the following data will show that for all of the lexical values that attend γραφή, *every instance surveyed, without exception, pertains to something physically written or drawn.*

Philo

Among the fifty-five instances assessed in Philo, γραφή may be translated as "charge (written)," "decree (written)" or "law (written)," "document," "design," "painting" or "picture," "Scripture" or "holy writing," "list,"[7] and "writing (in the sense of inscription, text, or written work)."[8] In Philo,

---

3. See, for instance, Collins, *Timothy and Titus*, 261–63; Johnson, *Letters to Timothy*, 419–24; Knight, *Pastoral Epistles*, 443–48; Mounce, *Pastoral Epistles*, 565–69; Marshall, *Pastoral Epistles*, 789–92; Quinn and Wacker, *Letters to Timothy*, 748–50, 756–62; Towner, *Letters to Timothy and Titus*, 58–59, 581–83; Witherington, *Letters and Homilies*, 359.

4. Unless otherwise noted, the translations provided in the samples below are the author's. The remaining instances of any given classification then will be listed by source. This approach provides, on the one hand, sufficient data to offer a fair sense of usage, thus accounting for any generalizations and conclusions appearing in this chapter, while on the other hand, avoiding so much detail that the point of the survey is lost. At the same time, there is enough documentation for follow-up or further examination, should that prove desirable.

5. This refers to the Masoretic principle of distinguishing carefully between *kethib* "what is written" and *qere* "what is read" (Morrow, "Kethib and Qere," 4:24–30).

6. While this proposal has been argued previously in chapter 4 relative to 2 Cor 8:18, the point here lies in drawing attention to specific additional texts that lend further support to the same argument in their use of γραφή.

7. One occurrence only, in *Flacc.* 185.

8. BDAG, 206b; Louw and Nida, *Greek-English Lexicon of the New Testament*, 33.53; Schrenk, "γράφω, γραφή, γράμμα, κ.τ.λ.," 749–51, 754–55. Generally speaking without respect to specific literary collections or writers, Schrenk includes among his possible renderings, "writing," "written characters," "the art of writing," "what is

the most numerous uses of γραφή are those instances best rendered as "Scripture." Also, when Philo uses γραφή to convey the notion of "Scripture," he usually modifies it with a form of ἱερά.[9]

γραφή = "Charge (Decree, Law)"

Post. 38

κἂν ἄρα τις γραφὴν ἀσεβείας ἐπενέγκῃ καθ᾽ ὑμῶν, ἀπολογούμενοι θαρρεῖτε. ("And if, then, anyone brings against you a charge of ungodliness, you are bold, as you defend yourself.")

Sacr. 71; *Decal.* 51; *Mos.* 2.203.

γραφή = "Painting (Picture, Design)"

Cher. 11

...ὡς γραφαί τε καὶ ἀνδριάντες ἀρχέτθποι γραφεῦσι καὶ πλάσταις. ("...as pictures and statues are patterns for painters and sculptors.")

Cher. 104; *Post.* 113; *Agr.* 168; *Ios.* 87; *Mos.* 1.158, 1.287; *Spec.* 1.33, 4.55; *Virt.* 51; *Prob.* 62, 94; *Prov.* 2.17; *Legat.* 148, 151, 365.

γραφή = "Scripture (Holy writing, Sacred writing)"[10]

Opif. 77*

ἐφ᾽ἅπασι γὰρ τοῖς ἄλλοις αὐτον ὁ ποιητὴς καὶ πατήρ, ὥσπερ αἱ ἱεραὶ γραφαὶ μηνύουσιν, εἰργάσατο. ("...for, after all other things, the Maker and Father [created] him, just as the *holy writings* make known.")

---

inscribed (inscription)," "copy," "drawing," "picture," "painting," "art," "written statement in personal or official dealings," "record," "document," "genealogy," "contract," "list," "decree," "edict," "published work," "written law or statute," "prescription," "Holy Scripture" (ibid., 749–50).

9. According to Helmut Burkhardt, Philo's concept of "Scripture" included non-canonical writings that he viewed as "divine," some of which originated in Greek mystery religions (Burkhardt, *Die Inspiration heiliger Schriften bei Philo von Alexandrien*, 73–149).

10. Instances in which γραφή is modified by ἱερά are marked with an asterisk.

Her. 106*, 159*, 286*; *Congr.* 34*, 90*; *Fug.* 4*; *Abr.* 4*, 61*, 68, 121*, 131, 236; *Mos.* 2.84*; *Decal.* 8*, 37*; *Spec.* 1.214*, 2.104*, 2.134*.

γραφή = "Writing (Document, Text, Inscription, Text, Work)"

Ebr. 11

τὰ μὲν οὖν ὡσανεὶ προοίμια τῆς γραφῆς ἀρκούντως λέλεκται. ("So then, it is as though the preface of this *work* stands told enough.")

Conf. 14; *Migr.* 34; *Her.* 167 (two occurrences), 266; *Somn.* 1.1; *Abr.* 11, 23; *Mos.* 2.40, 2.51, 2.74, *Spec.* 1.1; *Praem.* 65; *Legat.* 276.

Josephus

In the various works of Josephus, γραφή occurs twenty-six times and may be translated as "literature," "painting" or "picture," "report (written)," "Scripture" or "holy writing," "text" or "inscription," and "work (written)."[11] In Josephus, γραφή usually refers to specific writings (whether of reports, instructions, or books). Only in one of two instances in which Josephus uses γραφή to convey the idea of "Scripture" does he modify it with a form of ἱερά.

γραφή = "Painting (Picture, Design)"

A.J. 19.7

τῶν τε ἱερῶν τῶν Ἑλληνικῶν οὐδὲν ἔτι ἀσύλητον κατέλιπεν ὁπόσα γραφῆς ἢ γλυφῆς ἐχόμενα καὶ τὰς λοιπὰς κατασκευὰς ἀνδριάντων καὶ ἀναθημάτων ἄγεσθαι κελεύσας παρ' αὐτόν. ("Of the temples of the Greeks, he left none inviolate, commanding that as many *paintings* and sculptures and the remaining articles of statuary and dedicatory items which were had be brought to him.")

B.J. 7.159

11. Schrenk, "γράφω, γραφή, γράμμα, κ.τ.λ.," 750–51, 754–55.

γραφή = "Scripture (Holy writing, Sacred writing)"

C. Ap. 2.45*

ἐπιθυμητὴς ἐγένετο τοῦ γνῶναι τοὺς ἡμετέρους νόμους καὶ ταῖς τῶν ἱερῶν γραφῶν βίβλοις ἐντυχεῖν. ("He became one who desired to know our laws and to read the books of our *holy writings*.")

B.J. 5.20

γραφή = "Writing (Literature, Report, Text, Work)"

Vita 361

ὀυ μὴν ἐγώ σοι τὸν αὐτὸν τρόπον περὶ τῆς ἐμαυτοῦ γραφῆς ἔδεισα. ("I certainly had no fear of the same issue as yours relative to my *work*.")

Vita 358; *C. Ap.* 1.236, 2.147, 2.288; *A.J.* 1.3, 1.7, 1.129, 3.38, 3.74, 3.94, 3.101, 3.218, 3.223, 3.259, 4.197, 4.302, 8.132, 10.218, 12.226, 14.265, 15.417, 16.183, 16.185, 19.298.

LXX

Across the breadth of the LXX,[12] containing the thirty-seven instances that are assessed here, γραφή may be translated as "document (or record or report)," "letter (correspondence),"[13] "record" or "report," "roll" or "genealogy," or "Scripture."[14] Perhaps of greatest significance at this point is the fact that in the LXX, γραφή alone is used to refer to Scripture.[15]

γραφή = "Document (Report, Writing)"

Deut 10:4

12. For this study, information is drawn from both the LXX, Rahlfs edition and the LXX, Göttingen edition.

13. One instance only, in Ezra 4:7.

14. LEH, 124; Schrenk, "γράφω, γραφή, γράμμα, κ.τ.λ.," 749–50.

15. As opposed to the parallel use of γράμμα to denote Scripture, as occurs in the NT (e.g., 2 Tim 3:15). Also, the apocryphal (or deuterocanonical) books included in the LXX are listed after the canonical books and appear in italics.

καὶ ἔγραψεν ἐπὶ τὰς πλάκας κατὰ τὴν γραφὴν τὴν πρώτην τοὺς δέκα λόγους. ("And he wrote upon the tablets, according to the first *writing*, the ten words.")

Exod 32.16 (2 occurrences); 1 Chr 28:19; 2 Chr 2:10, 24:27, 35:4; Ezra 7:22; Ps 86:6; Dan 5:7, 5:8, 5:15, 5:16, 5:24, 5:25, 6:9, 10:21;[16] *1 Esd* 1:4; *1 Macc* 12:21, 14:27, 14:48; *2 Macc* 2:4; *3 Macc* 2:27; *Sir* 39:32, 42:7, 44:5, 45:11.

γραφή = "Genealogy (Roll)"

Ezra 2:62

οὗτοι ἐζήτησαν γραφὴν αὐτῶν οἱ μεθωεσιμ καὶ οὐχ εὑρέθησαν. ("These sought their *genealogy* recorded in a list, but they were not found.")

Neh 7:64; Ezek 13:9; *1 Esd* 5:39, 8:30.

γραφή = "Scripture"

1 Chr 15:15

καὶ ἔλαβον οἱ υἱοὶ τῶν Λευιτῶν τὴν κιβωτὸν τοῦ θεοῦ ὡς ἐνετείλατο Μωυσῆς ἐν λόγῳ θεοῦ κατὰ τὴν γραφήν. ("And the sons of Levi took the ark of God as Moses commanded in the word of God according to the *Scripture*.")

1 Chr 30:5, 30:18; Ezra 6:18; *4 Macc* 18:14.

16. The references shown from Daniel are taken from θ', the Theodotian text, which follows the MT much more closely at this point than the LXX text does (Rahlfs, LXX, 870–936; LXX, [16/2], 311–75). Its more conspicuous adherence to the Hebrew text should not be surprising, since the Theodotian version represents one of three distinctly Jewish translations offered as an alternative to the Alexandrian version that became so congenial to the Christian movement (Jellicoe, *Septuagint and Modern Study*, 83).

Masoretic Text

Apart from three instances in which γραφή translates מכתב, essentially a synonym of כתב,[17] two in which it translates a participial form of כתב,[18] and one in which it translates the infinitive of כתב,[19] every other incidence of γραφή in the canonical books of the LXX corresponds to an occurrence of כתב in the BHS.[20] In addition, כתב appears in the BHS in three passages that the LXX leaves untranslated,[21] and one in which כתב is translated by ἐπιστολή,[22] while the LXX features γραφή in one minor addition to material found in 1 Chr 15:15 in the BHS. Working from the opposite direction, there remain several occurrences of כתב in the MT that the LXX translates with expressions that are different from, though semantically equivalent with γραφή, such as γραπτόν, ἐγγραφή, and λέξις.[23] However, in the vast majority of instances in which כתב is used in the Hebrew text, its usage conforms precisely to that of γραφή in the Greek, and it *always* refers to something that assumes a physically written form. Specifically, as it occurs in the BHS, כתב may be translated,

17. Exod 32:16 (two occurrences) and Deut 10:4. For translations of כתב, Brown, Driver, and Briggs include "writing," "register," "mode of writing," "character," "letter," "edict," and "a book of truth," while for מכתב, "hand-writing," and "thing written" are added (BDB, 508). See also *TWOT*, 1:458–59; Schrenk, "γράφω, γραφή, γράμμα, κ.τ.λ.," 749–50.

18. 2 Chr 30:5 and 30:18.

19. Ps 87:6 (86:6 in the LXX).

20. As noted above (note 16), the instances in Daniel that correspond to the MT are drawn from the Theodotian version of the Greek OT, since the LXX departs from the MT significantly throughout Daniel (See Rahlfs, LXX, 870–936; LXX [16/2], 311–75). Nevertheless, Schrenk notes explicitly, "In the LXX γραφή is always the rendering of מכתב, כתב, כתוב, and once מדרש (2 Chron 24:27)" (Schrenk, "γράφω, γραφή, γράμμα, κ.τ.λ.," 749). However, in spite of the final point of Schrenk's observation here, as well as his assertion, " ספר is never γραφή but βιβλίον, βίβλος" (ibid.), it is somewhat unclear exactly what γραφή is intended to translate in 2 Chr in 2 Chr 24:27, it appears that it *may* translate ספר instead of מדרש, or that the one Greek word may be intended to translate the entire idea expressed in the construction, על־מדרש ספר. This impression is even stronger when one takes into consideration the absence of βιβλίον or βίβλος to translate ספר.

21. These are Esth 4:8, 8:9, and 9:27. Also, the BHS features one instance of מכתב in 2 Chr 35:4 that the LXX does not translate explicitly but may be understood as an elliptical instance of γραφή.

22. Esth 8:13 [12a] (Rahlfs, LXX, 967; LXX [8/3], 189).

23. Γραπτόν appears in Ezra 1:1 and 2 Chr 36:22, ἐγγραφή in 2 Chr 21:12, and λέξις in Esth 1:22, 3:12, and 8:9 (LEH, 124b, 167a, 370ab; Schrenk, "γράφω, γραφή, γράμμα, κ.τ.λ.," 769–70).

"decree (written)," "document (or record, report, or writing)," "letter (Correspondence),"[24] "roll" or "genealogy,"[25] or "Scripture."[26] The examples presented below are those that correspond to instances of γραφή in the LXX and that have not yet been discussed.

כתב = "Document (Inscription, Record, Report, Writing)"

1 Chr 28:19

הכל בכתב מיד יהוה עלי השכיל כל מלאכות התבנית ("All this in *writing*, from the hand of the Lord upon me, I was made to understand.")

1 Chr 28:19; 2 Chr 2:10, 35:4; Dan 5:7, 5:8, 5:15, 5:16, 5:17; 5:24, 5:2510:21; Ezra 4:7, 6:18, 7:22, 7:64.

כתב, γραφή, and the Principle of Kethib-Qere

The real significance of the preceding survey and comparison of כתב with γραφή becomes more apparent when one reflects as well upon rabbinic principles and practices that pertain to Scripture. In the case of letters written by Paul—including the letters to Timothy in this study—such a reflection is especially important since these principles and practices likely influenced Paul's perspective on the handling of Scripture. These standards take root in the rabbinic view of Torah. While the term "Torah," construed most narrowly, refers only to the Pentateuch, it also may be used to designate the whole of the Hebrew Scriptures, the "sacred Scriptures" of the Jews, or even "the whole of authoritative, sacred tradition" both written and oral.[27] At the same time, while the expression itself may convey a range of related ideas, the rabbinic convention concern-

24. One instance only, in Ezra 4:7.
25. Two instances only, in Ezra 2:62 and 13:9.
26. BDB, 508; *TWOT*, 1:458–59; Schrenk, "γράφω, γραφή, γράμμα, κ.τ.λ.," 742, 749–50.
27. Gerhardsson, *Memory and Manuscript*, 20–21; See also Soulen and Soulen, *Handbook of Biblical Criticism*, 198. Also, while Gerhardsson's work consists of a recent 1998 revision and integration of two works first published in 1961 and 1964, in a 2000 review Ellis affirms the continuing "fundamental importance" of this work "for a historical-literary understanding of the New Testament" (Ellis, "Review of Birger Gerhardsson," 98–99).

ing Torah maintained a strict distinction between the written and oral Torah, a distinction that may be traced at least as far back as the time of Hillel and Shammai, who laid the foundations for the Tannaitic tradition that prevailed in Judaism during the first two centuries A.D.[28] As a result of the distinction between written and oral authoritative traditions, according to Gerhardsson, "The text of the written Torah has, during the period with which we are concerned here, i.e., from the beginning of the Christian era, been preserved with remarkable precision."[29] Furthermore, Gerhardsson also writes,

> It is just because it is the Sacred Word, the source of endless riches, which is found in the Scriptures, that each and every syllable must be both preserved and used . . . The perception of the text as sacred leads partly to a desire to preserve the text without corruption . . . Furthermore, certainty that the sacred words of the text have in fact been preserved without distortion adds to the frankness with which the very letter of the text is drawn upon for teaching purposes.[30]

In time, preservation of the Divine Word (or word of God) itself apparently became an end in its own right, a chief point driving the effective formalization of the Tannaitic determination to replicate the text with exactitude.[31] Again, Gerhardsson maintains,

> Rabbinic Judaism had an emphatically repeated rule that the written Torah was *not* to be copied out from memory (כתב מלב, כתב מפה). The written Torah was to be passed on in written form, and must therefore, without question be copied from a written *Vorlage* (כתב מן הכתב). According to R. Johanan, not a single letter might be copied without having the text before one's eyes![32]

28. Gerhardsson, *Memory and Manuscript*, 21. Relative to the link between the Tannaitic tradition and Hillel and Shammai, see also Ferguson, *Backgrounds of Early Christianity*, 461–62; Soulen and Soulen *Handbook of Biblical Criticism*, 186–87.

29. Gerhardsson, *Memory and Manuscript*, 40. Gerhardsson adds that, since that time, "There has continually been a tendency to detailed, static reproduction of its wording" (ibid.). Arie Rubinstein similarly states that "long before the known schools of Masoretes a standard Hebrew text of the Old Testament had become dominant" (Rubenstein, "Kethib-Qere Problem," 127). See also Gordis, *Biblical Text in the Making*, xxxiii.

30. Gerhardsson, *Memory and Manuscript*, 41.

31. Ibid., 42.

32. Ibid., 46.

This earnest determination not to confuse or conflate the written Torah with oral Torah[33] (which eventually attained written form in the Mishnah)[34] long delayed the commitment to writing of Torah tradition that had been handed down orally. Eventually, in keeping with the need to preserve the uncorrupted written text, the Masoretes extended and formalized this concern so as to cover even the vocalized oral transmission of the written tradition, which had the additional effect of averting the transformation of memorized portions of Torah into Scripture (*kethib*), *ipso facto*.[35] This especially pertained to sections or passages in which the orthography of the vocalization (*qere*) could have modified the orthography of the written form. Accordingly, Robert Gordis points out that "the entire spirit of Masoretic activity" entailed "the preservation of the text as it reached them and not its correction or improvement."[36] Thus, while most maintain that the codification of *Kethib-Qere* did not occur until the Masoretic Period, the functional principle itself appears to have been operative during the Rabbinic age.[37]

33. Ibid., 46–47; Morrow, "Kethib and Qere," 24; Soulen and Soulen, *Handbook of Biblical Criticism*, 94, 113–14, 186.

34. Soulen and Soulen, *Handbook of Biblical Criticism*, 113–14, 186.

35. Gerhardsson, *Memory and Manuscript*, 47; Morrow, "Kethib and Qere," 24; Soulen and Soulen, *Handbook of Biblical Criticism*, 94. Gerhardsson adds, "The copyist who wanted to transmit the written Torah according to the 'orthodox' halakah thus had to have a written edition before him" (Gerhardsson, *Memory and Manuscript*, 47). In Aramaic, *Kethib* translates, "It is written," while *Qere* translates, "It is read" (Morrow, "Kethib and Qere," 24–30; Soulen and Soulen, *Handbook of Biblical Criticism*, 94). Jacob Neusner also observes, concerning the distinction between practice and codification of the Kethib/Qere, "The rabbis themselves formulated a number of rules on how to compose the material for successful transmission, how to proceed with teaching and transmission, how to retain memorized tradition in memory, and the like . . . Such rules normally codified an already existing practice. The rules themselves are thus later than a good deal of the transmitted material that appears to conform with them" (Neusner, preface to *Memory and Manuscript*, xi).

36. Gordis, *Biblical Text in the Making*, xiv–xv.

37. See for example, Costacurta, "Implicazioni semantiche in alcuni casi de qere-ketib," 227–39; Morrow, "Kethib and Qere," 27–28; Soulen and Soulen, *Handbook of Biblical Criticism*, 109. At the same time, while Harry Orlinsky asserts "the non-existence of the K-Q system prior to about the sixth to seventh century A.D." (Orlinsky, "Problems of Kethib-Qere," 44), Gordis maintains, with reference to the Tetragrammaton, "The antiquity of this *Kethibh-Qere* is attested by the fact that it was already evident in the Septuagint version of the Torah in the middle of the third century . . . An additional argument in favor of the reliability of [early sources] is the fact that they are attributed to Ezra and the early Sopherim, that is to say to the early Second Commonwealth period, before the destruction of the Temple, and obviously

Among the Tannaitic scholars of the first two centuries, one of the most renowned and revered was Gamaliel the Elder of the rabbinic school of Hillel, who also held a firm commitment to the sharp differentiation between the written Torah and oral Torah tradition.[38] Indeed, according to Gerhardsson, it is Gamaliel the Elder whom Rabbis credit with the origination of the rule and practice inscribed in b Git. 60b., to the effect: "You shall not deliver/transmit sayings (transmitted) in writing orally; you shall not deliver/transmit sayings (transmitted) orally in writing."[39] This same Gamaliel also appears twice in the book of Acts, first as the voice of reason in response to the emerging movement of followers of Jesus (Acts 5:33–40), and then as Paul's own teacher during his early years in Judea (Acts 22:3). The personal and pedagogical connection between

---

long before the Tannaim . . . It is clear that Ezra, or his successors, were concerned not only with establishing the Oral Law for their contemporaries, but with fixing the text of the written Torah as well" (Gordis, *Biblical Text in the Making*, xvii, xx). Emanuel Tov reflects a mediating position, noting, "The notation of the Ketib and Qere in the manuscripts of M derives from a relatively late period, but the practice was already mentioned in the rabbinic literature" (Tov, *Textual Criticism of the Hebrew Bible*, 59). Tov also notes, "Most scholars now adhere to the first intermediate view [that of Gordis]" (ibid., 63). See also Cowley, *Gesenius' Hebrew Grammar*, 65–66; Josephus, *Ant.* 13.297. What matters for the purposes of this study is the wide agreement that, while the actual codification of the K-Q system may not have taken effect until well into the Masoretic Period, there is good reason to suppose that the core principles, particularly zeal for preservation of the original written text of the Torah, were effectively in place and operative in the Rabbinic Age.

38. Concerning this, Gerhardsson writes, "It is clear that the targum was originally oral translation (and interpretation) of the written sacred text. The development which we see during the centuries about the beginning of the Christian era is that the targum begins to be stabilized and copied down. We see Gamaliel and other Pharisaic doctrinal authorities opposing these copies of the targum as *Scripture*, and opposing their use *inter alia* in public worship" (Gerhardsson, *Memory and Manuscript*, 69 n. 1). See also Chilton, "Gamaliel," 903–6; Ferguson, *Backgrounds of Early Christianity*, 462; Goodman, "Rabbis," 1,292; Morrow, "Kethib and Qere," 24; Soulen and Soulen, *Handbook of Biblical Criticism*, 186–87.

39. Gerhardsson, *Memory and Manuscript*, 69, 159. See also the translation provided by Isidore Epstein, "The words which are written thou art not at liberty to say by heart, and the words transmitted orally thou art not at liberty to recite from writing" (Epstein, *Babylonian Talmud*, 4:284). Cf. Epstein's translation of b Tem. 14b, "Those who write the traditional teachings (are punished) like those who burn the Torah, and he who learns from them (the writings) receives no reward . . . Thus teaching you that matters received as oral traditions you are not permitted to recite from writing and that written things (Biblical passages) you are not permitted to recite from memory" (Epstein, *Babylonian Talmud*, 3:98–99).

Gamaliel and Paul forges an additional link between כתב and γραφή that is particularly relevant to this study.[40]

As a former student of Gamaliel, Paul (then Saul of Tarsus) claimed to have acquired training κατὰ ἀκρίβειαν τοῦ πατρῴου νόμου (Acts 22:3), which suggests at least that he would have received instruction as a Tannaitic scholar in accordance with the Tannaitic traditions as understood and articulated by Gamaliel. Here is where the present consideration of γραφή and the Rabbinic principle codified in *Kethib-Qere* intersect, for if Paul were so instructed, and if he had in truth adopted the same zeal for literary exactitude as his teacher (and there is no reason to suppose otherwise), then he would have exhibited great sensitivity and discretion in his use of either כתב or γραφή, both of which function only as references to physically written material.[41] Furthermore, while some may point out that Paul explicitly rejected the τῶν πατρικῶν [αὐτοῦ] παραδόσεων (Gal 1:14), it also is undeniable that he in fact maintained the highest regard for the Law, Prophets, and Writings, and that he appealed to them fre-

---

40. Although, on the basis of a disturbance led by a certain Theudas during the procuratorship of Curspius Fadus, which begin in A.D. 44 after the death of Herod Agrippa I, Chilton seems to suggest that Gamaliel's remarks concerning the rebellions of Theudas and Judas of Galilee as recorded in Acts 5:33–39 exhibit an "inversion of chronological order" (Chilton, "Gamaliel," 904–5). Consequently, he believes this casts doubt upon "the historicity of the entire episode" in Acts, which leads him to view the account as crafted purely for the "programmatic purpose of Luke-Acts" (ibid.). See also Balsdon, Dacre, and Levick, "Claudius," 337–38; Josephus, *Ant.*, 19.343–53, 19.363, 20.97–98; Acts 12:20–23; Ferguson, *Backgrounds of Early Christianity*, 395; Rajak, "Gaius (1)," 619–20. However, while the account of which Chilton writes (and which Josephus reports) does occur sometime during or after A.D. 44, and might not fit the timeframe of Gamaliel's comments as recorded, Josephus also writes of ἕτερα μυρία θορύβων that occurred 3 to 5 years earlier, prior to the procuratorship of Sabinus which bridged the emperorships of Gaius Caligula and Claudius (Josephus, *Ant.*, 17.252, 17.269; Ferguson, *Backgrounds of Early Christianity*, 31–32; Suetonius, *Cal.* 4.58). As these would have been very recent history in Gamaliel's day, the rebellions of Theudas and Judas of Galilee to which he refers quite plausibly could have arisen during this period. Thus, while there is no independent corroboration for Gamaliel's remarks, neither is there any clear data that shows them to be implausible.

41. As Gordis observes, "Paul in his epistles has remarkably little to say about the oral Torah of Pharisaic (Rabbinic) Judaism" (Gordis, *Biblical Text in the Making*, xiv–v). However, Gordis also writes, "In certain situations, however, [Paul] has reason to remind his congregations anew [sic] that he was once a Pharisee, and that he had been exceedingly zealous for the traditions of his fathers (περισσοτέρως ζηλωτὴς ὑπάρχων τῶν πατρικῶν μου παραδόσεων, Gal 1.13 f., Phil 3.5 ff.), by which, as a former Pharisee, he meant both the oral and the written Torah—interpreted in Pharisaic fashion" (ibid.).

quently (and authoritatively) in his instructions to the church. Indeed, what Paul rejected was not Torah itself, but what he determined to have been the errant interpretations of Torah, much of which had become prevailing oral tradition within the Judaism of his day.[42] Thus, while Paul, in his zeal for his new understanding of Torah in light of his encounter with Christ, certainly challenged conventional Jewish understandings and interpretations, he nevertheless upheld the quality of Torah as God's sacred, inviolable, and authoritative word, and very likely retained his passion for the exacting preservation of the text by which that word was transmitted. Consequently, it is highly unlikely that he would have referred to any version of "Jesus sayings," or oral Christian παραδόσις, or indeed anything else not occurring in written form, as γραφή.

דבר־יהוה and ὁ λόγος τοῦ θεοῦ

In addition to the likely effect of the *Kethib-Qere* principle upon Paul's view of what exactly constitutes Scripture, and as argued previously through the analyses of chapters 3 through 6, Paul plainly ascribes to his own apostolic teaching (and to the teaching that Timothy has received) the status of ὁ λόγος τοῦ θεοῦ,[43] an expression that previously would have been reserved for the Torah. Indeed, Gerhardsson traces the connection between Torah and the apostolic tradition (or perhaps even a transition from Torah alone to Torah-and-Gospel) by postulating a common center from which each body of revelation proceeded. Specifically, he points out that the "word of

42. Gerhardsson writes, "Paul claimed, according to Luke: 'I believe everything laid down by the Torah or written in the Prophets' Acts 24.14. In the Apostle's own writings this belief is expressed with unmistakeable confidence: 'Whatever was written in former days (in the Holy Scriptures) was written for our instruction' (ὅσα γὰρ προεγράφη, εἰς τὴν ἡμετέραν διδασκαλίαν ἐγράφη), Rom 15.4; cf. 1 Cor 9.10, 10.11. According to Luke, Paul also confessed, 'I say nothing but what the Prophets and Moses said would come to pass,' Acts 26.22 . . . For Paul, the Scriptures are the words of God (τὰ λογία τοῦ θεοῦ, Rom 3.2). He is entirely in agreement with the opinion that they provide an inexhaustible source of revelation, comfort, teaching, instruction and discipline. It is unthinkable for him that the Scriptures should be dispensed with" (Gerhardsson, *Memory and Manuscript*, 283–84). See also Blum, "Apostles' View of Scripture," 41, 43–47; Fuller, *Gospel and Law*, 88–105; Quinn, "Epistles to Timothy and Titus," 561b; Rosner, "'Written for Us,'" 88–89, 92.

43. Gerhardsson, *Memory and Manuscript*, 214–15; Fitzmyer, "Memory and Manuscript," 452; Karris, "Polemic of the Pastoral Epistles," 558–59; Knight, *Faithful Sayings*, 14–15; Swinson, "Πιστὸς ὁ λόγος: An Alternative Analysis"; Towner, *Goal of Our Instruction*, 123–24.

the Lord," as codified in Deut 17:8, Isa 2:3, and Mic 4:2, always had its seat and point of origin in Jerusalem, "the place which the Lord your God chooses," whence that word would go out to the nation and the world.[44] Likewise, as Gerhardsson observes, "The Risen Lord directs that the Apostles' activity is to begin in Jerusalem" by proclaiming μετάνοιαν εἰς ἄφεσιν ἁμαρτιῶν (Acts 5:31).[45] Showing his own sense of continuity with the revelatory word of God, Paul writes of his gospel proclamation in 1 Corinthians, calling it λόγος . . . ὁ τοῦ σταυροῦ (1:18) and then ὁ λόγος μου καὶ τὸ κήρυγμά μου (2:4).[46] He later gives clear indications that his words are in fact God's words as taught to him by God's spirit (2:12–13).[47] Paul's self-consciousness of the divine source of his own teaching is reflected as well in the letters to Timothy, for as tracing the prominent semantic streams occurring in both 1 and 2 Timothy has shown, the designation or quality of ὁ λόγος τοῦ θεοῦ or ὁ λόγος τοῦ κυρίου pertains to at least seven of eight occurrences of ὁ λόγος in 1 Timothy, and at least five of seven occurrences in 2 Timothy,[48] all of which, it has been argued, refer to the gospel teaching authorized by God and entrusted to the apostolic company for them to preserve and disseminate. As a result, the various points of data presented in the present chapter not only support the notion that ὁ λόγος in 1 and 2

44. Gerhardsson, *Memory and Manuscript*, 214–15. Pao also notes, regarding Luke's "summary statements" in Acts, "Above all, the function of these thematic emphases is to portray the early Christian community as the continuation of the covenant people of the ancient Israelite traditions; and it is in them alone that the word of God is now deposited . . . The first appearance of 'the word' is in Jerusalem" (Pao, *Acts and the Isaianic New Exodus*, 150. See also Alfaro, *Justice and Loyalty*, 47–48; Blenkinsopp, *Isaiah 1–39*, 190–91; Childs, *Isaiah*, 30; Mays, *Micah*, 94. This position also may be implicit in Tigay (Tigay, *Deuteronomy*, 164).

45. Gerhardsson, *Memory and Manuscript*, 216. See also Bock, *Acts*, 63–67, 210, 248; Longenecker, *Acts*, 52–53, 105; Marshall, *Book of Acts*, 61, 107, 120; Moessner, "How Luke Writes," 153, 157, 163; Pao, *Acts and the Isaianic New Exodus*, 150. Accordingly, Wilder also affirms the continuity of the apostolic teaching with the Law and the Prophets, writing, "The NT apostles may best be thought of as the counterparts to the OT prophets" (Wilder, *Pseudonymity, the New Testament, and Deception*, 186).

46. Bachmann, *Der erste Brief des Paulus an die Korinther*, 81–82, 114–16; Schrage, *Der erste Brief an die Korinther*, 1:170–71, 235.

47. Kaiser, "A Neglected Text," 311; Swinson, "'We' Effect, and Its Implications."

48. This point also has been argued throughout chapters 3 to 6. The specific occurrences mentioned are 1 Tim 1:15 (πιστὸς ὁ λόγος), 3:1 (πιστὸς ὁ λόγος), 4:5 (λόγου θεοῦ), 4:6 (τοῖς λόγοις τῆς πίστεως), 4:9 (πιστὸς ὁ λόγος), 5:17 (οἱ κοπιῶντες ἐν λόγῳ καὶ διδασκαλίᾳ), 6:3 (ὑγιαίνουσιν λόγοις τοῖς τοῦ κυρίου ἡμῶν Ἰησοῦ Χριστοῦ); 2 Tim 1:13 (ὑγιαινόντων λόγων ὧν παρ᾽ ἐμοῦ), 2:9 (ὁ λόγος τοῦ θεοῦ), 2:11 (πιστὸς ὁ λόγος), 2:15 (τὸν λόγον τῆς ἀληθείας), 4:2 (κήρυξον τὸν λόγον).

Timothy originates with God and refers to the apostolic gospel proclamation; they also indicate that the stream of revelation that began with Torah reemerges in this very same gospel.

The New Testament and the Apostolic Fathers

By the time of the composition of the NT documents, γραφή seems to have attained a more technical and limited function in Christian writings. Accordingly, the fifty occurrences throughout the NT serve only as references to Scripture, most of which unambiguously pertain to the OT.[49] However, in addition to 1 Tim 5:18 and 2 Tim 3:16, the chief subjects of this study, 1 Cor 15:3–4 and 2 Pet 3:15–16 both exhibit usages of γραφή that may serve as references to authoritative apostolic writings that circulated during the life and ministry of Paul. These will be examined in some detail below.[50]

Throughout the writings of the Apostolic Fathers, nearly every one of the twenty-two instances of γραφή examined refers to Scripture,[51] with four exceptions occurring in Papias, and one other appearing in the Shepherd of Hermas, where they are construed as "book," "writing."[52] Among the explicit seventeen references to Scripture, 2 Clem. 2.4 leads directly into an exact citation of Jesus' words as found in Mark 2:17.[53]

49. Matt 21:42, 22:29, 26:54, 26:56; Mark 12:10, 12:24, 14:49; Luke 4:21, 24:27, 24:32, 24:45; John 2:22, 5:39, 7:38, 7:42, 10:35, 13:18, 17:12, 19:24, 19:28, 19:36–37 (two occurrences), 20:9; Acts 1:16, 8:32, 8:35, 17:2, 17:11, 18:24, 18:28; Rom 1:2, 4:3, 9:17, 10:11, 11:2, 15:4, 16:26; 1 Cor 15:3–4 (two occurrences); Gal 3:8, 3:22, 4:30; [1 Tim 5:18]; [2 Tim 3:16]; Jas 2:8, 2:23, 4:5; 1 Pet 2:6; 2 Pet 1:20, 3:16. See also Schrenk, "γράφω, γραφή, γράμμα, κ.τ.λ.," 749–61.

50. Jean Carmignac also proposes that 2 Cor 3:4–16 gives indications of a written καινὴ διαθήκη that stood alongside and indeed was superior to ἡ ἀναγνώσις τῆς παλαιᾶς διαθήκης. However, as attractive as this hypothesis may be, it is difficult to justify the reading as proposed by Carmignac (Carmignac, "2 Corinthiens 3. 6,14 et le Début de la Formation du Nouveau Testament," 384–86).

51. 1 Clem. 23.3, 23.5, 34.6, 35.7, 42.5, 45.2, 53.1; 2 Clem. 2.4, 6.8, 14.1, 14.2; Barn. 4.7, 4.11, 5.4, 6.12, 13.2, 16.5.

52. One instance occurring in Pap. 3.14, three in Pap. 2, and one in Herm. Vis. 6.1. See also BDAG, 206b; Schrenk, "γράφω, γραφή, γράμμα, κ.τ.λ.," 757–61.

53. 2 Clem. 2.4 reads, καὶ ἑτέρα δὲ γραφὴ λέγει ὅτι οὐκ ἦλθον καλέσαι δικαίους, ἀλλὰ ἁμαρτωλούς, while Mark 2:17 reads, καὶ ἀκούσας ὁ Ἰησοῦς λέγει αὐτοῖς ὅτι οὐ χρείαν ἔχουσιν οἱ ἰσχύοντες ἰατρους ἀλλ᾽ οἱ κακῶς ἔχοντες· οὐκ ἦλθον καλέσαι δικαίους ἀλλὰ ἁμαρτωλούς. Regarding this instance, Ehrman flatly states in his introductory comments, "The words of Jesus are actually called Scripture (2.40) but are nonetheless

1 Corinthians 15:3–5

In 1 Cor 15:1–2, one of the two texts noted above in which γραφή may refer to an early Christian writing, Paul reaffirms τὸ εὐαγγέλιον ὃ εὐηγγελισάμην ὑμῖν, ὃ καὶ παρελάβετε, ἐν ᾧ καὶ ἑστήκατε, δι' οὗ καὶ σῴζεσθε, as he prepares to answer those who claim ἀνάστασις νεκρῶν οὐκ ἔστιν.[54] In the process, he enumerates specific points of the one gospel message, in the cataloguing of which, he twice draws upon one phrase that bears significantly upon this study. 1 Cor 15:3–5 reads,

> παρέδωκα γὰρ ὑμῖν ἐν πρώτοις, ὃ καὶ παρέλαβον, ὅτι Χριστὸς ἀπέθανεν ὑπὲρ τῶν ἁμαρτιῶν ἡμῶν κατὰ τὰς γραφὰς καὶ ὅτι ἐτάφη καὶ ὅτι ἐγήγερται τῇ ἡμέρᾳ τῇ τρίτῃ κατὰ τὰς γραφὰς. καὶ ὅτι ὤφθη Κηφᾷ εἶτα τοῖς δώδεκα.

Twice, in the phrase κατὰ τὰς γραφὰς, Paul refers to αἱ γραφὰι, apparently so as to corroborate the preceding point of gospel teaching. Thus, the assertion, Χριστὸς ἀπέθανεν ὑπέρ τῶν ἁμαρτιῶν ἡμῶν reflects the witness of αἱ γραφὰι. Likewise, the assertion ἐγήγερται τῇ ἡμέρᾳ τῇ τρίτῃ also reflects the testimony of αἱ γραφὰι. This raises a question regarding the precise referent of αἱ γραφὰι. With respect to the first assertion, Χριστὸς ἀπέθανεν ὑπέρ τῶν ἁμαρτιῶν ἡμῶν, most commentators point to the general testimony of the OT as a whole, noting the implied lesson of the sacrificial system regarding the necessity of an atoning death, or to various OT prophecies, such as Isa 53:3–9, in which the servant of God suffers for the sake of the sins of the many.[55] However, while plausible, and while Isaiah certainly does testify to the atoning death of God's Servant, even these possibilities are uncertain and somewhat conjectural. With

---

drawn from oral traditions rather than written Gospels" (Ehrman, *Apostolic Fathers*, 159). However, as the results of this particular study suggest, such a position as that reflected in the last half of his remarks cannot be assumed safely.

54. Fee, *First Epistle to the Corinthians*, 718; Lenski, *Epistle to the Corinthians*, 626, 649; Morris, *Paul to the Corinthians*, 200–201; Thiselton, *First Epistle to the Corinthians*, 1,172, 1,183, 1,216; Thrall, *Paul to the Corinthians*, 103–4.

55. Thrall reflects the uncertainty surrounding these words, writing, "Both the death and the resurrection of Christ are said to have taken place *in accordance with the Scriptures*. If this refers to any specific passage in the Old Testament, perhaps the most likely one is the description in Isa 53 of the suffering and the subsequent exaltation of the Servant of the Lord. Alternatively, Paul's phrase may mean that these events happened in accordance with the fundamental significance of Scripture as a whole. This is little more than saying that Christ's death and resurrection were part of God's plan for mankind, a plan of which the earlier stages are recorded in the Old Testament" (Thrall, *Paul to the Corinthians*, 104).

respect to the second assertion, ἐγήγερται τῇ ἡμέρᾳ τῇ τρίτῃ, the situation grows more complicated, for there exists no specific corresponding OT passage or teaching that bears witness to the resurrection on the third day.[56] Nevertheless, to all appearances, Paul plainly adduces scriptural authority standing behind this confessional point. Several of the explanations offered have some merit and do warrant consideration as possible solutions to the construal of κατὰ τὰς γραφὰς. However, the great uncertainty and lack of consensus attending the discussion makes the endorsement of any one of them difficult, especially since Paul's remark seems so firm, as does the apparent expectation that it readily would be understood and heeded by his readers. Furthermore, considering the skepticism regarding the resurrection that Paul most obviously addresses among the Corinthians in 1 Cor 15, this assertion and its supporting data would seem to be most critical for Paul.[57] Consequently, it is difficult to accept that Paul would rely, as authoritative corroboration of this vital assertion, upon vague or uncertain sources called αἱ γραφαί, or upon a fairly technical interpretive scheme with which the Corinthians may not have been familiar.

Therefore, it is proposed here that the possibility of a circulating written gospel also must be taken into consideration so as to account for Paul's expression, κατὰ τὰς γραφὰς. Consistent with what has been proposed already, it is significant that Luke's gospel explicitly testifies to

56. Though several sources suggest the possibility of Jonah 1:7—2:1 or Hos 6:2, Collins takes an atypical approach, suggesting that the phrase κατὰ τὰς γραφὰς functions as a "hermeneutical key" insofar as it "points the direction in which the scriptural interpreter must go if he or she is to understand the death and resurrection of Christ" (Collins, *First Corinthians*, 530). Morris and others, wrestling with the uncertainty of these remarks, seek to detach ἐγήγερται from τῇ ἡμέρᾳ τῇ τρίτῃ so as to tie it with the phrase κατὰ τὰς γραφὰς, without having to contend with trying to find a scriptural reference to τῇ ἡμέρᾳ τῇ τρίτῃ. For instance, Morris writes, "It is likely that *according to the Scriptures* is to be taken with *was raised*, rather than *with on the third day* . . . There is little Old Testament evidence for a rising on the third day (though some suggest Hos 6:2, or Jonah 1:17), but Isaiah 53:10–12 may fairly be held to prophesy the resurrection" (Morris, *Paul to the Corinthians*, 202, emphasis Morris'). Michael Russell and Jens Christensen both see an OT motif built around "three days" behind Paul's remarks (Christensen, "He Rose on the Third Day," 101–13; Russell, "On the Third Day," 1–17). However, this solution can pertain only to the second instance of κατὰ τὰς γραφὰς.

57. As Christensen also affirms, "That Christ died for our sins and that he rose again the third day, is both singly and jointly the conclusive news, that therefore must be scripturally documented" (Christensen, "He Rose on the Third Day," 101). See also Fee, *First Epistle to the Corinthians*, 726.

most of the fundamental points of the gospel as reviewed by Paul in 1 Cor 15:3–5.[58] In addition, while these details also find some corresponding report in more than one of the canonical gospels, *only* Luke bears witness to four of the five points Paul itemizes in these verses, while Isaiah attests to the Servant's atoning death.[59] Thus, while these details in themselves do not necessarily *require* the existence of a written version of Luke's gospel, the plausibility of such a written source standing alongside the OT accounts for Paul's use of κατὰ τὰς γραφὰς, and it is consistent with the proposal that the two instances of γραφή in 1 Cor 15 in fact refer to an existing and authoritative apostolic writing.[60]

2 Peter 3:15–16

Of all the texts in the NT, the second text noted above, 2 Pet 3:16, provides the clearest testimony to the scriptural status attributed to the apostolic writings as well as to the apostles' awareness that their writings stood with those of the prophets as having the authority of God-given revelation. Indeed, in 1:21, Peter himself addresses the matter of inspiration when he states, οὐ γὰρ θελήματι ἀνθρώπου ἠνέχθη προφητεία ποτέ, ἀλλὰ ὑπὸ πνεύματος ἁγίου φερόμενοι ἐλάλησαν ἀπὸ θεοῦ ἄνθρωποι.[61] While this particular remark likely refers to the prophets of the OT, it also lays groundwork that may account for the utterances of the apostles, for later in 3:2, Peter exhorts his readers, μνησθῆναι τῶν προειρημένων ῥημάτων ὑπὸ τῶν ἁγίων προφητῶν καὶ τῆς τῶν ἀποστόλων ὑμῶν ἐντολῆς τοῦ κυρίου καὶ σωτῆρος. In this statement, Peter appears to draw a line, as it were, not to separate, but to link the prophetic utterances of old with the apostolic

58. Thrall, *Paul to the Corinthians*, 104–5.

59. Ibid., 104. In addition, it may be significant for this argument that Luke frequently uses the phrase ἄφεσις ἁμαρτιῶν as a cipher for the gospel message (Luke 1:77, 3:3, 24:47; Acts 2:38, 5:31, 10:43, 13:38, 26:18).

60. Anderson, in the midst of arguing that Theophilus (to whom Luke addresses his works) was in fact the lawyer who argued Paul's defense in Rome, states, "Luke wrote his gospel during the reign of Herod Antipas . . . Paul was in fact familiar with the Gospel of Luke" (Anderson, "Theophilus: A Proposal," 205–6). See also the discussion of 2 Cor 8:18 and Paul's reference to τὸν ἀδελφὸν οὗ ὁ ἔπαινος ἐν τῷ εὐαγγελίῳ διὰ πασῶν τῶν ἐκκλησιῶν in chapter 4.

61. Bauckham, *Jude, 2 Peter*, 233; Davids, *2 Peter and Jude*, 213–15; Schreiner, *1, 2 Peter, Jude*, 324; Senior, "1 Peter," in Senior and Harrington, *1 Peter, Jude and 2 Peter*, 209.

teaching of his day.[62] Thus, when one reads in 3:15–16 of ὁ ἀγαπητὸς ἡμῶν ἀδελφὸς Παῦλος, who ἔγραψεν ὑμῖν, ὡς καὶ ἐν πάσαις ἐπιστολαῖς, and whose writings οἱ ἀμαθεῖς καὶ ἀστήρικτοι στρεβλοῦσιν ὡς καὶ τὰς λοιπὰς γραφάς, it may be understood that Peter has now explicitly classified the Pauline writings as γραφή alongside "the rest of the Scriptures," referring at least to the OT and possibly including, by implication, all of the writings of the apostles extant in his day.[63]

Thus, in 1 Cor 15:3–5 as presented above, Paul uses γραφή in a manner that is at least equivocal, and at most is suggestive of Luke's gospel. Meanwhile, 2 Pet 3:15–16 indisputably asserts that Paul's writings are indeed γραφή. Accordingly, it is proposed here that the compound effect of the two texts, coupled now with 1 Tim 5:18 (and the testimony of 2 Cor 8:18, as discussed in chapter 4), results in the implication that Paul, the Corinthian believers, and Timothy all were aware of and familiar with a written and circulating version of Luke's gospel.

Summary of Findings

Upon review of the preceding survey, two details are immediately noticeable. First, the semantic domain of γραφή is broad enough that even when a given occurrence of γραφή plausibly may serve as a reference to Scripture, the immediate context in which it falls must confirm the construal; lexis alone is inadequate for making any firm determinations. While this is hardly surprising, it nevertheless serves as a caution against overly sanguine generalizations and hasty conclusions based upon word studies. Second, and more importantly, across the five different collections of Greek literature represented above, accounting for one hundred and ninety-five instances of γραφή, every occurrence refers to something physically recorded in writing or something drawn or inscribed. This same quality attends the corresponding Hebrew term, כתב. In addition,

62. Bauckham, *Jude, 2 Peter*, 288; Davids, *2 Peter and Jude*, 260–62; Harrington, "Jude and 2 Peter," in Senior and Harrington, *1 Peter, Jude and 2 Peter*, 281–82; Schreiner, *1, 2 Peter, Jude*, 370.

63. Davids, *2 Peter and Jude*, 307–9; Harrington, "Jude and 2 Peter," in Senior and Harrington, *1 Peter, Jude and 2 Peter*, 296; Schreiner, *1, 2 Peter, Jude*, 397–98. While R. M. Grant does not maintain the genuine Petrine authorship of 2 Peter, he does acknowledge, "When we find in 2 Peter clear references to 1 Peter (3:1) and to 'all' the letters of Paul (3:16), we are led to believe that something like a canon, at least of epistles, is being shaped" (Grant, "New Testament Canon," 288).

the conventional use of γραφή by the NT writers (and the typical use reflected in the Apostolic Fathers) narrows significantly as it assumes a virtually technical standing reserved for references to Scripture.

When taken together with the exegetical conclusions already offered in previous chapters, these last two observations make it very unlikely that ἡ γραφή in 1 Tim 5:18 is intended to refer to any kind of oral or detached "sayings" tradition, as several sources assert.[64] On the contrary, the findings of this survey indicate that 1 Tim 5:18 must refer to written text relative to *both* citations offered (Deut 25:4 and Luke 10:7), which supports the results of the discourse and exegetical analyses of 1 Tim 5:18, presented in chapters 3 and 4. This in turn provides corroboration for the proposal, also argued in chapters 3 and 4, that Paul consciously cites an already published version of the Gospel of Luke, to which he also ascribes scriptural standing. As for γραφή in 2 Tim 3:16, although there is little dispute that it probably refers to written material, nothing in the immediate literary context of 2 Timothy necessarily *requires* a written referent, apart from a firm sense of the lexical parameters of γραφή. However, as with 1 Timothy, the findings in this survey make it highly unlikely that Paul would use γραφή in 2 Timothy to refer to an oral gospel tradition, or merely the content of the apostolic proclamation without respect to form or medium. Rather, if Paul's usage is at all consistent, and if the conclusions drawn from the discourse and exegetical analysis for 2 Tim 3:16 as presented in chapters 5 and 6 are reasonable, the gospel proclamation to which Paul would be referring throughout 2 Timothy and which occupies the greater part of his attention in the letter most probably existed in a written form, which also must have been in circulation at least among the Galatian churches. As argued in chapter 4, this document most likely would have been a version of Luke's gospel, as the first impression of the citation in 1 Tim 5:18 suggests. Finally, in addition to the continuity between כתב and γραφή, the continuity between Torah and Gospel as traced and proposed by Gerhardsson and others further reinforces this argument, and along with it, advances the thesis of this study.

---

64. Such as Collins, *Timothy and Titus*, 146; Johnson, *Letters to Timothy*, 278; Mounce, *Pastoral Epistles*, 310–11; Oberlinner, *Zweiter Timotheusbrief*, 254–55; Roloff, *Der erste Brief an Timotheus*, 306; Witherington, *Letters and Homilies*, 275.

CHAPTER 8

Conclusion: γραφη in the Letters to Timothy

AT THE OUTSET OF this work, it was proposed that the broad literary schemes running through the letters to Timothy, the close analysis of 1 Tim 5:18 and 2 Tim 3:16 within their immediate literary contexts, and the available historical data concerning them all indicate that γραφή, as Paul uses it in each letter, serves as a term that includes as its referent both the OT writings and some of the apostolic writings that now comprise part of the NT. Over the course of the ensuing study, this claim has gained footing, having been examined along four different axes.

First, chapters 3 and 5 traced and evaluated both the lines of discourse and the predominant semantic streams running through 1 and 2 Timothy. In the process, it was shown that the overriding concern driving each letter's composition lay in Paul's determination to uphold, preserve, and advance the apostolic tradition that is the gospel message. Furthermore, over the course of each letter, Paul's references to this message assumed several forms. Specifically, among the various expressions that Paul uses to denote that message, this study identified ἡ ἀλήθεια, ἡ καλὴ διδασκαλία, ἀνάγνωσις (in company with both παράκλησις and διδασκαλία), ὁ λόγος τῆς ἀληθείας, ἡ παραθήκη, ὁ [πιστός] λόγος, ὁ λόγος τοῦ θεοῦ, τοῖς λόγοις τῆς πίστεως, τὸ εὐαγγέλιον, τὸ εὐαγγέλιον τῆς δόξης τοῦ μακαρίου θεοῦ, τὸ μαρτύριον, τὸ μυστήριον τῆς πίστεως, ἡ ὑγιαίνουσα διδασκαλία, ἡ πίστις, τὸ κήρυγμα, ὑποτύπωσις . . . ὑγιαινόντων λόγων ὧν παρ᾽ἐμοῦ ἤκουσας, ἃ ηκουσας παρ᾽ἐμοῦ, τὸ εὐαγγέλιόν μου, and οἷς ἔμαθες καὶ ἐπιστώθης, ὑγιαίνοντες λόγοι ὁι τοῦ κυρίου ἡμῶν Ἰησοῦ Χριστοῦ, and ἡ παραθήκη. Most of these interchangeable terms appear in both letters and perform the same functions.[1] Furthermore, while Paul affirms in both letters the continuing authority of the OT writings—either explicitly by declaration or implicitly through citations and allusion—the apostolic gospel teaching is treated as equally authoritative, serving as the object of Paul's most focused attentions as well as providing the basis for the imperatives given in the letters. As such, it holds a standing commensurate with the Law, Prophets, and Writings, with the result that both letters identify and uphold two distinct and compatible sources of authoritative teaching.

The observations adduced and conclusions drawn along this particular line of analysis find support among most of the scholarly sources consulted with respect to the letters to Timothy. However, whereas there exists wide agreement relative to the conclusions summarized thus far, only Towner and Van Neste among the sources consulted have sought to account for their positions by systematically tracking Paul's discourse.[2] Furthermore, few of the sources just mentioned seriously entertain the final implication for which this study argues, either because of assumptions that prematurely rule out otherwise arguable interpretive conclusions, or because the integration of γραφή into the prevailing discourse and semantic stream of each letter has gone unobserved or was not seen as a significant indicator of the intent behind Paul's use of this term.

Over the course of the discourse survey of 1 Timothy, three points that arise prior to 5:18 were identified as particularly important because they provide three instances in which the semantic stream pertaining to the gospel explicitly intersects with at least one existing written work. First, the only two occurrences of νομοδιδάσκαλος in the NT outside of 1 Timothy 1:7 appear in Luke 5:17 and in Acts 5:34. The second instance occurs in 4:1–5 and speaks of ὁ λόγος τοῦ θεοῦ in which believers, those who know ἡ ἀλήθεια, recognize the goodness of marriage and of all foods as blessings provided by God. With respect to both subjects, food and marriage, it was also observed that Jesus' teaching on both matters may

1. Specifically, such terms appearing in 1 Timothy include ἡ ὑγιαίνουσα διδασκαλία, τὸ εὐαγγέλιον τῆς δόξης τοῦ μακαρίου θεοῦ, ὁ λόγος, ὁ [πιστὸς] λόγος, λόγος θεοῦ, ἡ πίστος, τὸ μαρτύριον, ἡ ἀλήθεια, τὸ μυστήριον τῆς πίστεως, τοῖς λόγοις τῆς πίστεως, ἡ καλὴ διδασκαλία, ἀναγνώσις (in company with both παρακλήσις and διδασκαλία), ἡ διδασκαλία, ὑγιαίνοντες λόγοι ὁι τοῦ κυρίου ἡμῶν Ἰησοῦ Χριστοῦ, and ἡ παραθήκη, while those appearing in 2 Timothy include ἡ ἀλήθεια, οἷς ἔμαθες καὶ ἐπιστώθης, τὸ εὐαγγέλιον, τὸ κήρυγμα, ὁ λόγος τῆς ἀληθείας, ὁ λόγος τοῦ θεοῦ, ὁ [πιστὸς] λόγος, ἡ παραθήκη, ἡ πίστις, and ὑγιαινούσα διδασκαλία.

2. Towner, *Goal of Our Instruction*; Van Neste, *Cohesion and Structure*.

be found in Luke's gospel. Thus, based upon this text, it was argued that Paul at least plausibly draws upon the Gospel of Luke in order to commend the lessons concerning freedom regarding marriage and food as they are presented in that document.

The final such instance lies in 4:13, in which Paul urges Timothy to attend to ἡ ἀνάγνωσις, ἡ παράκλησις, and ἡ διδασκαλία. While there is broad consensus that ἡ παράκλησις and ἡ διδασκαλία are both terms that Paul uses to refer to the gospel, it was proposed here, in contradistinction from most other sources, that because of its place in the succession of elements to which Timothy is to attend, ἡ ἀνάγνωσις also functions as the initial basis for ἡ παράκλησις and ἡ διδασκαλία, and thus also most likely refers to that same message. However, the vital trait of ἡ ἀνάγνωσις lies in the fact that it must refer to a written source of instruction. As has been argued, this suggests a written gospel. In view of these details, among others, the impression that Paul cites Luke 10:7 as Scripture in 1 Tim 5:18 gained a fair degree of traction, though at this point in the study the assertion could not be pressed as certain.

With respect to 2 Tim 3:16, it was observed that Paul maintains his emphasis upon securing the apostolic gospel message, to which he refers in 3:14 as οἷς ἔμαθες καὶ ἐπιστώθης. When he also writes of τὰ ἱερὰ γράμματα in 3:15 as that body of instruction in which Timothy had been trained from infancy, τὰ ἱερὰ γράμματα refers to the second body of teaching mentioned in 3:14–17. Consequently, it was argued on the basis of the discourse and semantic streams of 2 Timothy that πᾶσα γραφή in 3:16 represents the integration of these two bodies of compatible teaching into one authoritative entity. However, as with the discourse and semantic analysis of 1 Timothy, not enough data emerged through this broad survey to do more than suggest that some apostolic writing or teaching had also attained the status of "Scripture."

Second, in chapters 4 and 6, γραφή was examined in its immediate literary context as it occurs in each letter, thus narrowing the scope of the examination compared to the discourse and semantic analysis. Rather than only seeking to determine the most prominent issue of the epistle or merely identifying the chief semantic stream, this assessment sought to determine as precisely as possible how each instance of γραφή functions within the immediate literary framework that contains it. With respect to 1 Tim 5:18, the fact that ἄξιος ὁ ἐργάτης τοῦ μισθοῦ represents an exact reflection of Luke 10:7 and the fact that this citation is the one more closely related to the point Paul is arguing in 5:17–18 by virtue of both lexis and syntax, are undeniable. With respect to 2 Tim 3:16, it was argued that construing γραφή as a reference that includes the apostolic gospel message corresponds more naturally to the content of 3:14–17 than reading it as a reference to the OT alone. In part, this rests upon the fact that both οἷς ἔμαθες καὶ ἐπιστώθης and τὰ ἱερὰ γράμματα already serve references to whole collections of material, as opposed to partial collections. Consequently, the use of πᾶς to modify γραφή becomes necessary and effective only if it implies a combination of two complete bodies of instruction. Conversely, πᾶς, if construed so as to refer to all of the OT writings alone (τὰ ἱερὰ γράμματα), becomes superfluous by virtue of redundancy. It was also argued that construing πᾶσα γραφή as a reference to the combination of OT writings with apostolic writings permits the most coherent integration of 3:14–17 with 3:10–13 and 4:1–4. In addition, considering the prevailing rhetorical scheme and overall agenda of 2 Timothy, it was argued that Paul would not commend τὰ ἱερὰ γράμματα alone as strongly as he commends πᾶσα γραφή with respect to its power to fully equip the man of God for godliness and service to the gospel.

Thus, while the more sweeping discourse and semantic surveys demonstrated that the thesis of this study is compatible with the broad rhetorical schemes of the letters, though not mandated by them, close analysis showed that in both instances, the most coherent reading of γραφή relative to the surrounding literary context construes it as a term by which Paul intends to refer to at least some of the apostolic writings alongside the OT: specifically, the Gospel of Luke along with some of Paul's own epistles.

Third, while in the case of 1 Tim 5:18, the very nature of the circumstances and context of λέγει γὰρ ἡ γραφή surely suggests that ἡ γραφή serves as a reference to a written source, the same could not be said in the case of 2 Tim 3:16. In fact, on a strictly exegetical basis, neither passage *must* refer to a written gospel source. Indeed, this point no doubt encourages the common inclination to posit a Logion source for the 1 Tim 5:18 assertion ἄξιος ὁ ἐργάτης τοῦ μισθοῦ αὐτοῦ that so precisely reflects Luke 10:7. Consequently, in an effort to determine the actual scope of the semantic options attending γραφή, chapter 7 featured a survey of its semantic domain based upon its usage in other texts. This survey spanned five different collections of literature: the writings of Philo, Josephus, the LXX, the NT, and the writings of the Apostolic Fathers. Parallel to the evaluation of γραφή in the LXX, chapter 7 also presented an evaluation of כתב, the Hebrew cognate of γραφή found in the MT. In the process, it was determined that both γραφή and כתב may be shown to refer *exclusively* to physically written or drawn material.

This point effectively rules out all hypotheses that seek to account for 1 Tim 5:18 or 2 Tim 3:16 as references to oral tradition or Logion sources, which in turn forces the decision: Either γραφή functions as an exclusive reference to the OT writings, or it is used by Paul in 1 and 2 Timothy to refer to the integration of the OT writings with apostolic gospel writings, some of which now appear in the NT. However, on the basis of the arguments and data summarized to this point, the first option is simply untenable in the case of 1 Tim 5:18, and while it remains possible for 2 Tim 3:16, it seems improbable and out of keeping with the course and emphasis of 2 Timothy as a whole. Specifically, the conventional treatment of 2 Tim 3:16 would result in a disruption of the rhetorical movement from 3:10–13, to 3:14–17, to 4:1–4. On the other hand, the construal of πᾶσα γραφή proposed in this study would maintain the high profile of the apostolic gospel message, thus permitting a more fluid line of discourse to be sustained through these consecutive literary units.

Fourth, in spite of the occasional acknowledgment of the possible existence of Christian writings that might have been viewed as "Scripture" in the first century,[3] there remains a wide resistance among scholars to the conclusions offered above, based largely upon assumptions regarding the dates associated with the composition of the NT writings. Therefore, it was deemed necessary to examine the most likely dating parameters of the composition, publication, and circulation of Luke's gospel, the bulk of which examination appeared in chapter 4. This analysis demonstrated the plausibility—even the probability—that Luke's gospel had been written and available to Timothy for his own instruction by as early as A.D. 52, well before Paul's correspondence with him, and that this gospel also could have received wide recognition as "Scripture" by A.D. 56. The importance of this assessment lies in the fact that the likely dating of the composition of Luke's gospel now makes the existence and circulation of such a written work prior to A.D. 56, known to Timothy and others, a probability rather than a mere possibility, which in turn elevates the likelihood that Paul would have referred to such a document as γραφή. This examination provides the final piece of data that permits the unhampered convergence of the results of all four lines of analysis presented in this study.

3. See, for instance, Guthrie, *Pastoral Epistles*, 117; Marshall, *Pastoral Epistles*, 615–16; Oberlinner, *Erster Timotheusbrief*, 254.

Taking all factors into consideration, the conclusions of this study may be summarized as follows. First, there remains virtually no justifiable doubt that γραφή must refer to a written body of authoritative teaching. Second, the importance of the gospel and of unfailing allegiance to it within the rhetorical schemes of 1 and 2 Timothy does not support the notion that Paul would lift up the OT writings alone as sources of teaching that could render the man of God ἄρτιος and πρὸς πᾶν ἔργον ἀγαθὸν ἐξηρτισμένος. Third, along with the citation of 5:18, four other plausible literary connections between 1 Timothy and the Gospel of Luke have been adduced that together increase the likelihood that Paul had Luke's gospel in mind while he wrote to Timothy. Fourth, common suppositions regarding the relatively late dating of Luke and Acts have been shown to be at best precipitous, if not improbable. Fifth, the same may be said of such widely held notions as the non-Pauline authorship of the PE or the incompatibility of the eschatology of the PE with that of the other Pauline writings. Sixth, while the two occurrences of γραφή in 1 and 2 Timothy have been examined and evaluated independently, the construals proposed in this work together present a consistent understanding and usage on the part of Paul, and thus suggest that γραφή represents a virtually technical term that referred to both OT and NT writings as early as the late apostolic age. Consequently, there exist neither lexical, nor exegetical, nor historical obstacles to the acceptance of the proposal offered in this study. For all of the above reasons, it is maintained here that the most reasonable and exegetically coherent construal of γραφή in 1 and 2 Timothy treats it as a signifier of the integrated body of instruction comprised of both the OT writings and the writings of the apostolic company.

Beyond the scope of the examination of γραφή in 1 and 2 Timothy that concerns this study are implications that affect the wider discussions of canon and biblical authority. Specifically, the sweeping denial advanced by Barr, Ehrman, and McDonald (among others) that members of the apostolic company were aware that their writings were "Scripture" even as the OT writings were "Scripture" is shown to rest upon incomplete data. Similarly, denials that the church had a clearly recognized orthodoxy, along with a sense of its own authoritative writings outside the OT prior to the second century, are also shown to rest upon thin evidence. In point of fact, the actual data suggest a reality that is quite to the contrary of these widely held notions. In conjunction with the evidence drawn from 1 Cor 2:12–13, 15:3, and 2 Pet 3:16, the combined witness of 1 Tim

5:1 and 2 Tim 3:16 testifies to an unambiguous sense among the apostolic company that they served as the new spokesmen, agents, and trustees of God's revelatory word to his people, an extension of "the word of the Lord." As a result, while many matters that still require attention relative to the larger questions of biblical authority and the biblical canon remain, Paul's use of γραφή in 1 and 2 Timothy nevertheless helps to guard, and perhaps even to advance, a high view of both OT and NT Scripture.

Bibliography

Aageson, James W. "The Pastoral Epistles, Apostolic Authority, and the Development of the Pauline Scriptures." In *The Pauline Canon*, edited by Stanley E. Porter, 5–26. Leiden: Brill, 2004.

Agnew, Francis H. "On the Origin of the Term *Apostolos*." *Catholic Biblical Quarterly* 38 (1976) 49–53.

Aland, Barbara, et al., eds. *The Greek New Testament*. 4th ed. Stuttgart: Deutsche Bibelgesellschaft, 2001.

————. *Nestle-Aland Novum Testamentum Graece*. 27th ed. Stuttgart: Deutsche Bibelgesellschaft, 1993.

————. *The Text of the New Testament: An Introduction to the Critical Editions and to the Theory and Practice of Modern Textual Criticism*. Translated by Erroll F. Rhodes. 2nd ed. Grand Rapids: Eerdmans, 1989.

Alexander, L. C. A. "Chronology of Paul." In *Dictionary of Paul and His Letters*, edited by Gerald F. Hawthorne and Ralph P. Martin, 115–23. Downers Grove, IL: InterVarsity, 1993.

Alfaro, Juan I. *Justice and Loyalty: A Commentary on the Book of Micah*. International Theological Commentary. Grand Rapids: Eerdmans, 1989.

Allert, Craig D. *A High View of Scripture? The Authority of the Bible and the Formation of the New Testament Canon*. Grand Rapids: Baker, 2007.

Anderson, Richard. "Theophilus: A Proposal." *Evangelical Quarterly* 69 (1997) 195–215.

"Aristides." In *The Oxford Dictionary of the Christian Church*, edited by F. L. Cross and Elizabeth A. Livingstone, 102. 3rd rev. ed. Oxford: Oxford University Press, 2005.

Artola, Antonio M. "El Momento de la inspiración en la constitución de las escritura según 2 Tim 3,16." *Estudios Bíblicos* 57 (1999) 61–82.

Bachmann, Phillipp. *Der erste Brief des Paulus an die Korinther*. Leipzig: A. Deichert, 1910.

Balla, Peter. *Challenges to New Testament Theology*. Peabody, MA: Hendrickson, 1997.

————. "Evidence for an Early Christian Canon (Second and Third Century)." In *The Canon Debate*, edited by Lee Martin McDonald and James A. Sanders, 372–85. Peabody, MA: Hendrickson, 2002.

Balsdon, John Percy, Vivian Dacre, and Barbara M. Levick. "Claudius." In *The Oxford Classical Dictionary*, edited by Simon Hornblower and Antony Spawforth, 337–38. 3rd rev. ed. Oxford: Oxford University Press, 2003.

Barr, James. *Holy Scripture: Canon, Authority, Criticism.* 1983. Reprint, New York: Oxford University Press, 2002.

Barrett, C. K. *The Pastoral Epistles in the New English Bible.* New Clarendon Bible. Oxford: Clarendon, 1963.

Barton, John. *Holy Writings, Sacred Text: The Canon in Early Christianity.* Louisville: Westminster John Knox, 1997.

Bassler, Jouette M. *1 Timothy, 2 Timothy, Titus.* Abingdon New Testament Commentaries. Nashville: Abingdon, 1996.

Bauckham, Richard. *Jesus and the Eyewitnesses: The Gospels as Eyewitness Testimony.* Grand Rapids: Eerdmans, 2006.

———. *Jude, 2 Peter.* Word Biblical Commentary 50. Waco, TX: Word, 1983.

Bauer, Walter. *Orthodoxy and Heresy in Earliest Christianity.* Edited by Robert A. Kraft and Gerhard Krodel. Translated by the Philadelphia Seminar on Christian Origins. Mifflintown, PA: Sigler, 1996.

Bauer, Walter F., et al., eds. *A Greek-English Lexicon of the New Testament and Other Early Christian Literature.* 3rd ed. Chicago: University of Chicago Press, 2000.

Belleville, Linda L. "Canon of the New Testament." In *Foundations for Biblical Interpretation,* edited by David S. Dockery, Kenneth A. Mathews, and Robert B. Sloan, 374–95. Nashville: Broadman and Holman, 1999.

Berding, Kenneth. "Polycarp of Smyrna's View of the Authorship of 1 and 2 Timothy." *Vigiliae Christianae* 53 (1999) 349–60.

Bernard, J. H. *The Pastoral Epistles.* Grand Rapids: Baker, 1980.

Birdsall, J. N. "The New Testament Text." In vol. 1 of *From the Beginnings to Jerome,* edited by P. R. Ackroyd and C. F. Evans, 308–77. The Cambridge History of the Bible. Cambridge: Cambridge University Press, 1993.

Birley, Anthony R. "Hadrian." In *The Oxford Classical Dictionary,* edited by Simon Hornblower and Antony Spawforth, 662–63. 3rd rev. ed. Oxford: Oxford University Press, 2003.

Blanchard, Yves-Marie. "'Toute écriture est inspiree' (2 Tim 3,16). Les problematiques de la canonisation et de l'inspiration, avec leurs enjeux respectifs." *Recherches de science religieuse* 93 (2005) 497–515.

Blenkinsopp, Joseph. *Isaiah 1–39: A New Translation with Introduction and Commentary.* Anchor Bible 19. New York: Doubleday, 2000.

Blevins, James L. "Acts 13–19: The Tale of Three Cities." Review and Expositor 87 (1990) 439–50.

Blum, Edwin A. "The Apostles' View of Scripture." In *Inerrancy,* edited by Norman L. Geisler, 39–53. Grand Rapids: Zondervan, 1980.

Bock, Darrell L. *Acts.* Baker Exegetical Commentary on the New Testament. Grand Rapids: Baker, 2008.

Bover, José M. "Fidelis Sermo." *Biblica* 19 (1938) 74–79.

———. "Uso de Adjetivo Singular πᾶς en San Pablo." *Biblica* 19 (1938) 411–34.

Bovon, François. "Canonical and Apocryphal Acts of Apostles." *Journal of Early Christian Studies* 11 (2003) 165–94.

Bray, Gerald. *Biblical Interpretation: Past and Present.* Downers Grove, IL: InterVarsity, 1996.

Brown, Francis, S. R. Driver, and Charles A. Briggs. *A Hebrew and English Lexicon of the Old Testament.* Oxford: Clarendon, 1951.

Brox, Norbert. *Die Pastoralbriefe*. Regensburger Neues Testament, 7.2. Leipzig: St. Benno, 1975.

Bruce, F. F. *Paul: Apostle of the Heart Set Free*. Grand Rapids: Eerdmans, 2000.

Burkhardt, Helmut. *Die Inspiration heiliger Schriften bei Philo von Alexandrien*. Monographien und Studienbücher 340. Basel: Giessen Brunnen, 1988.

Canoy, Robert W. "Teaching Eschatology and Ethics in the Thessalonian Letters." *Review and Expositor* 96 (1996) 249–60.

Carmignac, Jean. "2 Corinthiens 3. 6,14 et le Début de la Formation du Nouveau Testament." *New Testament Studies* 24 (1978) 384–86.

Carrington, Philip. "The Problem of the Pastoral Epistles: Dr. Harrison's Theory Reviewed." *Anglican Theological Review* 21 (1939) 32–39.

Carson, D. A., and Douglas J. Moo. *An Introduction to the New Testament*. 2nd ed. Grand Rapids: Zondervan, 2005.

Chadwick, Henry, and Mark Julian Edwards. "Polycarp." In *The Oxford Classical Dictionary*, edited by Simon Hornblower and Antony Spawforth, 1211. 3rd rev. ed. Oxford: Oxford University Press, 2003.

Childs, Brevard. *Isaiah*. Old Testament Library. Louisville: Westminster John Knox, 2001.

Chilton, Bruce. "Gamaliel." In vol. 2 of *The Anchor Bible Dictionary*, edited by David Noel Freedman, 903–6. New York: Doubleday, 1992.

Christensen, Jens. "And That He Rose on the Third Day According to the Scriptures." *Scandanavian Journal of the Old Testament* 2 (1990) 101–13.

Chrysostom, John. *Homilies on the Epistles of Paul to the Corinthians*. In vol. 12 of *Nicene and Post-Nicene Fathers*, Series 1, edited by Philip Schaff. 1886–1889. 14 vols. Reprint, Peabody, MA: Hendrickson, 1995.

Clarke, Kent D. "The Problem of Pseudonymity in Biblical Literature and Its Implications for Canon Formation." In *The Canon Debate*, edited by Lee Martin McDonald and James A. Sanders, 440–68. Peabody, MA: Hendrickson, 2002.

Collingwood, R. G. *The Idea of History*. Edited by Jan Van Der Dussen. Rev. ed. New York: Oxford University Press, 2005.

Collins, Raymond F. *1 and 2 Timothy and Titus: A Commentary*. New Testament Library. Louisville: Westminster John Knox, 2002.

———. *First Corinthians*. Sacra Pagina 7. Collegeville, MN: Liturgical, 1999.

Conybeare, William John, and John Paul Howson. *The Life and Epistles of Saint Paul*. New York: Horan, 1917.

Cook, David. "2 Timothy 4:6–8 and the Epistles to the Philippians." *Journal of Theological Studies* 33 (1982) 168–71.

———. "The Pastoral Fragments Reconsidered." *Journal of Theological Studies* 35 (1984) 120–31.

Cook, Donald E. "Scripture and Inspiration: 2 Timothy 3:14–17." *Faith and Mission* (1984) 56–61.

Costacurta, Bruna. "Implicazioni semantiche in alcuni casi de qere-ketib." *Biblica* 71 (1990) 227–39.

Cothenet, Éduard. "Directives pastorales dan les Épîtres a Timothée." *Esprit et vie* 114 (2004) 17–23.

Cowley, A. E., ed. *Gesenius' Hebrew Grammar*. 2nd ed. Oxford: Clarendon, 1985.

Craigie, Peter C. *The Book of Deuteronomy*. New International Commentary on the Old Testament. Grand Rapids: Eerdmans, 1976.

Davids, Peter H. *The Letters of 2 Peter and Jude*. Pillar New Testament Commentary. Grand Rapids: Eerdmans, 2006.

De Boer, Martinus C. "Paul, Theologian of God's Apocalypse." *Interpretation* 56 (2002) 21–33.

De Virgilio, Giuseppe. "Ispirazione ed efficacia della Scrittura in 2 Tm 3, 14–17: In occasione del XXV anno della promulgazione dell Costituzione Dogmatica Dei Verbum." *Rivista Biblica Italiana* 38 (1990) 485–94.

Dibelius, Martin, and Hans Conzelmann. *A Commentary on the Pastoral Epistles*. Translated by Philip Buttolph and Adela Yarbro. Philadelphia: Fortress, 1972.

Driver, S. R. *A Critical and Exegetical Commentary on Deuteronomy*. International Critical Commentary. Edinburgh: T. & T. Clark, 1896.

Dunbar, David G. "The Biblical Canon." In *Hermeneutics, Authority and Canon*, edited by D. A. Carson and John D. Woodbridge, 295–360. Grand Rapids: Baker, 1995.

Easton, Burton Scott. *The Pastoral Epistles: Introduction, Translation, Commentary and Word Studies*. New York: Scribner's, 1947.

Edwards, B. B. "The Genuineness of the Pastoral Epistles." *Bibliotheca sacra* 150 (1993) 131–39.

Ehrman, Bart D. *The Orthodox Corruption of Scripture: The Effect of Early Christological Controversies on the Text of the New Testament*. Rev. ed. New York: Oxford University Press, 2011.

———. *Lost Christianities: The Battles for Scripture and the Faiths We Never Knew*. New York: Oxford University Press, 2003.

———. *Lost Scriptures: Books That Did Not Make It into the New Testament*. New York: Oxford University Press, 2003.

———, ed. and trans. *The Apostolic Fathers*. 2 vols. Loeb Classical Library. Cambridge: Harvard University Press, 2005.

Elliger, K., and W. Rudolph, eds. *Biblia Hebraica Stuttgartensia*. 5th rev. ed. Stuttgart, Germany: Deutsche Bibelgesellschaft, 1997.

Ellingworth, Paul. "The 'True Saying' in 1 Timothy 3,1." *The Bible Translator* 31 (1980) 443–45.

Elliott, J. Keith. "Absent Witnesses? The Critical Apparatus to the Greek New Testament and the Apostolic Fathers." In *The Reception of the New Testament in the Apostolic Fathers*, edited by Andrew F. Gregory and Christopher M. Tuckett, 47–58. Oxford: Oxford University Press, 2007.

Ellis, E. Earle. *Paul and His Recent Interpreters*. 1961. Reprint, Eugene, OR: Wipf & Stock, 2004.

———. "Review of Birger Gerhardsson, *Memory and Manuscript*." *Southwestern Journal of Theology* 43 (2000) 98–99.

Engberg-Pedersen, Troels, ed. *Paul Beyond the Judaism/Hellenism Divide*. Louisville: Westminster John Knox, 2001.

Epp, Eldon Jay. "The Papyrus Manuscripts of the New Testament." In *The Text of the New Testament in Contemporary Research: Essays on the Status Quaestionis*, edited by Bart D. Ehrman and Michael W. Holmes, 3–21. Grand Rapids: Eerdmans, 1995.

Epstein, Isidore, ed. *The Babylonian Talmud. Seder Kodashim*. Vol. 3. London: Soncino, 1961.

———. *The Babylonian Talmud. Seder Nashim*. Vol. 4. London: Soncino, 1961.

Eusebius, of Caesarea. *Ecclesiastical History*. Translated by Kirsopp Lake. Vol. 1. Loeb Classical Library. Cambridge: Harvard University Press, 2001.

———. *Ecclesiastical History*. Translated by J. E. L. Oulton. Vol. 2. Loeb Classical Library. Cambridge: Harvard University Press, 2000.

Evans, C. F. "The New Testament in the Making." In vol. 1 of *The Cambridge History of the Bible: From the Beginnings to Jerome*, edited by P. R. Ackroyd and C. F. Evans, 232–84. Cambridge: Cambridge University Press, 1993.

Fairbairn, Patrick. *A Commentary on 1 and 2 Timothy and Titus*. Edinburgh: Banner of Truth Trust, 2002.

Fee, Gordon D. *1 and 2 Timothy and Titus*. New International Biblical Commentary 13. Peabody, MA: Hendrickson, 1988.

———. *The First Epistle to the Corinthians*. New International Commentary on the New Testament. Grand Rapids: Eerdmans, 1987.

Ferguson, Everett. *Backgrounds of Early Christianity*. 2nd ed. Grand Rapids: Eerdmans, 1993.

———. "Factors Leading to the Selection and Closure of the New Testament Canon." In *The Canon Debate*, edited by Lee Martin McDonald and James A. Sanders, 295–320. Peabody, MA: Hendrickson, 2002.

Fiore, Benjamin. *The Pastoral Epistles*. Sacra Pagina 12. Collegeville, MN: Liturgical, 1991.

Fitzmyer, Joseph A. "Memory and Manuscript: The Origins and Transmission of the Gospel Tradition." Review of *Memory and Manuscript: The Origins and Transmission of the Gospel Tradition*, by Birger Gerhardsson. *Theological Studies* 23 (1962) 442–57.

Fuller, Daniel P. *Gospel and Law: Contrast or Continuum? The Hermeneutics of Dispensationalism and Covenant Theology*. Pasadena, CA: Fuller Seminary Press, 1982.

———. *The Unity of the Bible: Unfolding God's Plan for Humanity*. Grand Rapids: Zondervan, 1992.

Furnish, Victor Paul. *2 Corinthians: A New Translation with Introduction and Commentary*. Anchor Bible 32a. New York: Doubleday, 1984.

Geldenhuys, Norval. *The Gospel of Luke*. New International Commentary on the New Testament. Grand Rapids: Eerdmans, 1983.

Gerhardsson, Birger. *Memory and Manuscript: Oral Tradition and Written Transmission in Rabbinic Judaism and Early Christianity*. Rev. ed. Grand Rapids: Eerdmans, 1998.

Goodman, Martin David. "Rabbis." In *The Oxford Classical Dictionary*, edited by Simon Hornblower and Antony Spawforth, 1292. 3rd rev. ed. New York: Oxford University Press, 2003.

Gordis, Robert. *The Biblical Text in the Making: A Study of the Kethib-Qere*. 2nd ed. Jersey City, NJ: Ktav, 1971.

Grant, Robert. "Aristides." In vol. 1 of *The Anchor Bible Dictionary*, edited by David Noel Freedman, 382. New York: Doubleday, 1992.

———. "The New Testament Canon." In vol. 1 of *The Cambridge History of the Bible: From the Beginnings to Jerome*, edited by P. R. Ackroyd and C. F. Evans, 282–308. Cambridge: Cambridge University Press, 1993.

Green, Eugenio. "La muerte y el poder del Imperio—1 Tesalonicenses 4:13–18." *Kairós* 40 (2007) 9–26.

Guthrie, Donald. *The Pastoral Epistles*. Tyndale New Testament Commentaries 14. 2nd ed. Grand Rapids: Eerdmans, 1990.

———. *The Pastoral Epistles and the Mind of Paul*. London: Tyndale, 1955.

Hafemann, Scott. "Eschatology and Ethics: The Future of Israel and the Nations in Romans 15:1–13." *Tyndale Bulletin* 51 (2000) 161–92.

Hanson, Anthony Tyrrell. *The Pastoral Letters: Commentary on the First and Second Letters to Timothy and the Letter to Titus*. Cambridge Bible Commentary. Cambridge: Cambridge University Press, 1966.

———. *Studies in Paul's Technique and Theology*. Grand Rapids: Eerdmans, 1974.

Harding, Mark. "Disputed and Undisputed Letters of Paul." In *The Pauline Canon*, edited by Stanley E. Porter, 129–68. Leiden: Brill, 2004.

Harl, Marguerite, Gilles Dorival, and Olivier Munnich. *La Bible Grecque Des Septante du Judaïsme Hellénistique au Christianisme Ancien*. Paris: Cerf, 1994.

Harris, Murray J. *The Second Epistle to the Corinthians: A Commentary on the Greek Text*. New International Greek Testament Commentary. Grand Rapids: Eerdmans, 2005.

Harris, R. Laird, Gleason L. Archer Jr., and Bruce K. Waltke, eds. *Theological Wordbook of the Old Testament*. 2 vols. Chicago: Moody, 1980.

Harrison, J. R. "Paul and the Imperial Gospel at Thessaloniki." *Journal for the Study of the New Testament* 25 (2002) 71–96.

Harrison, P. N. *The Problem of the Pastoral Epistles*. London: Oxford University Press, 1921.

Hasler, Victor. *Die Briefe an Timotheus und Titus (Pastoralbriefe)*. Zürcher Bibelkommentare 12. Zürich: Theologischer, 1978.

Hemer, C. J. *The Book of Acts in the Setting of Hellenistic History*. Winona Lake, IN: Eisenbrauns, 1990.

Hentschel, Anni. *Diakonia im Neuen Testament. Studien zur Semantik unter besonderer Berücksichtigung der Rolle von Frauen*. Wissenschaftliche Untersuchungen Zum Neuen Testament 2. Tübingen: Mohr Siebeck, 2007.

Hirsch, E. D., Jr. *Validity in Interpretation*. New Haven: Yale University Press, 1967.

Holtz, Gottfried. *Die Pastoralbriefe*. Theologischer Handkommentar zum Neuen Testament 13. Berlin: Evangelische, 1986.

House, H. Wayne. "Biblical Inspiration in 2 Timothy 3:16." *Bibliotheca sacra* (1980) 54–63.

Irenaeus, Saint, Bishop of Lyon. *Against Heresies*. In vol. 1 of *Ante-Nicene Fathers*, edited by Alexander Roberts and James Donaldson, 1885–87. Peabody, MA: Hendrickson, 1995.

Jellicoe, Sidney. *The Septuagint and Modern Study*. Winona Lake, IN: Eisenbrauns, 1993.

Johnson, Luke Timothy. *The First and Second Letters to Timothy: A New Translation with Introduction and Commentary*. Anchor Bible 35a. New York: Doubleday, 2001.

Johnston, J. William. *The Use of Πᾶς in the New Testament*. Edited by D. A. Carson. Studies in Biblical Greek 11. New York: Lang, 2004.

Josephus, Flavius. *Josephus*. Translated by H. St. J. Thackeray et al. 10 vols. Loeb Classical Library. Cambridge: Harvard University Press, 1926–1965.

Kaiser, Walter C., Jr. "The Current Crisis in Exegesis and the Apostolic Use of Deuteronomy 25:4 in 1 Corinthians 9:8–10." *Journal of the Evangelical Theological Society* 21 (1978) 3–18.

———. "A Neglected Text in Bibliology Discussions: 1 Corinthians 2:6–16." *Westminster Theological Journal* 43 (1981) 301–19.

Kalland, Earl S. "Deuteronomy." In *Deuteronomy–2 Samuel*, edited by Frank E. Gaebelein, 3–238. Expositor's Bible Commentary 3. Grand Rapids: Zondervan, 1992.

Karris, Robert J. "The Background and Significance of the Polemic of the Pastoral Epistles." *Journal of Biblical Literature* 92 (1973) 549–64.

———. *The Pastoral Epistles*. New Testament Message 17. Wilmington, DE: Glazier, 1979.

Kelly, J. N. D. *The Pastoral Epistles*. Black's New Testament Commentary 14. Peabody, MA: Hendrickson, 1998.

Kittel, Gerhard. "λέγω, λόγος, λαλέω, ῥῆμα, κ.τ.λ." In vol. 4 of *Theological Dictionary of the New Testament*, edited by Gerhard Kittel, translated by Geoffrey W. Bromiley, 91–143. Grand Rapids: Eerdmans, 1983.

Knight, George W. *The Faithful Sayings in the Pastoral Epistles*. Nutley, NJ: Presbyterian & Reformed, 1979.

———. *The Pastoral Epistles: A Commentary on the Greek Text*. New International Greek Testament Commentary. Grand Rapids: Eerdmans, 1999.

Koester, Helmut. "Writings and the Spirit: Authority and Politics in Ancient Christianity." *Harvard Theological Review* 84 (1991) 333–72.

Kuck, Daivd W. "The Freedom of Being in the World 'As If Not.'" *Currents in Theology and Mission* 28 (2001) 585–93.

Kümmel, Werner Georg. *Introduction to the New Testament*. Rev. ed. Translated by Howard C. Kee. Nashville: Abingdon, 1984.

Ladd, George Eldon. *A Theology of the New Testament*. Edited by Donald A. Hagner. Rev. ed. Grand Rapids: Eerdmans, 1993.

Lee, G. M. "Studies in Texts: 1 Corinthians 9:9–10." *Theology* 71 (1968) 122–23.

Lenski, R. C. H. *The Interpretation of St. Paul's Epistles to the Colossians, to the Thessalonians, to Timothy, to Titus and to Philemon*. Columbus, OH: Wartburg, 1946.

———. *The Interpretation of St. Paul's First and Second Epistle to the Corinthians*. Columbus, OH: Wartburg, 1946.

Lightfoot, J. B., ed. and trans. *The Apostolic Fathers*. 2nd ed. 5 vols. Peabody, MA: Hendrickson, 1989.

Lindemann, Andreas. *Der Erste Korintherbrief*. Handbuch zum Neuen Testament 9. Tübingen: Mohr-Siebeck, 2000.

Lock, Walter. *A Critical and Exegetical Commentary on the Pastoral Epistles*. International Critical Commentary. Edinburgh: T. & T. Clark, 1978.

Longenecker, Richard N. *Acts*. The Expositor's Bible Commentary 9. Grand Rapids: Zondervan, 1995.

———. *Biblical Exegesis in the Apostolic Period*. 2nd ed. Grand Rapids: Eerdmans, 1999.

Louw, Johannes P., and Eugene A. Nida, eds. *Greek-English Lexicon of the New Testament Based on Semantic Domains*. 2nd ed. 2 vols. New York: United Bible Societies, 1989.

Lust, J., E. Eynikel, and K. Hauspie, eds. *Greek-English Lexicon of the Septuagint*. Rev. ed. Stuttgart: Deutsche Bibelgesellschaft, 2003.

Marcheselli-Casale, Cesare. *Le Letter Pastorali. Le due Lettere a Timoteo e la Lettera a Tito: Introduzione, versione, commento.* Scritti delle origini cristiane 15. Bologna: Dehoniane, 1995.

Marshall, I. Howard. *The Book of Acts: An Introduction and Commentary.* Tyndale New Testament Commentary 5. Grand Rapids: Eerdmans, 1980.

———. *The Pastoral Epistles: A Critical and Exegetical Commentary.* International Critical Commentary. London: T. & T. Clark, 2004.

Martin, Ralph P. *2 Corinthians.* Word Biblical Commentary 40. Nashville: Nelson, 1986.

Matera, Frank J. *2 Corinthians: A Commentary.* New Testament Library. Louisville: Westminster John Knox, 2003.

Mays, James Luther. *Micah.* Old Testament Library. Philadelphia: Westminster, 1976.

McDonald, Lee Martin. *The Biblical Canon: Its Origin, Transmission, and Authority.* Peabody, MA: Hendrickson, 2007.

McDonald, Lee Martin, and Stanley E. Porter. *Early Christianity and Its Sacred Literature.* Peabody, MA: Hendrickson, 2000.

McGowan, A. T. B. "The Divine Spiration of Scripture." *Scottish Bulletin of Evangelical Theology* 21 (2003) 199–217.

Merrill, Eugene H. *Deuteronomy.* New American Commentary 4. Nashville: B. & H., 1994.

Merz, Annette. "The Fictitious Self-Exposition of Paul: How Might Intertextual Theory Suggest a Reformulation of the Hermeneutics of Pseudepigraphy?" In *The Intertextuality of the Epistles: Explorations of Theory and Practice,* edited by Thomas L. Brodie, Dennis R. MacDonald, and Stanley E. Porter, 113–32. Sheffield: Sheffield Phoenix, 2006.

Meier, John P. "2 Timothy 1:1–14; 3:14–17: The Inspiration of Scripture: But What Counts as Scripture?" *Midstream* (1999) 71–78.

Metzger, Bruce M. "A Reconsideration of Certain Arguments against the Pauline Authorship of the Pastoral Epistles." *Expository Times* 70 (1958) 91–94.

———. *The Text of the New Testament: Its Transmission, Corruption, and Restoration.* 3rd ed. New York: Oxford University Press, 1992.

———. *A Textual Commentary on the Greek New Testament.* 2nd ed. Stuttgart, Germany: Deutsche Bibelgesellschaft, 2001.

Miller, James D. *The Pastoral Letters as Composite Documents.* Society for New Testament Studies Monograph, Series 93. Cambridge: Cambridge University Press, 1997.

Moessner, David P. "How Luke Writes." In *The Written Gospel,* edited by Marcus Bockmuehl and Donald A. Hagner, 149–70. New York: Cambridge University Press, 2005.

Morris, Leon. *The First Epistle of Paul to the Corinthians: An Introduction and Commentary.* Tyndale New Testament Commentaries 7. Leicester: InterVarsity, 1996.

Morrow, William S. "Kethib and Qere." In vol. 4 of *The Anchor Bible Dictionary,* edited by David Noel Freedman, 24–30. New York: Doubleday, 1992.

Moule, C. F. D. *The Birth of the New Testament.* 3rd ed. London: Continuum, 2002.

———. "The Problem of the Pastoral Epistles: A Reappraisal." *Bulletin of the John Rylands Library* 47 (1965) 430–52.

Mounce, William D. *The Morphology of Biblical Greek.* Grand Rapids: Zondervan, 1994.

———. *Pastoral Epistles.* Word Biblical Commentary 46. Nashville: Nelson, 2000.

Murphy-O'Connor, Jerome. "2 Timothy Contrasted with 1 Timothy and Titus." *Revue Biblique* 98 (1991) 401–18.

Needham, Nick. "Tradition in 2 Timothy." *Evangel* 17 (1999) 6–9.

Neusner, Jacob. Preface to *Memory and Manuscript: Oral Tradition and Written Transmission in Rabbinic Judaism and Early Christianity*, by Birger Gerhadsson. Rev. ed. Grand Rapids: Eerdmans, 1998.

Niell, Stephen, and Tom Wright. *The Interpretation of the New Testament: 1861–1986.* 2nd ed. New York: Oxford University Press, 1988.

Nielsen, Charles M. "Scripture in the Pastoral Epistles." *Perspectives in Religious Studies* 7 (1980) 4–23.

Nolland, John. *Luke.* 3 vols. Word Biblical Commentary 35. Dallas: Word, 1993.

Oberlinner, Lorenz. *Die Pastoralbriefe: Erster Timotheusbrief.* Herders theologischer Kommentar zum Neuen Testament XI/2 Erste Folge. Freiburg im Briesgau, Germany: Herder, 1994.

———. *Die Pastoralbriefe: Zweiter Timotheusbrief.* Herders theologischer Kommentar zum Neuen Testament XI/2 Zweite Folge. Freiburg im Briesgau, Germany: Herder, 1995.

Orlinsky, Harry M. "Problems of Kethib-Qere." *Journal of the American Oriental Society* 60 (1940) 30–45.

Pagels, Elaine. *The Gnostic Gospels.* New York: Random House, 1989.

Pao, David W. *Acts and the Isaianic New Exodus.* Wissenshaftlich Untersuchungen zum Neuen Testament 2. Reihe 130. 2000. Reprint, Grand Rapids: Baker, 2002.

Philo, of Alexandria. *Philo.* Translated by F. H. Colson and G. H. Whitaker. Loeb Classical Library. 10 vols. Cambridge: Harvard University Press, 1929–1962.

Piñero, Antonio. "Sobre El Sentido de Θεοπνευστοσ: 2 Tim 3,16." *Filologia Neotestamentaria* (1988) 143–53.

Pirot, Louis, and Albert Clamer. *La Sainte Bible: Texte Latin et Traduction Française d'Après Les Textes Originaux avec Commentaire Exégétique et Théologique.* Vol. 12. Paris: Letouzy et Ané, 1946.

Plummer, Alfred. *A Critical and Exegetical Commentary on the Gospel according to Saint Luke.* 5th ed. International Critical Commentary. Edinburgh: T. & T. Clark, 1953.

Quinn, Jerome D. "Epistles to Timothy and Titus." In vol. 6 of *The Anchor Bible Dictionary*, edited by David Noel Freedman, 560–71. New York: Doubleday, 1992.

Quinn, Jerome D., and William C. Wacker. *The First and Second Letters to Timothy: A New Translation with Notes and Commentary.* Eerdmans Critical Commentary. Grand Rapids: Eerdmans, 2000.

Rahlfs, Alfred, ed. *Septuaginta.* Stuttgart, Germany: Deutsche Bibelgesellschaft, 1979.

Rajak, Tessa. "Gaius (1)." In *The Oxford Classical Dictionary*, edited by Simon Hornblower and Antony Spawforth, 619–20. 3rd rev. ed. New York: Oxford University Press, 2003.

Ramsay, William M. *Historical Commentary on the Pastoral Epistles.* Edited by Mark Wilson. Grand Rapids: Kregel, 1996.

Reck, Reinhold. "2 Tim 3,16 in der altkirchlichen Literatur: Eine wirkungsgeschichtliche Untersuchung zum Locus classicus der Inspirationslehre." *Wissenschaft und Weisheit* 53 (1990) 81–105.

Reed, Jeffrey T. "Cohesive Ties in 1 Timothy: In Defense of the Epistle's Unity." *Neotestamentica* 26 (1992) 131–47.

————. "Discourse Features in the New Testament Letters with Special Reference to the Structure of 1 Timothy." *Journal of Translation and Textlinguistics* 6 (1993) 228–52.

Rendall, F. "Faithful Is the Word." *The Expositor* 3/5 (1887) 314–20.

Richards, E. Randolph. *Paul and First-Century Letter Writing: Secretaries, Composition and Collection.* Downers Grove, IL: InterVarsity, 2004.

Ridderbos, Herman. *The Authority of the New Testament Scriptures.* Philadelphia: Presbyterian & Reformed, 1963.

————. *Paul: An Outline of His Theology.* Translated by John Richard DeWitt. Grand Rapids: Eerdmans, 1979.

————. *Redemptive History and the New Testament Scriptures.* 2nd ed. Phillipsburg, NJ: Presbyterian & Reformed, 1988.

Roberts, J. W. "The Bearing of the Use of Particles on the Authorship of the Pastoral Epistles." *Restoration Quarterly* 1 (1957) 132–37.

Robertson, A. T. *A Grammar of the Greek New Testament in the Light of Historical Research.* Nashville: Broadman, 1934.

Robinson, James M., and Helmut Koester. *Trajectories through Early Christianity.* Philadelphia: Fortress, 1971.

Robinson, John A. T. *Redating the New Testament.* Philadelphia: Westminster, 1976.

Roloff, Jürgen. *Der erste Brief an Timotheus.* Evangelisch-Katholischer Kommentar zum Neuen Testament 15. Zürich: Benziger, 1988.

Rosner, Brian S. "'Written for Us': Paul's View of Scripture." In *A Pathway into the Holy Scripture,* edited by Philip E. Satterthwaite and David F. Wright, 81–105. Grand Rapids: Eerdmans, 1994.

Rubenstein, Arie. "A Kethib-Qere Problem in the Light of the Isaiah Scroll." *Journal of Semitic Studies* 4 (1959) 127–33.

Russell, Michael. "On the Third Day, According to the Scriptures." *Reformed Theological Review* 67 (2008) 1–17.

Schlatter, Adolf. *Die Kirche der Griechen im Urteil des Paulus: Eine Auslegung seiner Briefe an Timotheus und Titus.* 2nd ed. Stuttgart, Germany: Calwer, 1958.

Schnabel, Eckhard J. *Early Christian Mission.* 2 vols. Downers Grove, IL: InterVarsity, 2004.

————. "History, Theology and the Biblical Canon: An Introduction to Basic Issues." *Themelios* 20 (1995) 16–24.

————. *Inspiration und Offenbarung: Die Lehre vom Ursprung und Wesen der Bibel.* Wuppertal, Germany: R. Brockhaus, 1997.

Schrage, Wolfgang. *Der Erste Brief an die Korinther (1 Kor 1,1–6,11).* Evangelisch-Katholischer Kommentar zum Neuen Testament 7/1. Zürich, Switzerland: Benziger, 1991.

Schreiner, Thomas R. *1, 2 Peter, Jude.* New American Commentary 37. Nashville: B. & H., 2003.

————. *Paul, Apostle of God's Glory in Christ: A Pauline Theology.* Downers Grove, IL: InterVarsity, 2001.

Schrenk, Gottlob. "γράφω, γραφή, γράμμα, κ.τ.λ." In vol. 1 of *Theological Dictionary of the New Testament,* edited by Gerhard Kittel, translated by Geoffrey W. Bromiley, 742–73. Grand Rapids: Eerdmans, 1983.

Scott, E. F. *The Pastoral Epistles.* London: Hodder & Stoughton, 1957.

Senior, Donald P., with Daniel J. Harrington. *1 Peter, Jude and 2 Peter*. Edited by Daniel J. Harrington. Sacra Pagina 15. Collegeville, MN: Liturgical, 2003.

Septuaginta. Vetus Testamentum Graecum auctoritate Academiae Scientiarum Gottingensis editum. Göttingen: Vandenhoeck & Ruprecht, 1931–2008.

Shepherd, Norman. *The Call of Grace: How the Covenant Illuminates Salvation and Evangelism*. Phillipsburg, NJ: Presbyterian & Reformed, 2000.

Sherwin-White, A. N., and Andrew William Lintott. "Praefectura." In *The Oxford Classical Dictionary*, edited by Simon Hornblower and Antony Spawforth, 1238. 3rd rev. ed. New York: Oxford University Press, 2003.

Soulen, Richard N., and R. Kendall Soulen. *Handbook of Biblical Criticism*. 3rd ed. Louisville: Westminster John Knox, 2001.

Spicq, C. *Saint Paul: Les Épitres Pastorales*. Paris: LeCoffre, 1947.

Stanley, Christopher D. *Paul and the Language of Scripture: Citation Technique in the Pauline Epistles and Contemporary Literature*. Society for New Testament Studies Monograph, Series 69. Cambridge: Cambridge University Press, 1992.

Stonehouse, Ned B. *Origins of the Synoptic Gospels: Some Basic Questions*. Grand Rapids: Eerdmans, 1963.

———. *The Witness of Luke to Christ*. Grand Rapids: Eerdmans, 1951.

Suetonius, Gaius Tranquillus. *Suetonius*. Translated by J. C. Rolfe. Rev. ed. 2 vols. Loeb Classical Library. Cambridge: Harvard University Press, 2001.

Swinson, L. Timothy. "Πιστὸς ὁ λόγος: An Alternative Analysis." Presentation at the annual meeting of the Society of Biblical Literature, New Orleans, Louisianna, November 22, 2009.

———. "'In Words Taught by the Spirit': An Exegetical Study of 1 Corinthians 2:6–16." ThM diss., Trinity Evangelical Divinity School, 2001.

———. "Textual Criticism and Authorship Traditions: An Examination of the Superscriptions in 1 and 2 Timothy." Presentation at the annual meeting of the Evangelical Theological Society, Washington, DC, November 16, 2006.

———. "The 'We' Effect, and Its Implications for Scripture and the Church: An Examination of First Corinthians 2:12–13." Presentation at the annual meeting of the Evangelical Theological Society. Valley Forge, Pennsylvania, November 17, 2005.

Thiselton, Anthony C. *The First Epistle to the Corinthians: A Commentary on the Greek Text*. New International Greek Testament Commentary. Grand Rapids: Eerdmans, 2000.

Thomas, Robert L. "Imminence in the NT, Especially Paul's Thessalonian Epistles." *The Master's Seminary Journal* 13 (2002) 191–214.

Thrall, Margaret E. *The First and Second Letters of Paul to the Corinthians*. Cambridge Bible Commentary. Cambridge: Cambridge University Press, 1990.

Tigay, Jeffrey H. *Deuteronomy*. JPS Torah Commentary. Philadelphia: Jewish Publication Society, 1996.

Tov, Emanuel. *Textual Criticism of the Hebrew Bible*. 2nd ed. Minneapolis: Fortress, 1992.

Towner, Philip H. "The Goal of Our Instruction: The Structure of Theology and Ethics in the Pastoral Epistles." *Journal for the Study of the New Testament*, Supplement Series 34. Sheffield, England: Sheffield Academic, 1989.

———. *The Letters to Timothy and Titus*. New International Commentary on the New Testament. Grand Rapids: Eerdmans, 2006.

Van Bruggen, Jakob. "Vaste grond onder de voeten. De formule pistos ho logos in de Pastorale Brieven." In *Bezield verband: Opstellen aangeboden aan prof. J. Kamphuis bij gelegenheid van zijn vijfentwintig-jarig ambtsjubileum als hoogleraar aan de Theologische Hogeschool van De Gereformeerde Kerken in Nederland te Kampen op 9 april 1984*, edited by J. Kamphuis, 38–45. Kampen: Uitgeverij Van den Berg, 1984.

Van Neste, Ray. *Cohesion and Structure in the Pastoral Epistles*. London: T. & T. Clark, 2004.

Warren, David. "Who Originated the Term 'Gospel' as a Genre?" Presentation at the annual meeting of the Evangelical Theological Society, Atlanta, Georgia, November 20, 2003.

Weiser, Alfons. *Der Zweite Brief an Timotheus*. Evangelisch-Katholischer Kommentar zum Neuen Testament 16. Zürich, Switzerland: Benziger, 2003.

Wenham, John W. *Redating Matthew, Mark and Luke: A Fresh Assault on the Synoptic Problem*. Downers Grove, IL: InterVarsity, 1992.

Westcott, Brooke Foss. *A General Survey of the History of the Canon of the New Testament*. 6th ed. Grand Rapids: Baker, 1980.

Wilder, Terry L. *Pseudonymity, the New Testament, and Deception: An Inquiry into Intention and Reception*. Lanham, MD: University Press of America, 2004.

Witherington, Ben, III. *Letters and Homilies for Hellenized Christians: A Socio-Rhetorical Commentary on Titus, 1–2 Timothy and 1–3 John*. Downers Grove, IL: InterVarsity, 2006.

———. *The Paul Quest: The Renewed Search for the Jew of Tarsus*. Downers Grove, IL: InterVarsity, 1998.

Wolfe, B. Paul. "The Place and Use of Scripture in the Pastoral Epistles." PhD diss., University of Aberdeen, 1990.

———. "The Sagacious Use of Scripture." In *Entrusted with the Gospel: Paul's Theology in the Pastoral Epistles*, edited by Andreas Köstenberger and Terry L. Wilder, 199–218. Nashville: B. & H. Academic, 2010.

———. "Scripture in the Pastoral Epistles: Premarcion Marcionism?" *Perspectives in Religious Studies* 16 (1989) 5–16.

Wolter, Michael. *Die Pastoralbriefe als Paulustradition*. Göttingen, Germany: Vandenhoeck & Ruprecht, 1988.

Yarbrough, Robert W. "The Theology of Romans in Future Tense." *The Southern Baptist Journal of Theology* 11 (2007) 46–60.

Zahn, Theodor. *Geschichte des Neutestamentlichen Kanons*. 2 vols. 1888–1892. Reprint, Chestnut Hill, MA: Adamant Media, 2005.

———. *Introduction to the New Testament*. Translated by John Moore Trout, et al. 3 vols. Grand Rapids: Kregel, 1953.

Author Index

CPSIA information can be obtained
at www.ICGtesting.com
Printed in the USA
FSHW012019291019
63549FS